MIGHT of the LIVING GOD

MIGHTY SERVANTS OF THE LIVING GOD

Children's Bible Stories

May our Lord bless you as you read this book.

Lois M. Bitler

LOIS M. BITLER

TATE PUBLISHING
AND ENTERPRISES, LLC

Mighty Servants of the Living God
Copyright © 2015 by Lois M. Bitler. All rights reserved.

No part of this publication may be reproduced, stored in a retrieval system or transmitted in any way by any means, electronic, mechanical, photocopy, recording or otherwise without the prior permission of the author except as provided by USA copyright law.

This book is designed to provide accurate and authoritative information with regard to the subject matter covered. This information is given with the understanding that neither the author nor Tate Publishing, LLC is engaged in rendering legal, professional advice. Since the details of your situation are fact dependent, you should additionally seek the services of a competent professional.

The opinions expressed by the author are not necessarily those of Tate Publishing, LLC.

Published by Tate Publishing & Enterprises, LLC
127 E. Trade Center Terrace | Mustang, Oklahoma 73064 USA
1.888.361.9473 | www.tatepublishing.com

Tate Publishing is committed to excellence in the publishing industry. The company reflects the philosophy established by the founders, based on Psalm 68:11,
"The Lord gave the word and great was the company of those who published it."

Book design copyright © 2015 by Tate Publishing, LLC. All rights reserved.
Cover design by Kristina Angela Igot
Interior design by Gram Telen
Illustrations by Kenneth Rede Rikimaru

Published in the United States of America
ISBN: 978-1-63367-360-1
Religion / Christian Education / Children & Youth
15.02.10

To my dear parents, Paul and Margaret Bitler,
former missionaries and faithful mighty
servants of the living God
and
To my very best friend, the Lord Jesus Christ,
who does all things well.

CONTENTS

Adam and Eve 11
Noah 17
The Tower of Babel 23
Job 27
Abraham 33
Sodom and Gomorrah 39
Joseph 47
Baby Moses 69
Moses 73
Balaam 91
Joshua 95
Judge Deborah 101
Gideon 107
Samson 113
Ruth 125
Hannah 133
King Saul 139
David and Goliath 145
Elijah: Challenge of Baal 149
Widow's Oil 153
The Kind Woman 155
Naaman 161
Elisha: God's Army Protects 165
Jehoshaphat 169
Josiah 173
Heroes of God 189
Wanted by God 193
Daniel 197

Jonah	201
Queen Esther	207
Baby Lord Jesus	219
Jesus in the Temple	223
Follow Me: Fishers of Men	227
You Must Be Born Again!	231
The Persistent Four	235
The Call of Matthew	239
Powerless Man	243
Feeding of Multitude	245
Peter's Walk of Faith	249
Blind Man	253
Jairus's Daughter	259
The Great Supper	261
The Lost Son	265
He Makes the Deaf to Hear	269
Healing of a Centurion's Servant	271
Healing of a Leper	273
The Son of Man is Lord Also of the Sabbath	275
Healing of Blind Bartimaeus	279
Jesus Loves the Little Children	281
Widow of Nain	283
The Master Speaks!	287
The Ten Lepers	289
The Power of Prayer	293
Zaccheus	295
The Good Samaritan	299
The Woman at the Well	303
The Raising of Lazarus from the Dead	307
The Widow's Mites	311
Worshipping the Lord Jesus Christ	315
My Savior, My Lord, the King	319
Death, Burial, and Resurrection of the Lord Jesus Christ	323
The Road to Emmaus	335

Walking and Talking and Praising God!................................ 339
Rejoicing all the Way!.. 341
Saul of Tarsus Becomes Paul the Apostle.............................. 345
Dorcas: A True Friend of Widows... 349
God's Answer to Prayer 353
A Changed Heart.. 357

ADAM AND EVE

"In the beginning, God created the heaven and the earth." This is how the Bible begins. The first book of the Bible is called Genesis. *Genesis* means "beginnings." From the book of Genesis, we shall learn how God made the first man and the first woman.

Let us begin: It took God six days to create or make all that we see today and also the things that we cannot see. Some of the things that we cannot see are all the stars, all the planets, and even the wind. The Bible tells us that on the first day, God made light, and he called the light "Day." He called the darkness "Night."

On the second day, God made the heavens or skies. The heavens divided the water from above the skies and below the skies.

On the third day, God made the dry land and called it "Earth." He brought together all the waters and called the waters "Seas." He also made all the plant life such as grass, trees, flowers, and much, much more.

On the fourth day, God made the sun, moon, and stars. He placed them in the sky. He made the sun to shine in the day and the moon and stars to shine in the night.

On the fifth day, God made animal life. He made all the animals that live in the sea and all the flying insects and birds that fly in the sky. He blessed these animals and told them to multiply and fill the whole earth.

On the sixth day, God made all the land animals. These are the animals that live on the earth such as cows, horses, elephants, lions, and tigers. Can you think of any more? He also made every little bug and every little worm that creeps along the earth or lives in the ground.

God saw that everything he created was good. God also created something else on the sixth day that was very, very special. Do you know what that was? He created man in his likeness. That means he gave men some things like he has—things such as feelings, a mind to think, a willingness to do many different things, and so much more. He gave the man power over all the fish in the sea, the birds in the air, the animals on the earth, and every little bug, insect, and worm that creeps, crawls, or flies. He gave to man all the plants that give fruit or seed. God put man in charge of everything on the earth.

On the seventh day, the Lord God rested from all his work. He blessed the seventh day and made it a holy day of rest. God was very pleased with everything he created. When the Lord God made man, he made him from the dust of the ground. God breathed into man the breath of life, and man became a living soul.

God brought all the animals to Adam to see what Adam would call them. God wanted Adam to name the animals and gave him power over all the animals. The Lord God planted a garden in the eastern part of Eden, and that is where he placed the man. In the middle of the garden, there was a tree called the Tree of Life and another tree called the Tree of Knowledge of Good and Evil. There was also a river which flowed out of this garden of Eden, and it divided into four parts: Pison, Gihon, Hiddekel, and Euphrates.

He put the man in this garden of Eden to take care of it. He commanded the man, "Out of every tree of the garden, you may eat. But of the Tree of Knowledge of Good and Evil, you will not eat. In the day you eat of this Tree of Knowledge of Good and Evil, you will surely die."

Boys and girls, we can see so far that because there is no sin, there is no death. The man was going to live forever in this garden of Eden. The Lord God said, "It is not good that the man should be alone. We will make him a help meet." God was going to make a friend and helper for Adam. God put Adam in a very deep sleep. While Adam was sleeping, God took one of Adam's ribs and closed it up with skin. God then took Adam's rib and from the rib, he made a woman.

God brought the woman to Adam.

Adam said, "This is now bone of my bones and flesh of my flesh. She shall be called 'Woman' because she was taken from man. Now shall a man leave his father and mother and shall cling to his wife and they shall be one flesh." That is how the first marriage began.

God likes marriage. Adam named his new wife "Eve," for she is mother of all living.

Now the man and the woman had no clothes on, and they were not ashamed. (Because there was no sin yet, they had nothing to be ashamed of.)

There was an animal in the garden that was very beautiful and delicate. This animal was called snake. The devil came into the snake. The snake said to the woman, "Did God *really* say 'Do not eat of every tree in the garden?'"

The woman answered, "We may eat of the fruit of the trees in the garden, but the tree that is in the middle of the garden God said, 'You shall not eat or touch it or else you will die.'"

The snake said, "You will not die. God knows that in the day you eat of that tree, your eyes will be opened and you will be like God. You will know good and evil."

When the woman saw that the tree was good for food, that it looked good to her eyes, and that it could make her know all things, she took the fruit from the tree and ate it. She gave the fruit to her husband and he ate it also. They believed the devil's lies more than they believed what God their Creator said.

The eyes of Adam and his wife, Eve, were opened, and they knew that they had no clothes on. They felt ashamed, and they quickly sewed together leaves from the fig tree and made aprons for themselves.

They heard the voice of God walking in the garden during the cool part of the day. Adam and Eve hid themselves among the trees. They did not want God to find them. God knows exactly where you are at all times—you cannot hide.

The Lord God called out to Adam, "Where are you?" Adam said, "I heard your voice in the garden, and I was afraid because I had no clothes on, and I hid myself." God said, "Who told you that you are not wearing any clothes? Did you eat of the tree that I told you not to touch or eat?" The man said, "The woman that you gave me, she gave me some fruit from that tree and I ate it."

The Lord God said to the woman, "What is this that you have done?"

The woman answered, "The snake tempted me, and I ate it."

Do you remember who entered into the snake? The devil can do a lot of different things to make you think that he is good, but the Bible tells us many, many times that the devil is evil. He is the father of lies.

The Lord God said to the snake, "Because you have done this, you are cursed above all the animals of the earth. You will crawl on your belly, and the dirt that you crawl upon will be your food."

The Lord God said these words to the devil, "You will be the enemy of all mankind. You will be the enemy of all those who love me. In the end, Satan, you will lose!"

God said unto the woman, "I will greatly add to your troubles. In pain, you will have children and your desire will be to your husband, and he shall rule over you."

God said to Adam, "Because you listened to your wife and ate of the tree that I told you not to eat, in sadness and pain you will work the ground. For now, the ground is cursed, and you will have to work very, very hard in order to eat and live on this earth. The earth will now bring out thorns and thistles. You will work with sweat and pain all the days of your life until you die. When you die, you will return to the ground; for dust is what you are made of and dust is what you will return to."

(Here, the Lord God is speaking of the body, not the soul. The Bible teaches us that your soul lives forever either in heaven or hell. The choice is yours to make.)

God still loved Adam and Eve very much. He made them each a coat from the skins of animals. God killed the animals to clothe Adam and Eve. The Lord God said, "Look, the man is become like us. Now he knows good and evil. If he eats of the Tree of Life he will live forever."

The Lord God sent Adam and Eve away from the garden, and he placed a cherubim with a flaming sword that turned in every direction to guard the way of the Tree of Life.

It must have hurt the Lord God to have to send Adam and Eve away. But Adam and Eve made the choice to disobey God even though God gave them everything they would ever want or need.

The Lord God loves each one of us so very much too. That is why he sent his Son, his only Son, to die for us upon a cross. He carried our sins on the cross so that we may live forever with him in heaven. Just like Adam and Eve, the choice is yours to make.

> For God so loved the world, that he gave his only begotten Son, that whosoever believeth in him should not perish, but have everlasting life.
>
> John 3:16 (AKJV)

How many days did it take God to create everything?
Can you name some things God made?
Was God happy with everything he created?
On what day did God make Adam?
How did God create Eve?

NOAH

The thrilling story of Noah and the great flood took place during the earlier part of the Bible (Genesis). Even then, sin was everywhere. Darkness and wickedness had covered the land. God looked down from heaven, and when he saw what the people were doing, he repented or had a change of mind that he had made man on earth. It brought sadness to his heart to see the evil things the people were doing. The Lord said, "I will destroy man whom I have created, the beasts and the animals from the earth."

Out of all the people, there was one man that found grace or mercy in the eyes of the Lord. He followed the Lord God perfectly. He was a just man and the Bible states, "He walked with God." Can you tell me what his name is? That's correct, Noah. Yes, Noah was a true friend of God. If God looked down from heaven today, could He say the same thing about you? Do you love him so much that you would live your life for him? Noah did.

Noah had three sons. Their names were Shem, Ham, and Japheth. His wife, most likely, was a woman who loved both God and her husband. God said to Noah one day, "The earth is filled with violence and sin. There is not one good person. They have all turned from me and my ways to a life filled with evil deeds which I can not stand for any longer. The sin has filled all the earth. You are to make an ark out of gopherwood. You will put tar inside and outside the ark to keep it together." God then gave Noah instructions and directions on how to build this ark. He told Noah, "I am going to bring a great flood of waters that will cover the whole earth. This flood will destroy all people, and everything that is in the earth shall die. But with you, Noah, I will make and begin my covenant. You and your sons and your wife and your sons' wives shall all enter into the ark and shall be saved from my judgment. You alone have followed after my ways and have lived a life full of goodness and truth.

"You centered your life around me, and because of this, I will save you and your family. I will keep you safe and will love you."

Boys and girls, the Lord Jesus Christ loves all those who belong to him. The book of John chapter 10 verses 27 and 28 tells us that the Lord Jesus says, "My sheep hear my voice, and I know them, and they follow me. And I give unto them eternal life, and they shall never perish, neither shall any man pluck them out of my hand." Do you know the Lord Jesus Christ? Are you one of his sheep?

God then instructed Noah to bring into the ark two of every animal, male and female, whether they be birds of every kind, cattle, every creeping thing of the earth and all the rest of all the living animals. God also told Noah to gather all the food together and bring it also into the ark. Noah did everything God said.

If we say we love the Lord Jesus Christ, we should keep his Ten Commandments, which are written in the Bible. We should do this out of love for God. Everything God has done for us was done with a perfect love.

After the ark was finished, the Lord God said to Noah, "Come thou and all thy house into the ark, for I have seen righteousness before me in this generation." This verse means that Noah was allowed to enter into the ark because he loved and obeyed the Lord God. He put his trust in God, knowing God would send the flood. He never argued with God; he was always willing to do what God asked. The people must have made fun of Noah while Noah was building the ark—for, you see, boys and girls, it had never rained before. The water came out of the ground each morning. But that did not stop Noah from doing God's will. It took Noah one hundred twenty years to finish building the ark. Noah wanted to obey God. It is not our good deeds that get us into heaven; it is our willingness to give our heart and life to the Lord Jesus Christ, fully trusting in Him. This is what God calls righteousness. This is what Noah did.

Everyone entered the ark—Noah, his wife, his sons and their wives, and all the animals (two of every kind, male and female)—as God commanded. God closed the door of the ark himself!

After seven days had passed, the flood began. That day, all the deepest parts of the earth were broken up, and the waters gushed out! The heavens were opened up, and the waters poured out in tremendous amounts! What a miracle that must have been! It rained straight for forty days and forty nights. The waters kept getting higher and higher, and the ark floated. Everything was covered—trees, hills, and mountains. You couldn't see a thing. Everyone and everything that was not in the ark had died. But Noah and those with him in the ark were alive. After forty days and forty nights, the rain stopped, but the waters stayed on the earth for one hundred fifty days. That is quite a long time when you are in the ark wondering when this will all come to an end. But the Bible states, "And God remembered Noah and every living thing and all the cattle that was with him in the ark."

Yes, God knows everything that happens to each of his little lambs. He never forgets.

God made a wind to pass over the earth, and the waters began to go down. After one hundred fifty days, the ark rested on the Ararat Mountains. There they waited forty more days. Then Noah opened the window of the ark, and he let a raven fly out.

He also sent a dove, but the dove found no resting place and returned to the ark. After another week, he sent the dove out again, and this time, the dove came back with an olive leaf in her mouth. Noah knew it soon would be time for them to leave the ark. After another week had passed, Noah again sent the dove out, and this time, she found a place in the earth to live and never returned to the ark.

Noah then removed the covering of the ark and looked all over the new ground.

He saw that the earth was dry. God spoke to Noah and said, "Go out from the ark, you and your wife and your sons and your sons' wives. Bring out with you all the animals that they may keep having more and more animals on the earth." Noah and his family and all the animals came out of the ark.

Noah built an altar to the Lord God and offered sacrifices on the altar to God. The Lord God was very pleased with Noah's offerings, and the Lord God said in his heart, "I will never again destroy the earth with water." God remembered his promise to Noah, which he had made to Noah before the flood began.

He spoke to Noah, "I will begin my agreement with you, Noah, and with all your children and with your future children. I will never send another flood upon the earth. Behold, whenever I bring a cloud over the earth, you will see a rainbow. I will look upon that rainbow, and I will remember the everlasting covenant between God and every living creature on the earth. This rainbow is my promise of the agreement between you and I and all living creatures."

God blessed Noah and his family and told them to have more and more families and fill the earth. Still today, God has remembered his promise to Noah, and we often see the rainbow after a rain. He has also sent his Son, the Lord Jesus Christ, to earth to die for our sins and to save us from destruction. He promised us eternal life and a home in heaven if we tell our sins to him, give our life to him, and put our trust in him. This is the *everlasting* part of the agreement that God promised to Noah, and we can have it today freely. God is so good.

> Therefore if any man be in Christ, he is a new creature; old things are past away; behold, all things are become new.
>
> 2 Corinthians 5:17 (KJV)

How many sons did Noah and his wife have?
What did God tell Noah to build?
How many days and nights did it rain on the earth?
What bird came back to Noah with an olive leaf in its mouth?
What did God promise Noah he would put in the sky after the rain?

THE TOWER OF BABEL

Do you remember the story of Noah and the ark? That is when the Lord God opened the heavens, and for forty days and forty nights, the rains came in tremendous amounts and poured down upon the earth. Everything and everyone had died, that is, except for Noah and his family. They were kept safe inside the ark. It took Noah one hundred twenty years to build the ark, and all the people of the earth had a chance to be saved, but they did not want God to come into their hearts.

Still, today, many people do not want God in their hearts, even though they have heard how the Lord Jesus Christ died for their sins.

Do you know why *all* people on the earth had a chance to be saved when Noah was building the ark? It was because everyone lived in the same part of the earth. They all lived near each other, and no one thought of moving to another part of the earth.

When the flood was over, Noah and his family came out of the ark and settled, once again, in a certain part of the earth. This is where the story of the Tower of Babel begins.

Noah had three sons: Shem, Ham, and Japheth. From these three sons, many different types of people were born, for example the Greeks, the Syrians, the Armenians, the Germans, the Russians, etc. Each race or type of people had their own king and nation. Although there were many different types of people, they all spoke the same language. That is because, as we read before, they all lived near each other.

One of these kings was named Nimrod. The Bible tells us that King Nimrod was a wicked king and rebelled against God.

We can begin to see that after the flood, *sin* has once more come into the world and into the hearts and minds of everyone. The Bible tells us that there is only one way to get rid of sin. That is by asking the Lord Jesus Christ to come into your heart and to take away your sin, for you see the Lord Jesus Christ is the perfect Son of God who came to earth to die for your sins in order that you may be able to enter heaven. If he didn't die on the cross for your sins, you could never go to heaven. You would still be full of sin, and there is no sin in heaven. Romans 3:23 tells us, "For all have sinned and fall short of the glory of God," and Romans 5:8 tells us, "But God shows his own love for us in this way: While we were still sinners, Christ died for us." Can you see how much God loves you and wants to have you go to heaven?

But King Nimrod hated God, and he made his people do terrible things while God was watching. He was a proud king, and he really thought he was just like God. He thought he could do the same things that God could do. Yes, King Nimrod had a plan, and he was going to show God he was greater than God.

He had all the people on earth, including all the kings and himself move to a flat piece of land in the country of Shinar. After all the people on the earth, including all the kings and himself moved to this place in the country of Shinar, King Nimrod put his plan into action.

He had all the people say, "Come, let us make brick. We will burn the brick and make stone and tar. Then we will build a city and a tower. The top of this tower will reach heaven. After we build this gigantic city and tower, we will think of a great name for ourselves. In this way, if anything happens to us, no one will forget our great name. We will be just like God."

King Nimrod really knew how to make the people "feel good," and did they begin to build! But they forgot the most important part of all—God. The Word of God tells us in Psalms 127:1, "Unless the Lord builds the house, its builders labor in vain."

In other words, the house will never be built no matter how hard you try if you leave God out of your plans. That is exactly what King Nimrod did. He left God out of his plan. (Remember, King Nimrod hated God.)

The Bible states, "And God came down to see the city and tower, which the people were building," and God said to the Lord Jesus Christ and to the Holy Spirit, "Everyone speaks the same language. Look what all the people of the earth are doing. Now they will continue to have even more evil ideas, and they will not stop their wickedness. Come, let us go down and let us confuse their language so that they will not understand what each person is saying."

What a miracle God did that day! He gave each person a different language to speak. That day, the work on the building stopped because no one knew what the next person was saying. The people began to move away, and they began to live in different parts of the earth. That is why, today, we see many different people with many different languages all over the world.

God called the tower that King Nimrod and all the people built The Tower of Babel. The word *Babel* means "The Lord confused the language of all the earth." From that one area or place where all the people lived, God scattered them all over the face of the earth.

You cannot leave God out of your life. He sees and knows everything you do and say. Let us read Isaiah 40:21–31: "Do you not know? Have you not heard? Has it not been told you from the beginning? Have you not understood since the earth was founded? He sits upon a throne above the circle of the earth, and its people are like grasshoppers. He stretches out the heavens like a canopy and spreads them out like a tent to live in. He brings princes to nothing and reduces the rulers of this world to nothing. No sooner are they planted, no sooner are they sown, no sooner do they take root in the ground, then he blows on them and they dry up, and a whirlwind sweeps them away like chaff. 'To whom will you liken me? Or who is my equal?' says the Holy One. Lift up your eyes and look to the heavens, who created all these things? He who brings out the starry host one by one and calls them each by name. Because of his great power and mighty strength, not one of them is missing. Why do you say, O Jacob and complain, O Israel, 'My way is hidden from the Lord; my cause is forgotten by my God?' Do you not know? Have you not heard? The Lord is the everlasting God, the Creator of the ends of the earth and his understanding no one can understand. He gives strength to the weary and increases the power of the weak. Even youths grow tired and weary, and young men stumble and fall, but they that wait upon the Lord shall renew their strength. They will soar on wings like eagles, they will run and not grow weary, they will walk and not be faint."

Thank you dear heavenly Father for sending us your Son to die on the cross for our sins and giving us everlasting life so that we may spend forever with you in heaven. Thank you for loving us so very much.

> Look unto me and be ye saved all the ends of the earth; for I am God and there is none else.
>
> Isaiah 45:22 (AKJV)

What was the name of the wicked King that rebelled against God?
Where did this King move all the people to?
What did the people use to build this city and high tower?
What was the name of the tower?
Who came down to see what they were doing?

JOB

There was a man who lived in the land called Uz. His name was Job. He obeyed, loved, and respected God. He stayed away from evil. Job was a very, very rich man. God had truly blessed Job. He was married and had seven sons and three daughters. He also owned seven thousand sheep, three thousand camels, five hundred bulls, and five hundred donkeys. He had many, many servants and a very big house. The Bible tells us that he was the greatest of all the men that lived in the East.

One day, his sons had a big party in each of their houses, and they invited their sisters to "Come eat and drink with us." When the party was over, Job sent for all of his children. They stood before their father, Job, and he would offer up sacrifices to God for them. He rose up early in the morning and offered a burnt offering to the Lord God. He offered one for each of them. Job did this because he said, "Maybe my children have sinned and cursed God in their hearts." The Word of God tells us that he did this many times, just as many times as his children had parties.

A burnt offering is when one would build an altar, which was usually made of stone. Wood would be placed on the top of this altar. The animal would become the sacrifice, and it would be offered up to God as the "burnt offering" for the forgiveness of one's sins.

Job really loved and obeyed the Lord God. Job knew the One who had given him blessings on earth, and he wasn't afraid to let others know how much he loved God.

Still, today, God has done so much for us. God sent his only Son to become our "burnt offering" for sin. He died on that rough, wooden cross. He took away our sins.

Do we remember to thank him for all he has done for us? Job never forgot to thank God.

Do you know, boys and girls, who Satan is? He is also called the devil. He is very evil. He hates God very much, and he hates those who have put their trust in God. Do you think Satan hated Job? He certainly did!

One day, the Bible tells us that Satan stood before God. God asked Satan, "Where have you been?" Satan answered, "I have been all over the Earth. I have been walking up and down the Earth."

The Lord said, "Have you noticed my servant Job? He respects and loves me. There is none like him."

Satan answered, "Do you know why he loves you? You have protected him from danger. You have given him everything. But if you would put out your hand and take away all that he has, he would curse you."

God replied, "Everything he has is in your power, but don't touch him. Don't touch my servant, Job." With that, Satan went out from the presence of God.

Truly, God holds all things in his hand. God truly has power over all. On a certain day when all of Job's children were having a big party or feast in the oldest brother's house, a messenger came to Job and said, "The bulls were in the fields plowing the dirt, and the donkeys were feeding besides them when all of a sudden, out of nowhere, the Sabeans came and took them all away. They killed the servants. I alone escaped to tell you this terrible news."

Before the servant finished, another servant came running to Job and said, "Fire came down from heaven and burnt up all the sheep and the servants. I alone escaped to tell you the news."

Again, before the servant could finish, another servant came to Job running as fast as he could, saying, "Another people, the Chaldeans, came and took all of your camels away and killed the servants. I am the only one who was able to escape, Master."

Before he could get the last sentence out, another servant of Job came up to him and said, "There came a great wind from the wilderness. It destroyed all the houses where your sons and daughters were having their party. The four corners of the house fell on all your children, and now they are all dead. I am the only one alive, and I ran as quickly as I could to bring you this horrible, horrible news."

Then Job, servant of God, got up and tore his clothes (a sign of deep sadness). He fell upon the ground and worshipped God. He said, "I was born naked. I had nothing when I came into this world, and when I die, I cannot take anything with me. The Lord gives and the Lord has taken away, blessed is the name of the Lord." Not once, not once did Job curse or find anything wrong with God. Would we have done the same? I wonder myself.

There came another day when Satan stood before God, and the Lord God said to Satan, "Where have you been?"

Satan answered, "I have been walking up and down the earth. I have been all around the earth."

The Lord asked Satan, "Have you watched my servant, Job? There is no man like him in all the earth. He fears God and stays away from evil. Even though I let you destroy his children, house, and animals, he stayed true to me."

Satan responded, "If you would harm his body, then he would curse you. A man would do anything in order to save his life."

The Lord God replied, "I give him over to you, but his life, you will not touch." With that, Satan was gone from God.

Immediately, Satan struck Job with open sores from the bottom of Job's feet to the top of Job's head. Poor Job, in such pain and agony, sat down amongst the ashes and took a piece of broken pottery to scratch himself with. Job's wife seeing him suffering said, "Why don't you curse God and die?"

He answered, "Now you are speaking as a foolish woman. What? Shall we only receive good things from God all of our life and never receive the evil things?"

In all of his pain, in all of his sadness, and in all of his loneliness, Job *never* cursed God, not in his thoughts and not with his lips.

Job had three friends who, when they heard of his suffering, came to visit him. Their names were Eliphaz, Bildad, and Zophar. They wanted to visit Job so that they could share his sadness and try to make him feel better.

When they arrived near Job's house, they looked at him, and they did not know that this man was Job. After they saw that this man was Job, they lifted up their voices and cried. They tore their clothes (a sign of deep sadness) and sprinkled dust on their heads. They sat down with Job for seven days and seven nights. No one spoke a word. They could not say one word, for they saw that Job was in great pain and sadness.

After the seven days past, Job spoke. When he finished speaking, the three men all took turns talking to Job. They tried to tell Job that he must have done something wicked in order for this to happen to him. They went on and on for many days telling Job, "You have to confess your sin to God. God is punishing you for the wicked thing you have done."

Job, all alone, sat there in his pain, listening and answering his three friends. He knew he had done nothing wrong.

After a long, long time, a fourth man, very young, came to see Job. He wanted to offer some comfort for him. His name was Elihu. Elihu was very angry with the three men because they had no answer for Job, yet they sat there trying to find things that were wrong with Job.

When they all finished speaking, Elihu spoke. Out of respect, he waited for his turn. He spoke softer words to Job than the other three men. The three men spoke very roughly to Job.

Still, I am sure Job felt so lonely through his grief. His wife let him down, and his friends let him down. Boys and girls, the Bible tells us in Psalms 118:8, "It is better to trust in the Lord than to put your trust in man."

After the young man, Elihu, finished speaking, do you know who spoke next? It was God himself! He doesn't need a man to speak for him. The Lord God spoke directly to Job, and he told Job all about his greatness, his power, and his glory. Here is a little example of what God said to Job, "Who is it that is speaking words without knowing what he is talking about? Strengthen yourself now like a man, for I will demand of you and you will answer me. Where were you when I laid the foundations of the earth? Who has measured the earth? Who set the doors upon the sea so that it would not overflow? Do you know when the wild goats, who live in the mountains, give birth to their little ones? He that correcteth God, let him answer me."

Job answered, "Lord, I am a man of unclean lips. I will put my hand over my mouth. I have spoken once too much. I will not answer you anymore."

Even though he had done no wrong, Job still saw himself as a man full of sin next to God, who is holy and true.

The Lord God continued his talk with Job. He wanted to let Job know that all things are under God's power.

At the end of God's conversation, Job answered, "Forgive me, Lord, for not trusting you. I repent of my sins in this dust and ashes where I sit." Then the Lord God said to Job's friend, Eliphaz, "My anger is very great against you and your two friends, for you have not spoken the right thing about me the way my servant, Job, has. Now, take seven bulls and seven male goats and go to my servant, Job, and offer up a burnt offering for your sins. My servant Job shall pray for you. I will accept his prayer. If you don't, I will deal with you for your sins because you have not spoken right about me the way my servant, Job, has."

Immediately Job's three friends, Eliphaz, Bildad, and Zophar did as the Lord God commanded. The Lord also accepted Job.

When Job prayed for his three friends, the Lord God took away the pain and suffering from Job. The Lord then gave Job twice as much as he had before.

All of Job's relatives and friends came to his house and ate with him. They all gave Job a piece of money and an earring made of gold. The Lord blessed Job more in the end than in the beginning. He now had fourteen thousand sheep, six thousand camels, one thousand bulls, and one thousand donkeys. He had seven sons and three daughters. The three daughters were the prettiest in all the land.

After all of this sadness, Job lived one hundred forty years, and he saw his children grow up, his grandchildren grow up, his great-grandchildren grow up and his great, great-grandchildren grow up. He died a very happy man in the Lord.

> Choose you this day whom ye will serve, but as for me and my house, we will serve the Lord.
>
> Joshua 24:15 (AKJV)

> O taste and see that the Lord is good. How happy is the man who trusts in Him!
>
> Psalms 34:8 (NLV)

Who is this story written about?
Did this man love God?
How many men came to see him when he was sad?
Did God bless this man at the end?
Did God love this man?

ABRAHAM

Two thousand years after the flood, Abram was born in the city of Ur. Abram lived with his wife, Sarai, his two brothers, and his father, Terah. They neither worshipped nor believed in God. Instead, they bowed down to idols made of stone and clay.

God spoke to Abram and told him to leave the city of Ur near the Persian Gulf. Abram obeyed God even though Abram didn't know who God was. Abram and his whole family packed away everything they had, and Abram led them out of the city. It was very hard for them to leave all their friends, knowing they may never see them again.

But God told Abram he would become a great nation and that God would bless him and make his name famous. God moved them from a busy city called Ur to a quiet place called Haran. But again, God wanted Abram, his wife Sarai, his nephew Lot, and the rest of the family, and all the servants to keep on going. So on they went believing in God. They passed the desert to a land called Canaan. There were many people in this land, but God told Abram that he was going to give all this land to him and his children.

It was a beautiful land, with trees and mountains and valleys and dark-green grass. It was here that Abram built his first altar to God, and for the first time, Abram worshipped God and believed on him.

God moved Abram and his family to the hills east of Bethel, and with each day, his faith in God grew stronger. He also built an altar here and worshipped and bowed down to God. It is in this place called Bethel that Abram called on the name of God.

The Lord God found a friend on earth and loved his new friend very much. As he and his wife and Lot moved on, there was a great famine in the land, and it made them go to Egypt.

Now Sarai was very beautiful, and Abram knew this, so when they came into Egypt, Abram made Sarai tell the Egyptians that she was his sister. This was a lie, but Abram thought that if she said this, then no harm would come to him.

One day, Pharaoh, king of Egypt, saw Sarai and called her into his palace. He thought she was so beautiful, and he wanted to keep her for himself. After all, she did say she was Abram's sister.

Suddenly, everyone in the palace became very sick. Pharaoh finally found out the truth and called for Abram. When Abram stood before Pharaoh, Pharaoh said, "She is your wife, why did you lie to me? Take her and get out of here." But Pharaoh did give them many beautiful gifts, including an Egyptian servant girl named Hagar for Sarai. But God still loved Abram. When the famine was over, Abram and his family went back to Canaan. When he was in Canaan, Abram built an altar and asked God to forgive him for what he did in Egypt. God did forgive Abram.

It took a lot of faith for Abram to obey God and leave his own country and his family and friends and begin wandering over the earth. His faith was growing stronger each day as they settled down in Canaan.

Now Lot was with them since the beginning of the journey. By this time, it was getting pretty crowded with Abram's sheep and goats and cattle and family and Lot's family, sheep, goats, and cattle. The servants of Abram and the servants of Lot began to fight because there was just no room for both of them.

One day, Sarai said to Abram, "There is just too much fighting going on here between our family and Lot's family. Abram, you must do something!"

Abram and Lot went to look at all the land surrounding them (and there was certainly a lot of land), and Lot chose to go to the Jordan Valley area. It was a beautiful piece of land with its dark-green grass, rivers of water, trees, and more trees. Abram stayed where he was.

When Abram was ninety-nine years old, the Lord God spoke to him again. What he heard really surprised him! God once more made the promise to Abram to make a very great nation of his children and all who would be born into his family.

God also changed his name from Abram to Abraham. We are told that *Abraham* means "father of a multitude." God said to Abraham, "As for Sarai, your wife, do not call her Sarai, for her name shall be Sarah. I will bless her, and I will give you and Sarah a son. You will call his name Isaac."

It was very hard for them to believe that at their age, they would have a child, but God never lies. Exactly one year later, as God promised, a baby boy was born to Sarah, and Abraham named the baby boy Isaac.

There was a great celebration that day in Abraham's household. They had a big feast for everyone. As the years went by, Isaac brought joy and laughter into his parents' lives. One night, God spoke to Abraham outside his tent. The next day, Abraham told Sarah all about the talk God had with him the night before and that he and his son must go on a trip together.

Early the next morning, Abraham and Isaac began the journey. Two of their servants went with them to help out. Sarah made sure there was enough food for all of them. It took three days and two nights to reach where they were going.

On the third day, Abraham looked up at one of the mountains and told his two servants, "Stay here with the donkeys. I and the boy will go up to worship, and then we will return to you."

Abraham and Isaac began the hard, long climb up to the top of the mountain. They took wood with them so that when they came to the top of the mountain, they could build an altar.

Finally, they climbed to the top of the mountain. There Abraham began looking for rocks to build an altar. Isaac said, "Father, we have the fire and the wood and the knife, but where is the lamb for the burnt offering?" Abraham told his son, "God will provide himself the lamb for the offering."

They continued to build the altar, and after the altar was finished, Abraham put the wood on the altar just right. He then took Isaac by the hand and led him to the altar. Isaac said nothing. He obeyed his father.

Abraham took his only son and put him on the altar on top of the wood. It was very hard for Abraham to do what he had to do next, but he knew he had to obey God. He took the knife in his hand, raised it into the air, ready to make the deep death thrust quick and sure.

Suddenly, a voice from heaven thundered with command and said, "Abraham! Abraham! Do not lay hands on the boy. Do nothing to him! For now I know you love and respect me and will always obey me because you did not hold back from me your only dear son."

Instantly, there was a strange noise in the bushes. Abraham turned around and saw a ram in the bushes. It was stuck there. God had supplied the sacrifice! For a moment, Abraham could not move, and then he fell to the ground, hugged his son, kissing him and praising God.

After Abraham and Isaac had sacrificed the ram on the altar, the Lord spoke to Abraham. This time, he said, "Because you have not held back your son, your only one, I will bless you beyond words.

"I will greatly multiply your generations so that they will be like the stars of heaven and the sand on the seashore. There will be too many to count. And through them, all the peoples of the earth shall be blessed."

God kept his promise to Abraham, and when Isaac was older, he married Rebekah, and they had two sons. One son was named Esau, and the other one was called Jacob.

It is through Jacob that God increased the families just as he promised Abraham. Today, this large number of people are called the Hebrew people.

> Blessed are they that hear the word of God, and keep it.
> Luke 11:28 (KJV)

Was Abraham a friend of God?
What was Abraham's wife name?
What was Abraham's son's name?
Did God bless Abraham just as he promised?
Did God love Abraham?

SODOM AND GOMORRAH

This is a very sad story. The people in this story hated God. They did not want anything to do with God and his ways. Instead, they chose to live wicked, evil lives apart from God. Sodom and Gomorrah are the names of the cities in this story.

Boys and girls, do you remember the story of Abraham? Abraham was called the friend of God. God gave Abraham that name. Abraham had a nephew called Lot. Lot and his wife and family lived in Sodom and Gomorrah.

The Bible tells us, boys and girls, that on a certain day, the Lord Jesus Christ and two angels came to visit Abraham. Abraham walked and talked with God. God loved Abraham. The Lord said to Abraham, "Because the cry of Sodom and Gomorrah is very great and because their sin is very heavy on my heart and very wicked, I will go down to them and see if they are doing everything that I have heard in heaven. If so, I will destroy them!"

Boys and girls, what exactly was Sodom and Gomorrah's great sin that God found to be very wicked—so evil that he would destroy Sodom and Gomorrah from the face of the earth forever?

The great sin that made God so very sad was with the men of Sodom and Gomorrah. The men of Sodom and Gomorrah loved each other in the wrong way. Instead of the men having wives and children and loving them as God had planned from the beginning of time, the men had other men as their boyfriends and as their lovers in a very sinful way. Their ways were so evil that God Himself could no longer stand it—the cry of their sin reached God's ears, and he was now going to destroy Sodom and Gomorrah from the face of the earth!

Abraham had a talk with God about Sodom and Gomorrah. God told Abraham that he could not find as many as ten people in all of Sodom and Gomorrah who loved and served the one true living God. God said to Abraham, "If there are ten people who love and serve me, I will not destroy Sodom and Gomorrah."

Abraham accepted what God said to be true. But there was one little problem, and that was Lot and his family who lived in Sodom and Gomorrah. Abraham feared that God would destroy them also.

But God who knows all things had other plans for Lot and his family. Because Abraham was God's friend on earth, God would save Lot and his family from destruction!

The Word of God tells us, boys and girls, that two angels came to the cities of Sodom and Gomorrah at evening time. The two angels came to see Lot. Lot was sitting at the gate of Sodom as you would come into the city. The gate is a very important place. The leaders and judges of Sodom and Gomorrah would sit at the gate. If anyone needed help or had a problem, the people would go to the gate of the city of Sodom and Gomorrah and speak to the leaders and judges there.

Boys and girls, how sad to find Lot sitting there at the gate with the leaders and judges of Sodom. Here are two cities ready to be destroyed by God due to a horrible sin called homosexuality (men loving other men), and here is Lot helping them as if all is well with Sodom and Gomorrah. No wonder Abraham was worried about his nephew Lot! Lot knew the commandments of the Lord God, and it makes you think how much Lot had forgotten them and it showed in Lot's life that he had forgotten God's laws!

As Lot sat in the gate of the city of Sodom, he looked up and saw two angels. Lot got up and went to meet them. He bowed his head and said to them, "My lords, I pray you, come into your servant's house and stay the night. You will have your feet washed [that shows the "dirt" of the city], and you may rise up and leave in the morning."

The angels answered, "No, we will stay in the street all night." However, Lot kept begging them to come into his house, and they did. He made them a feast and baked unleavened bread, and they ate. Before they went to sleep that night, the men of Sodom and Gomorrah went all around Lot's house. Some of the men were old, and some of the men were young. The Bible tells us that they came from every part of Sodom and Gomorrah.

These men called to Lot, "Where are the men who came to your house this night? Bring them out to us that we can have sex with them! We want them!"

Lot went out of his house to talk with the men of Sodom and Gomorrah. Lot said to them, "I pray you, brethren, do not do this evil thing. Look, I have two daughters who were never married. I will give them to you. You do to them as you wish—only don't do anything to these men."

Boys and girls, Lot's answer about giving his two daughters to these men was just as sinful and evil as the men of Sodom and Gomorrah's sin was!

How wicked were their thoughts! God tells us in his Word, in Isaiah 55:8, "For my thoughts are not your thoughts neither are your ways my ways, saith the Lord."

The men of Sodom and Gomorrah said to Lot, "Stand back. You came here as a stranger to live, and now you want to be our judge?" Remember, boys and girls, Lot sat at the gate of the city! "We will do worse with you than we will do to the two men in your house!"

The men of Sodom and Gomorrah pressed hard against Lot as they were going toward the door to Lot's house. They were going to break down the door to get to the two men! But the two angels in Lot's house put out their hands and grabbed Lot and pulled him into the house and shut the door!

The angels of God struck the men of Sodom and Gomorrah with total blindness from the most powerful man in Sodom and Gomorrah to the very least of the men in Sodom and Gomorrah. All were struck with blindness! God has no favorites—sin is sin!

The Bible says that they wore themselves out trying to find the door!

The angels said to Lot, "Is there anyone else in Sodom and Gomorrah who belongs to you? Go and get them now, and get out of Sodom and Gomorrah, for we will destroy this place because the cry of them has become great before the face of the Lord. The Lord has sent us to destroy Sodom and Gomorrah!"

Lot went to speak to his sons-in-law and said to them, "Get up and get out of this place, for the Lord God will destroy it."

But his sons-in-law laughed at Lot and stayed in Sodom and Gomorrah.

Boys and girls, because of the way Lot lived his life in Sodom and Gomorrah, he could not talk about the one true God. Who would have believed Lot now about God after living the way he did in Sodom and Gomorrah?

When the morning came, the angels made Lot hurry, saying, "Arise, take your wife and your two daughters and go. If you don't go now, you will be destroyed along with the homosexuals of these cities!"

After seeing all of this, Lot still wanted to stay, but the angels took hold of Lot's hand and the hand of Lot's wife and the hand of Lot's two daughters, the Lord God being full of mercy and compassion toward them. And the angels led them out of the cities and set them outside of Sodom and Gomorrah.

When the angels led Lot, Lot's wife, and his two daughters out from Sodom and Gomorrah, the angels said to them, "Run, escape for your life! Do not look back! Escape to the mountain! If you don't do this, you will be destroyed along with Sodom and Gomorrah!"

But Lot did not want to go to the mountain where the angels of God had told him to go. He wanted to go to a little city called Zoar.

Boys and girls, the kindness of God! God permitted Lot and his wife and two daughters to flee to the little city of Zoar!

It was morning, and the sun rose upon the earth when Lot entered the city of Zoar.

The Bible tells us after Lot and his family were in the city of Zoar that the Lord God rained down from heaven fire and brimstone upon Sodom and Gomorrah! Imagine, boys and girls, the Lord God opening up the heavens and fire and brimstone (which has a terrible smell), pouring down all over Sodom and Gomorrah! It was the holy anger of God coming down in judgment upon the men of Sodom and Gomorrah!

The Bible tells us that while these cities were being totally destroyed by God, Lot's wife looked back. She missed the things and the way of life that Sodom and Gomorrah had offered to her. She missed them so much that she disobeyed the Word of God and turned back and looked upon the destruction of Sodom and Gomorrah. The angels said to them, "Do *not* look back!" No one would want to see the holy anger of the Lord God, but she did not obey. She had to look back for her whole life, and all her things of this world were found in Sodom and Gomorrah.

Because Lot's wife disobeyed and *chose* to look back once more on Sodom and Gomorrah, the Bible tells us that she turned into a pillar of salt!

Boys and girls, did you know that when the Lord Jesus Christ walked upon this earth, he spoke about Lot's wife? He told his twelve followers, "Remember Lot's wife." The world has nothing to offer you compared to everything the Lord God can give you!

Abraham, Lot's uncle, got up early in the morning and went to the place where he stood before the Lord. Abraham looked toward Sodom and Gomorrah and toward all the land of the plain which belonged to Sodom and Gomorrah, and Abraham saw with his own eyes the smoke of the country going up as the smoke of a great fire—a smoking furnace!

Boys and girls, the Bible tells us that when God destroyed Sodom and Gomorrah, God remembered Abraham and sent Lot out of Sodom and Gomorrah before he destroyed Sodom and Gomorrah.

What the Lord wouldn't do for you! How he loves you!

Boys and girls, the Bible tells us that God's holy anger was upon Sodom and Gomorrah *only*. God did not destroy any other city, place, or person. All these years Sodom and Gomorrah had! All these chances Sodom and Gomorrah had to turn from their sin of men loving men and men having sex with other men to obeying the Lord God! How sad! But the men of Sodom and Gomorrah *chose* the way they wanted to live, and God permitted it while all the time God was putting out his hand of mercy and love toward the people of Sodom and Gomorrah. The day finally came when God, yes God himself, walked away from them! The smell and filth of their sin had reached heaven. The holiness of God could not allow the sinfulness of homosexuality to go on any longer.

How long will it take you, boys and girls, to come to the Lord Jesus Christ? God loves you. God hates your sin, but God loves you! Sin is evil. Sin is of the devil who is totally evil. There is no good in the devil. God is Good. There is no evil in God! God is holy. God wants you to be on the right side of life. That right side of life is God's side—the winning side! God's side can give you joy and everlasting life! The other side, the devil's side, will only bring you misery and a terrible ending to your life just like the sad story we just read! Don't let the devil fool you!

If you ask the Lord Jesus Christ into your heart and into your life, he will come in and give you a clean heart and a new life! The Lord Jesus Christ will be the captain of your life, and he will put you on the right road of life, and after your life on earth is over, the Lord Jesus Christ himself will receive you into heaven to live with him forever and ever!

Yes, boys and girls, the death of the Jesus Christ on that hard, cruel cross of Calvary that dark day where he shed His Blood for you and for me makes this all possible now! What will you do with the Lord Jesus Christ?

> Behold! The Lamb of God who takes away the sin of the world!
>
> John 1:29 (NKJV)

What are the names of the two cities in this story?
How many angels came to see Lot?
How did God destroy Sodom and Gomorrah?
What happened to Lot's wife when she looked back?
What little city did Lot and his daughters run to for safety?

JOSEPH

The story of Joseph is found in Genesis. Joseph came from a very large Hebrew family. He had eleven brothers. These are their names in the order of their birth beginning from oldest to youngest: Reuben, Simeon, Levi, Judah, Dan, Naphtali, Gad, Asher, Issachar, Zebulun, Joseph, Benjamin.

His father's name was Jacob (God gave him the name of Israel). His mother's name was Rachel. His mother passed away while she gave birth to Joseph's younger brother, Benjamin. They all lived in the land called Canaan.

The life of Joseph begins when Joseph was seventeen. He helped to take care of his father's sheep. He was a shepherd, as many young Hebrew boys were. One day, he was with his half brothers feeding the flock of sheep, and when he arrived home, his father asked him how his brothers were acting. Joseph reported to his father of their wickedness. It made the father very sad to hear of how wicked his sons were.

Now Israel loved Joseph more than all his children. He made Joseph a coat of many colors. When Joseph's brothers saw that their father gave Joseph this coat, they became very jealous and hated Joseph so much that they treated Joseph very cruelly.

One night, Joseph had a dream, and he told the dream to his brothers. Joseph said, "Please listen, I pray, to the dream. We were tying up the wheat in the field, and my wheat arose and stood up, and all your wheat stood around my wheat and worshipped my wheat."

His brothers said, "You really think you will reign over us and be our leader?" His brothers hated him even more.

Joseph then dreamed another dream and not only did he tell his brothers about this second dream, but he also told his father.

He said, "I dreamt that the sun and the moon and the eleven stars bowed down before me."

His father said, "Shall I and your mother and your eleven brothers bow down before you?"

His brothers became very jealous, but his father was going to make sure he would remember Joseph's dream.

One day, his brothers went to a place called Shechem to feed their father's sheep. Israel said to his son, Joseph, "Aren't your brothers in Shechem? Please go and see if your brothers and the sheep are doing well. Then come back and tell me."

Joseph obeyed his father.

When Joseph came to Shechem, a certain man asked him, "Are you looking for someone?"

Joseph said, "I am looking for my brothers. Please tell me where they are feeding the sheep."

The man said, "They are not here. They left Shechem. I heard them say they were going to go to Dothan." Joseph went to Dothan and found his brothers there. When his brothers saw Joseph from far away, they said to each other, "Look, the dreamer is coming. Let's kill him and throw him into some pit. We will tell our father that some evil animal killed him. Then we will see what becomes of his dreams."

The oldest brother, Reuben, heard the plan and said, "Let us not kill him. Instead, let's throw him into this pit." (Reuben was planning later on to take Joseph back home safely to his father. He didn't want the other brothers to harm him.)

When Joseph came to the place where his brothers and the sheep were feeding, his brothers took off Joseph's coat of many colors and threw Joseph into the pit. (The pit was used to store water, but there was no water in this pit.) They all sat down to eat, and as they were eating, they lifted up their eyes and saw a group of people called Ishmaelites and/or Midianites. They were carrying spices, balm (which is a sweet-smelling oil from a small evergreen tree), and myrrh (a plant that is used to make perfume). They were going to Egypt, the most powerful country on earth.

Judah (the fourth oldest of the brothers) said to his brothers, "What good would it do us to kill our brother and then hide his body? Let's sell him to the travelling Ishmaelites and/or Midianites. This way, we have cleaned our hands of him.

"We'll be free of him, and we won't be found guilty of murder, for after all, he is our brother." All the brothers agreed except for Reuben (the oldest). He was not there when the rest of the brothers had planned this.

When the merchants came by, they took Joseph out of the pit, and then they sold their own brother for twenty pieces of silver to the merchantmen. The travelling merchants brought Joseph to Egypt. There is someone else in the Bible who was sold for silver coins. Do you know who that person was? It was the Lord Jesus Christ.

He was sold for thirty pieces of silver by his own Hebrew people, and then they handed him over to the Romans. He then died on a cross for our sins. In many ways, Joseph is an example of the Lord Jesus Christ.

Joseph was greatly loved by his father and forgotten by his own brothers. The Lord Jesus Christ was greatly loved by his Father and forgotten by his own Hebrew people.

When Joseph's oldest brother, Reuben, returned and looked down into the pit and saw that Joseph was not there, he tore his clothes. (It was the custom in those days to tear your clothes when in deepest sorrow or pain.)

He went to his brothers and said, "Where is Joseph, where is he?" The brothers explained to Reuben what was done to Joseph, and then they all thought of a way to "hide" their sin. They killed a baby goat and took Joseph's beautiful, handmade coat of many colors and dipped it in the blood of the goat. They brought it to their father and said, "Father, we found this coat with blood all over it, and we do not know if this is your son's coat or not."

But Israel knew. He knew right away and said, "It is my son's coat. An evil animal killed him. Without a doubt, Joseph has been torn into pieces." Then Israel tore his clothes and put sackcloth on. (Sackcloth was worn when in deepest sorrow.) The father cried and cried for many days over his son's death. Oh, how he wished Joseph was alive.

All of Israel's sons and daughters tried to comfort their father, but he refused to feel better. He said, "I will go down to the grave weeping for my son." Those brothers of Joseph never thought their father would weep so much for Joseph and for so long.

But Joseph was not dead. Instead, he was in Egypt and had just been sold to Potiphar, who was an officer, captain of the guard, to Pharaoh.

Joseph became a slave at the age of seventeen. Joseph has many more things to suffer for God, which we shall soon see. The Lord Jesus Christ suffered much for us in order that we may enter heaven to live with him forever.

The Lord God was with Joseph, and the Lord God blessed Joseph while he served his master, Potiphar.

Potiphar noticed that God was with Joseph because everything that Joseph did turned into good. Potiphar thought well of Joseph and gave Joseph power over all things belonging to Potiphar and his house. From the first time Potiphar put Joseph in charge of his home and his things, the Lord blessed this Egyptian's house and his land as well.

Now Joseph was a handsome man and well-liked. In the meantime, Potiphar's wife had other plans for Joseph, evil plans. She had been looking at Joseph and thinking of Joseph in a way that God would not like.

One day, she said to Joseph, "Lie with me." She wanted Joseph to be her boyfriend even though she was married to Potiphar. But Joseph refused. He said to her, "My master, Potiphar, has trusted me with everything in his house and field. I am in charge of everything. The only thing that does not belong to me is you because you are his wife. Tell me how can I do this great wickedness and sin against God?" But day after day, she kept bothering Joseph. She would not leave Joseph alone.

One day, Joseph was all alone (all the other men servants were out of the house), and Potiphar's wife came to Joseph. She grabbed hold of his clothing and said to him again, "Lie with me."

Joseph ran away from her, leaving his clothes in her hand. He got away from her as quickly as he could.

When she saw she had his clothes in her hand, she ran to the men who were outside and said, "This Hebrew man who was brought into our house, look how he makes fun of us! He came to me and wanted to lie with me, and I screamed with a loud voice. When he heard me scream, he left his clothes with me and ran."

Potiphar's wife kept Joseph's clothing with her until Potiphar came home. When her husband came home, she said to him, "That Hebrew servant who has come to live with us has made fun of me. He came to me, and I screamed and cried with all my strength, and then he ran and left his clothing with me."

That was all Potiphar needed to hear! He was angry! When he heard those words from his wife, he became very angry!

He himself took Joseph and put him in prison, the same prison where they kept the king's prisoners. There was Joseph, not guilty of any crime, locked up in prison!

But God was with Joseph. Yes, even though Joseph was in the king's prison, God was there right beside him. God did not forget Joseph. God had great plans for Joseph. God needed Joseph, and Joseph needed God.

The Lord God showed kindness to Joseph, and Joseph became well-liked in the eyes of the jailkeeper. The jailkeeper gave Joseph charge of all the king's prisoners. That was quite a big job! The prisoners did whatever Joseph told them to do. The jailkeeper did not have to worry about Joseph's work; he knew he could trust Joseph. Everything that Joseph did was found to be excellent.

As time passed, Joseph remained in prison. It seemed as if he had been forgotten. One day, two new prisoners were sent to the king's prison where Joseph was. One of the prisoners was the chief baker for Pharaoh, and the other prisoner was the chief butler for Pharaoh.

Pharaoh was very angry with them. The captain of the guard put these two prisoners under Joseph's power.

One night, each of these two men had a dream. In the morning, Joseph came to see how they were doing—they looked so sad.

Joseph asked them, "Why are you sad?"

They answered, "We each have dreamed a dream, and there is no one here who can tell us what the dreams mean."

"The meaning of dreams belong to God. Please tell me your dreams."

The chief butler said, "In my dream, I saw a vine. The vine had three branches on it. It also had budded, and blossoms came out, and all the blossoms brought out ripe grapes. Pharaoh's cup was in my hand, and I took the grapes and squeezed them into Pharaoh's cup, and I gave the cup to Pharaoh."

"This is what your dream means. The three branches are three days. Within the next three days, Pharaoh will give you your job back. You will be chief butler again, and as his butler, you will again hold his wine cup in your hand. When everything is going well with you, please think about me and remember me before Pharaoh, I pray, to bring me out of this place. I was stolen from my country, and I have been put here in the king's prison although I have done nothing wrong."

When the chief baker saw that the meaning of the chief butler's dream was good, he said to Joseph, "I was also in my dream, and I had three white baskets on my head. The top basket had many different kinds of food in it for Pharaoh, but the birds kept eating the food out of the top basket on my head."

"This is the meaning of the dream: The three baskets are three days. Within the next three days, Pharaoh will call you out of prison, and he shall hang you on a tree, and the birds will eat your flesh."

Sure enough, in three days was Pharaoh's birthday, and he made a feast for all of his servants. He made the chief butler and the chief baker stand before him. He made the butler his chief butler again and the butler put Pharaoh's wine cup into Pharaoh's hand, but Pharaoh hanged the chief baker just as Joseph said. Instead of the chief butler remembering Joseph, he forgot all about him, and Joseph was left in prison.

After two years passed, Pharaoh had a dream, and in this dream, Pharaoh stood by the river. Out of the river came seven fat healthy cows, and they ate grass in the meadow. While the fat healthy cows were eating, out of the river came seven skinny sickly cows, and they stood by the seven fat healthy cows. The seven sickly cows ate up the seven fat cows. With that, Pharaoh awoke from his dream!

He fell asleep again, and this time, he dreamt he saw seven ears of grain. (Ears of grain are the parts that hold the grain.) These seven ears of grain were all on one stalk. They were full and good.

After that, he saw seven thin ears ripped apart by the east wind. They came up after the seven good ears of grain. The seven thin ears of grain ate up the seven good ears of grain. Pharaoh suddenly woke up and realized that it was all a dream.

These two dreams left Pharaoh very upset, and in the morning, he called for all the magicians in the land of Egypt and all the wise men. Pharaoh told them his dreams, but not one of them could tell Pharaoh what the dreams meant.

The chief butler then remembered Joseph and said to Pharaoh, "I remember what happened to the chief baker and me and how we were put in prison and we each had a dream. Only one young man who was in charge of us told us what our dreams meant. Everything happened exactly as he said it would. I was given my job back, and the chief baker was hanged."

Then Pharaoh sent for Joseph, and they quickly brought him out of jail. He shaved and changed his clothes and then went to see Pharaoh. Pharaoh said to Joseph, "I have dreamed two dreams, and there is no one here who is able to tell me what the dreams mean. I have heard of how you are able to tell the meaning of dreams."

Joseph answered Pharaoh, "It is not in me to tell the meaning of dreams. God shall give Pharaoh the right answer." Pharaoh then told Joseph the two dreams. Pharaoh said, "I have told these dreams to the magicians and the wise men of Egypt, but they could not tell me the answer."

Joseph said to Pharaoh, "The two dreams have one meaning: God has shown to Pharaoh what he is going to do. The seven good cows and the seven good ears of grain are seven years, the dreams are one. The seven sickly and skinny cows and the seven thin, empty ears of grain, which have been ripped by the east wind, are seven years of famine.

"This is what God is showing to Pharaoh: Look! There is going to be seven years of much food throughout all the land of Egypt. After those seven years are finished, there shall be seven years of famine throughout all the land of Egypt. People will soon forget about all the food that was easy to get in Egypt, for the famine will be very bad. Since you dreamt this dream twice, it has been settled before God. God will bring this to pass shortly. Now let Pharaoh find a truly wise man full of wisdom and let Pharaoh set him over the land of Egypt. Let Pharaoh also choose officers over the land. Let them set aside one-fifth of all the land of Egypt during the seven good years and let the officers set aside all the crops on this land. Let them store the food away in the different cities so that when the seven bad years come, we will have food for all the people. In this way, the land of Egypt will not be destroyed when the famine comes."

Pharaoh and his servants found this advice from Joseph to be very good. Pharaoh said to his servants, "Is there a man like this man, where the spirit of God is in him?" Pharaoh said to Joseph, "Because God has shown you this, there is no one as wise as you. Therefore, you shall be over my house, and all my people shall do as you say. Only in the throne shall I be greater than you."

Pharaoh made Joseph second-in-command over all the land of Egypt. Quite a promotion from being in prison!

Pharaoh said to Joseph, "See, I have set you over all the land of Egypt." Pharaoh took off his royal ring from his hand and put it on Joseph's hand. He put beautiful royal clothes of fine linen on Joseph, and then he put a gold chain around Joseph's neck. Pharaoh made Joseph ride in his own second chariot, and the people cried and bowed the knee before Joseph. Yes, Pharaoh made Joseph ruler in all the land, and Pharaoh said to Joseph, "I am Pharaoh, and no man shall lift his hand or foot in all the land of Egypt without your knowledge and approval."

Pharaoh gave Joseph an Egyptian name of Zaphenathpaneah, and Joseph's wife was named Asenath. She was the daughter of Potiphera, priest of On. Joseph ruled over all the land of Egypt. Joseph was thirty years old when he stood before Pharaoh.

In the next seven years, the earth brought forth much grain and fruit by the handfuls. Joseph got together all the food of the seven years and stored it in the cities. He gathered so much grain; it was as the sand of the sea. There was so much grain that the Word of God tells us you couldn't even number it.

In the meantime, Joseph had two sons who were both born before the famine came.

Joseph called the first son, *Manasseh,* which means "God has made me forget all my hard times and all my father's house." The name of the second son was *Ephraim* which means "God has made me rich and successful in the land of my suffering."

After the seven years of much food had passed, along came the seven years of famine. God never lies. The famine was in all the lands. They had no food, but in the land of Egypt, there was bread. When all the people became so very hungry, they cried to Pharaoh for bread, and Pharaoh said to his Egyptian people, "Go to Joseph and do whatever he tells you."

The famine spread itself all over the face of the earth. Joseph opened all the storehouses in all the cities and sold the food to the Egyptians. The famine was very bad in Egypt. It was so terrible in all the lands that all the people in all the countries came to Egypt to buy food.

Do you see how very much God needed Joseph? Joseph was a true servant of God. Do you remember the part when Joseph was younger and he dreamt that his brothers would bow down to him? Now we shall see how God will bring all of this to happen.

When Israel, Joseph's father, saw that there was grain in Egypt, he said to his sons, "Why are all of you just standing around? I have heard that there is grain in Egypt. Go down there, and buy us some grain so that we will live and not die."

Joseph's ten brothers prepared themselves and went to Egypt to buy grain, but Benjamin (Joseph's younger brother and the youngest of all the brothers), stayed with his father. Jacob did not want Benjamin to go with the others for he was afraid something terrible might happen to him.

The ten brothers traveled through all the land of Canaan and arrived in Egypt to buy grain.

Joseph was governor over all the land, and it was Joseph's job to sell the food to all the people of the land. Along came Joseph's brothers, and they bowed before Joseph with their faces down to the earth. Joseph saw his brothers, and he knew them, but he pretended not to know them. He spoke very roughly to them. He said, "Where do you come from?" They answered, "From the land of Canaan. We are here to buy food." Joseph knew who his brothers were right away, but they had no idea that this man, governor and second-in-command over all the land of Egypt, was their brother.

Then Joseph remembered the dreams and said to them, "You are all spies. You are here to see how the famine has left our land empty." They said, "No, my lord, we are here to buy food. That is the only reason your servants are here. We all belong to the same father. We are not spies. We are your servants." But Joseph said, "No, you came to see how empty our land looks."

They answered, "We are twelve brothers, the sons of one man in the land of Canaan. The youngest has stayed with our father, and one brother is gone."

Joseph answered, "I have said you are spies. Now we shall see. By the life of Pharaoh, none of you shall go from here until your youngest brother comes here. One of you will go and get your brother, and the rest shall be kept in prison. We will see whether you are all telling the truth. If you are not telling the truth, you are all certainly spies."

He put them all in prison for three days. On the third day, Joseph said unto them, "Obey and live, for I respect God. If you are true men, let one of the men stay bound in prison. The rest will carry grain to your house. You will bring your youngest brother to me, and then I will know that your words are true, and none of you shall die."

They all agreed to what Joseph had said. As of yet, they still had no idea this was their brother. They turned to each other and said in their Hebrew language, "Truly, we are guilty for what we did to Joseph. We threw him in that pit, and he cried out to us, but we would not listen to him. This is our punishment."

Reuben said, "Didn't I tell you not to harm this child? But none of you would listen!

Now we are paying for what we all did to Joseph."

Joseph heard them speaking to each other. He understood each word. They did not know that Joseph understood the

Hebrew language, for Joseph used a person who can speak different languages to speak to his brothers.

After hearing what his brothers said, Joseph turned away from them and began to cry. He then came back and spoke with them and took Simeon (the second oldest), and bound him before their eyes. Simeon would be kept in prison until the brothers came back with Benjamin, the youngest.

Joseph commanded the servants to fill his brothers' sacks with grain and put all their money into each of their sacks. He also commanded the servants to give the men food and water for the trip back to Canaan. The ten men loaded the donkeys with grain and departed from Egypt. When they arrived at an inn (place to rest), one of the brothers opened his sack to give his donkey some food, and was he surprised with what he saw! He said to his brothers, "Look! My money is in the sack." They all felt like fainting. They became very afraid. They said to each other, "What is this that God has done to us?"

When they arrived home in Canaan and saw their father, they said to him, "The man who is lord over all the land of Egypt spoke very roughly to us and said that we are spies. We said to him, 'We are not spies. We are twelve brothers, all sons of one father. The youngest is home with our father and one is no longer with us.' And the man, the lord of the country, said to us, 'This is how I'll know you are telling the truth: leave one of your brothers here with me and take food back with you to your land because of the famine and go. Bring your youngest brother to me, then I will know you are not spies, but honest men. I will then return Simeon to you, and you will be able to go about your business here in Egypt.'"

Then all the brothers emptied their sacks of grain and found that in all of their sacks, their money was returned to them. When all of them and their father saw the money, they became very afraid. Jacob said to his sons, "You are taking away my children, first Joseph, then Simeon, and now Benjamin. All these things are against me."

Reuben said to his father, "You can kill my two sons if I don't bring Benjamin back to you." But the father said, "Benjamin, my son, will not go with you, for his brother is dead, and he is left alone. Should some terrible thing happen to him on the way, I will go down to the grave with great sadness."

The famine became much worse in the land of Canaan, and when they ran out of the grain which they had bought in Egypt, their father said to them, "Go again and buy us some food."

Judah said, "The governor, lord of the land, told us very seriously that we will not see his face unless our youngest brother is with us. If you let us take our brother with us, we will go and buy food in Egypt; but, if you don't let us take Benjamin, we will not go because the man said, "You will not see me unless your youngest brother is with you."

The father said, "Why did you tell this man you had a brother?" They answered, "Because this man very carefully asked us about our family life, our father, and if we had a brother. We told him the truth. How did we know he would tell us to bring our youngest brother to him?"

Judah said to his father Israel, "Send the boy with me, and we will go that we may live so that neither us nor you nor the little ones may die. I will be responsible for Benjamin's safety. If I don't bring him back to you, then you can put the blame on me forever. Let us go now. We waited so long already. We could have been there and back."

Their father said, "If it must be this way, then do this: Take the best fruits that we have and put them in your vessels. Take some balm, honey, spices, myrrh, nuts, and almonds, and give them as a present to this man. Take twice as much money with you plus the money that was found in your sacks, for perhaps, it was a mistake. Now take your brother and go again to see this man, and God Almighty give you mercy when you stand before this man so that I may see your brothers, Simeon and Benjamin again. If my children are taken away from me, then my children will be taken away."

The brothers did as their father said. They took the presents, doubled the money plus the money found in the sacks, and of course, most importantly, Benjamin. They went to Egypt, and they are now standing before Joseph.

When Joseph saw Benjamin with them, he said to the ruler of his house, "Bring these men to the house, kill an animal, for all these men will have dinner with me today. His servant obeyed Joseph. The men became afraid when they were brought to Joseph's house. They said to each other, "He will use us as his slaves because of the money they found in our sacks."

When they came to the door of Joseph's house, they spoke to the steward of the house (a steward was a supervisor of the house). They said to him, "Sir, when we came the first time to Egypt, we certainly came to buy food, but when we came to the inn and opened our sacks, we looked and saw that all our money was returned to us in our sacks. We now have the money in our hands, and we want to give it back to you. We have other money with which to buy more food. We do not know who put our money into our sacks."

The steward of the house answered, "Peace be to you. Do not be afraid. Your God and the God of your father have given you treasure in your sacks. I had your money." The steward then brought Simeon, who was kept bound, to his brothers. The steward brought the men to Joseph's house and gave them water, washed their feet, and fed their donkeys. Joseph would be coming at noon. The brothers made sure they were ready, for they would be eating with Joseph.

When Joseph arrived at home, they gave him their presents, and they bowed themselves before him to the earth. Joseph asked them, "Is your father well? Is he still alive?" They answered, "He is still alive and in good health." Again, they bowed themselves before Joseph.

Joseph lifted up his eyes and saw his brother Benjamin and said, "Is this your youngest brother? May God be kind and loving to you, my son."

Joseph ran out of the room as fast as he could. He ran to his room and cried because he missed them so much. He wanted so much to hug his brother Benjamin. He loved him so much—all of them.

He washed his face and controlled himself. He went to the table and said, "Bring out the bread." He sat at a separate table, and the eleven brothers sat at a separate table. The other Egyptians ate at a separate table also. This was because it was considered an awful thing for an Egyptian to eat with a Hebrew person.

They were seated at the table according to their birth. This amazed the brothers because they didn't think that Joseph knew who was the oldest, who was the second oldest, who was the third oldest, and all the way down to the youngest, Benjamin. He set before them huge plates of food, but he gave Benjamin five times more food than the others. They all drank and ate and were very happy.

Joseph commanded the steward of the house saying, "Fill the men's sacks with food as much as they can carry, and put each man's money back into their sacks. Take my cup, my silver cup and open up the youngest brother's sack and lay it on the top of his sack with his grain money." The steward obeyed Joseph.

As soon as morning came, the men went away. When they were out of the city, but not too far away, Joseph said to his steward, "Follow those men. When you overtake them, say to them, 'Why have you rewarded evil for good? Why have you taken his silver cup?'" The steward obeyed and overtook them and said those exact words to the men.

They answered, "My lord, why do you say these things? It would be against God that your servants would do such a thing.

Look! The money that we found in our sacks, we gave it back to you. Why should we steal silver or gold from your lord's house? If you find this silver cup with one of us, that one will die, and the rest of us will be your servants."

The steward said, "Let it be according to your words. Whoever has this cup will be my servant, and the rest will be found blameless."

Quickly, they each brought their sacks to the ground and opened them up. The steward searched. He began at the oldest brother's sack and stopped at the youngest brother's sack, Benjamin. He found the cup in Benjamin's sack. All the brothers tore their clothes. They were both shocked and afraid. They loaded up their sacks again and returned with the steward back to Egypt.

When Judah and all the brothers came to Joseph's house, they fell before him on the ground. Joseph said to them, "What is this that you have done? Don't you know the power I have as governor of all the land of Egypt?"

Judah answered, "What can we say to you? How can we show you we are not guilty? God has found out our sin. Behold, we are your servants, all of us."

Joseph answered, "It would be against God to make all of you my servants. Only the one in whose hand the cup is found shall be my servant. The rest of you can go home to your father."

Judah answered, "O, my lord, please let your servant say a word, and please don't become angry, for you have as much power as Pharaoh. You asked us if we have a father or a brother. We answered, 'We have a father, an old man, and a young brother named Benjamin. He is the son of our father's old age. His older brother is dead, and so is his mother. Our father loves Benjamin so very much.' You said for us to bring Benjamin to you so that you may meet him and look upon him. We answered, 'The boy cannot leave his father, for if he leaves him, our father might die.' But you said, 'Unless you bring him here, none of you shall see me anymore.' When we arrived home, we told our father everything you said to us, and our father said, 'Go again to Egypt, and buy more food.' We said, 'We cannot go there unless Benjamin comes with us, for we will not be able to buy food unless Benjamin is with us.' Our father said, 'All of you know how my wife, Rachel, had two sons. One of them, Joseph, has been torn in pieces, and I see him no more, and now you have to take this one from me also. Should something terrible happen to him, you shall all make me to go down to my grave with much crying and sadness.'

"Now, my lord, if I go to my father and Benjamin is not with me, my father will die. His life is wrapped up in Benjamin's life. All of us shall be the cause of our father's death. There will be much crying and sadness. I, Judah, am personally responsible for making sure Benjamin returns home safely to our father.

"I told my father, 'If I do not bring the boy back to you, I will carry the blame forever.' Now, please I beg of you let me, your servant, stay here instead of the boy and let the boy return to my father with my brothers. How can I go home to my father without Benjamin and then watch my father slowly die?"

Joseph could no longer control himself before his brothers, and he began to cry. He made everyone leave the room until he stood there alone with his brothers. He then told them how he was their brother, Joseph, and he cried as he told them.

All of the Egyptians and all of the house of Pharaoh heard him.

Joseph said to his brothers, "I am Joseph. Does my father still live?" His brothers could not answer him, for they were very much afraid. Joseph was second-in-command to Pharaoh. He was very powerful. He could have them killed.

Instead, Joseph said to them, "Come close to me, please. I am Joseph, your brother whom you sold into Egypt. Don't be sad or angry with yourselves that you sold me. God sent me here to Egypt before any of you came here to preserve life. The famine has been here two years, and it will continue for five more years. The land cannot be plowed or harvested. God sent me here to make sure our Hebrew lives and the lives of others are kept alive in the earth. We are saved by God's great deliverance. None of you sent me here to Egypt. God sent me here. He has made me a father to Pharaoh and lord of all his houses and a ruler throughout all of Egypt. Go now to my father and say, 'Thus saith your son, Joseph, God has made me lord of all Egypt. Come down. Do not stay in Canaan. You will live in the land of Goshen. You shall be near to me, you and your children and your children's children and your flocks and herds and everything you have. I will take care of you, for there will be five more years of famine. I want you here. I do not want any harm to happen to you because of this famine.'"

Joseph then said to his brothers, "You see with your eyes, and Benjamin also sees with his eyes that it is me speaking all these things to you in the Hebrew language. You shall tell my father about all of my glory in Egypt and all that you have seen. Now go and bring my father here."

He hugged his brother Benjamin and wept upon Benjamin's neck. Benjamin cried upon Joseph's neck. Joseph then hugged each of his brothers and cried with them. Afterward, they all talked with each other.

Everyone in Pharaoh's house soon found out that Joseph's brothers came to Egypt. This pleased Pharaoh and the servants very much. Pharaoh said to Joseph, "Tell your brothers to load the donkeys and go to the land of Canaan. Take your father and the things of your home and come to me. I will give you the good of the land of Egypt. You shall have the best that Egypt has. Take our wagons for your little ones and for your wives and bring your father and come. Do not worry about your furniture, for everything in Egypt is yours."

Joseph's brothers did as Pharaoh commanded. Joseph gave them wagons and food for the trip as Pharaoh commanded. He gave each of them a set of clothing but to Benjamin, Joseph gave three hundred pieces of silver and five sets of clothing. To his father, Joseph gave:

ten donkeys loaded with the good things of Egypt, ten female donkeys loaded with grain and food for his father's trip back. Then he sent them away saying, "Make sure you take the most direct road home."

All the brothers left Egypt and came into the land of Canaan to Israel. They said to their father, "Joseph is alive, and he is governor of all Egypt!" Israel's heart fainted. It was as if his heart stopped beating, for he could not believe their words. But they told him all that Joseph asked them to say, and when Israel saw all seven wagons which Joseph had sent for him, Israel's spirit was lifted. He felt like a new man. He said, "It is enough. Joseph, my son, is still alive. Yes, I will go and see him before I die."

Their father took everything he had and went with them on their trip back to Egypt to see Joseph. On the way, they stopped at a place called Beersheba, and he offered sacrifices to the God of his father, Isaac.

God spoke to Israel and said, "Israel, Israel," and Israel answered, "Here I am." God answered, "I am God, the God of your father. Do not be afraid to go down into Egypt, for from you, I will make a great nation. I will go down with you into Egypt, and I will bring you out again. Joseph shall put his hand upon your eyes."

Israel then left the place called Beersheba. His sons carried Israel, their father, their little children, and their wives in the wagons Pharaoh sent them. They took their cattle and belongings from Canaan and came into Egypt. There was Israel coming into Egypt with all his children and grandchildren and over all of them was God, watching and protecting each step of their way.

The God of Israel is the same God that lives today. He never changes. It is a beautiful thing to have God watching and protecting you over each step of your life. All the people that came with Israel out of the land of Canaan were sixty-six people. Just think of how God promised Israel that he was going to make a great nation out of him. Did he? God certainly did! The Hebrew race. Nothing is impossible with God!

Israel had Judah go first and lead the way for the trip to Goshen. They arrived safely to Goshen. In the meantime, Joseph got his chariot ready and went out to meet Israel, his dear father.

When Joseph presented himself to his father, he hugged his father and cried upon his father's neck for a long time. Israel said to Joseph, "Now I can die because I have seen you and I truly know you are alive."

Joseph said to his brothers and to all the people with them, "I will now go to Pharaoh and say to him, 'My brothers and my father and all my father's house who lived in Canaan are now here. These men are shepherds. Their life is spent taking care of cattle and sheep. They have brought their flocks and herds and everything with them. When Pharaoh asks you, 'What do you do for a living?' you shall answer, 'Your servants' work has always been taking care of cattle and sheep. From the time we were young, even until today, we have been shepherds. May we live in the land of Goshen?'" (Joseph wanted them to live in Goshen, for the Egyptians thought it a terrible thing to be a shepherd.)

Then Joseph came to Pharaoh and said, "My father and my brothers and all their flocks and herds with everything they have from the land of Canaan are here now in the land of Goshen." Joseph then presented five of his eleven brothers to Pharaoh.

Pharaoh said to them, "What do you do for a living?"

They answered, "Your servants are shepherds, and so were our fathers. We have come here to live because there is no longer any grass for our flocks and herds to eat due to the famine. May we live in the land of Goshen?"

Pharaoh spoke to Joseph, saying, "Your father and your brothers came to you. All the land of Egypt is before you. Give them the best of the land. Let them live in the land of Goshen. Should any of them be excellent shepherds, make them rulers over my cattle also."

Then Joseph brought in his dear father to meet Pharaoh, king of all Egypt. (Remember, Egypt at that time was the most powerful and richest country on earth.) As Israel stood before Pharaoh, Israel blessed Pharaoh.

Pharaoh said to Israel, "How old are you?" Israel answered, "The days of my life are a hundred thirty years." Israel then blessed Pharaoh again.

Joseph placed his father and brothers in the best part of the land of Egypt. He placed them in Rameses of Goshen as Pharaoh had commanded. Joseph took good care of his father and brothers and all of their wives and children. He made sure they had enough food and clothing.

Israel lived seventeen years in the land of Egypt, and he died at the age of one hundred forty-seven. He lived to see Joseph again and Joseph's wife and two sons: Ephraim and Manasseh. He made Joseph promise to bury him where his fathers were buried, not in Egypt. Joseph promised his father he would do this.

Before Israel died, he blessed Joseph's sons (giving the greater blessing to Joseph's younger son). He then called all his sons to be with him, and after speaking with them, he passed away. He died a joyful man. Joseph lived to the age of one hundred ten. He was a great-great-grandfather. Before Joseph passed away, he said to his brothers, "God will visit the Hebrew people here in Egypt, and God will bring them out of Egypt. I want my bones to be carried out of Egypt when God delivers them." They promised Joseph it would be done. Joseph then died.

What a beautiful example Joseph is to us. When we trust and obey God, God does reward us. He will not forget us because he truly does love all of those that belong to him. Do you belong to him? Are you sure? If you are not sure, would you like to be sure that you belong to him? You can ask him right now to live in your heart and take away all your sins.

He will give you a clean heart and a new life. That is why God's Son died on the cross. He died so that you would be able to live forever in heaven with him. There is no other way.

> The things which are impossible with men are possible with God.
>
> Luke 18:27 (KJV)

What was the name of Joseph's father?
How many sons were in the family?
What was the name of the youngest son?
Why were Joseph's brothers jealous of him?
How old did Joseph live to?

BABY MOSES

Boys and girls, have you ever heard the story of Baby Moses? Baby Moses was born in a most amazing way. The Hebrew people were living in the land of Egypt. From seventy people, they have now become hundreds. They filled the entire land of Egypt!

They also had a new Pharaoh. He was not a very nice Pharaoh. He said to his Egyptian people, "Look! The people and children of Israel are more and mightier than we are. Come and let us think of a wise plan so that we may rule them. If we don't think of a plan to rule them, they will become too many for us, and then they will join our enemies and fight against us. They will take away our land and everything that belongs to us."

Their "wise plan" was not wise at all; instead, it turned out to be a very mean plan. Pharaoh set taskmasters over the Hebrew people. The Hebrew people became slaves of the Egyptians, and the taskmasters made sure the Hebrew people did their work or else they would be severely punished.

The Hebrew people had to build cities for Pharaoh. That was hard work! But the Bible states that the harder the Hebrew people worked, the more they grew in number. They had many more children! This angered the Egyptians, and they made the Hebrew peoples' lives miserable. Pharaoh kept the Hebrew people bound in chains and made them make tar and bricks. He also had them working in the fields. He made sure they did all the hard work. One day, Pharaoh went to speak with the two Hebrew midwives. One was named Shiphrah, and the other was named Puah. (When a woman was ready to have a baby, a midwife would help to deliver the baby just as a nurse would help to deliver a baby today.)

Pharaoh said to the two midwives, "When you help to deliver the Hebrew women's children, if it is a baby boy, I want him killed. If it is a baby girl, she shall live."

But these two midwives respected the Lord God, and they would not kill the little Hebrew boy babies. Children, the Bible teaches in 1 Samuel 2:30, "Those that honor me, I will honor."

Then Pharaoh called for the two midwives and said unto them, "Why have you done this? Why have you saved the Hebrew boy babies?"

They answered, "The Hebrew women are not like the Egyptian women, for the Hebrew women are strong and quick. The babies are born before we can get to their homes to help them."

The Hebrew people became more and more, and they became very mighty.

The Lord God blessed the two midwives, and he gave them families of their very own.

But Pharaoh was not happy. He then commanded all the Egyptian people, "Every son that is born to the Hebrew people shall be thrown into the river where they will drown and die. Every daughter shall be kept alive."

Now a certain Hebrew man named Amram from the Tribe of Levi married a woman named Jochebed, who was also from the same tribe. (There are twelve tribes of Israel. Levi is the name of one of the twelve tribes of Israel. It is the "priestly" tribe. The Hebrew priests were chosen from this tribe.)

After being married for a while, they had children. After Pharaoh gave this command of death for Hebrew boy babies, this certain man and woman had a baby boy. He was a beautiful baby boy. The mother hid him for three months. When she could no longer keep him hidden, she made a little boat with a cover over it. It was made from bulrushes (bulrushes are tall plants that look like grass. They grow in water). She used thin, sticky mud and tar to keep the bulrushes together.

When she finished making the little boat, she placed her beautiful baby boy into her homemade boat where it stayed tucked away among the water plants along the river's edge.

Her little daughter, Miriam, stood a little distance away from the boat to see what would happen. The little baby boy was sleeping quietly in his new little home.

God also had his eyes on the little boat, for it held a precious little person inside.

And sure enough, something did happen. There was a visitor at the river. Do you think you can guess who the visitor was? It was Pharaoh's daughter! What would she be doing at the river?

Why, she came to take a bath, of course! Her servants walked along the river's edge while she was in the water.

Suddenly, to her surprise, she discovered the little boat and called for her servants to help lift it out of the water. She had to know what was in that little boat! When she opened it and saw the child, the baby began to cry. She had pity on the little baby boy and said to her servants, "This is one of the Hebrews' children."

Then the little baby boy's sister, Miriam, said to Pharaoh's daughter, "Shall I go and get a Hebrew nurse for the child?" Pharaoh's daughter said, "Go." Who do you think the little girl ran to get?

No sooner was the little girl gone, then she was back with her mother. (Pharaoh's daughter did not know that this was the baby's real mother.) God knew. He knows everything.

Pharaoh's daughter said to the woman, "I want you to take care of this child for me. I will pay you money for doing this." The woman happily took care of the baby boy. She gave him the very best care.

The child grew, and when he became a certain age, the mother took him to Pharaoh's daughter. The boy became Pharaoh's daughter's son. Pharaoh's daughter named the little boy Moses. The name of *Moses* means "I drew him out of the water."

This was the just the beginning of Moses's amazing life. God had great plans for him. From the beginning of Moses's life to the end, God never left Moses. If you let the Lord Jesus come into your life and you give him first place in your life, then he will tell you the same words that he said to Moses, "Certainly, I will be with you." Exodus 3:12 (NASB)

God never lies.

What was the name of the country where this story takes place?
What did they call the king of this country?
What was the name of the people who became slaves?
Who was hiding in a little boat in the bulrushes?
Who was watching over the little boat until the princess found the little boat?

MOSES

Do you remember the story of Baby Moses? Do you remember how his mother hid him in a little boat in the river? Do you know why she hid him? It was because they were Hebrews. The Egyptians were told to kill any Hebrew boy baby by order of Pharaoh, king of Egypt!

Who found the baby in the river? Correct. Pharaoh's daughter. She called the baby *Moses* which means "I drew him out of the water." She took care of Moses, and he grew up to be a very smart and strong young man.

While he was growing up in Pharaoh's palace in Egypt, there was a group of people who were suffering in Egypt. They were called the Hebrew people. They were made slaves under the Egyptians. They were beaten many times by the Egyptians. Day and night, they cried out to God, asking God to send them a deliverer, someone to save them from the Egyptians.

Moses knew he was Hebrew. One day after he was grown, he left the palace and went out to see the Hebrew people. He saw the heavy loads they were carrying. He saw how they were forced to make bricks for Pharaoh so that he could have his magnificent buildings.

While Moses was watching his Hebrew people working so hard, he saw an Egyptian killing a Hebrew. That made Moses very angry. He looked this way, and then he looked that way, and when he saw that no one was watching, he killed the Egyptian and buried him in the sand.

The next day, Moses went out again, and this time, he saw two Hebrew men fighting. He said to one of them, "Why must you two fight like this?" The man answered, "Who made you to be a judge over us? Are you going to kill me the same way you killed that Egyptian?"

Moses stood still. Total fear came over him. He thought to himself, *Everyone knows what happened.*

When Pharaoh heard about this, he sent men to look for Moses. He wanted Moses killed! But Moses ran away from Pharaoh and from Egypt. He went to live in the land of Midian, which is in the desert.

When he came to Midian, he sat down by a well of water. There he saw seven daughters of a priest trying to give their animals water. They were having a hard time because shepherds came and drove them away. The shepherds were all men, and they drove the women away. They wanted to be first. Moses saw this, and he stood up and helped the women give their animals water to drink. The women invited him to their home and told their father how Moses helped them at the well.

The father told Moses, "You may live with us." Moses married one of the daughters named Zipporah, and they had a little boy named Gershom. *Gershom* means "I have been a stranger in a strange land."

After some time had passed, Pharaoh died. But they still kept the Hebrew people as slaves. The Hebrew people cried and cried to the Lord God of Israel, asking him to please save them from the Egyptians.

And God heard their prayers, and God heard their cries, and God remembered his promise to Abraham, Isaac, and Israel. God looked on his people, and he knew all about their suffering. He did not forget them.

Moses was now a shepherd, and it was his job to make sure the sheep had enough to eat and drink. One day, while he was out with the sheep, he saw something that was so amazing—he couldn't believe his eyes! He was on the west side of the desert, and when he came to the mountain of God, Mt. Horeb, the angel of the Lord came to him in a flame of fire out of the middle of a bush! He looked and saw that the bush was burning with fire, but the fire never destroyed the bush! That's a miracle! Moses wanted to turn and look at this little tree burning.

Who is the only person we know of that can do miracles? God! God is going to speak to Moses now. Let's listen to what God is going to say!

When God saw that Moses was going to turn and look at this bush, God called him from the middle of the burning bush and said, "Moses, Moses." And Moses answered, "Here I am."

God replied, "Do not come near here. Take your shoes off your feet, for the place where you are now standing is holy ground. I am the God of your father, the God of Abraham, the God of Isaac, and the God of Israel."

Moses was afraid to look at God, so he hid his face. The Lord God continued speaking and said, "I have certainly seen the suffering of my people in Egypt. I have heard their cries.

"I know the Egyptians are hurting them very much. I have come down to save them from the hand of the Egyptians. I will bring them into a land running over with milk and honey.

"Come Moses, I am going to send you to Pharaoh, king of Egypt. You are going to be the man who will save my people from the Egyptians. You will lead them out of Egypt and to the promised land."

Moses said, "Me? Who am I, Lord, that I should go to Pharaoh and take the Hebrews away from him and from Egypt?"

The Lord God answered, "Certainly, I will be with you. This is my promise that I am with you: when you take the people out of Egypt, you shall serve God on this mountain where we are right now."

Moses answered, "What shall I say? What shall I do when the Hebrews ask your name?"

God said, "You say, his Name is 'I AM THAT I AM'. You are to say, 'I AM' has sent me to you. Go, and get the wise men of Israel and tell them that I have surely visited you, and I have seen what is going on in Egypt. I will take you from the suffering and bring you into a promised land that is running over with milk and honey.

"They will listen to your voice. They will go with you to see Pharaoh, and you will say to him, 'The Lord God of the Hebrews has met with us. Let us go, we ask, for three days so that we can go into the wilderness to sacrifice to the Lord, our God.'

"And I am sure that Pharaoh will not let you go. He will make it very hard. But I will stretch out my hand, and I will kill Egypt with my wonders and miracles. I will do it right in front of him. The Egyptians will respect and like the Hebrew people. And when it is time for my people to leave Egypt, they will not leave empty. They will be given silver, gold and clothing. They will leave the Egyptians with nothing!"

Moses kept making excuses to God. He kept telling God why he couldn't do what God wanted him to do. He said, "They will not hear my voice." So God put a rod (large stick) in Moses's hand, which would turn into a snake and then back again into a stick. God told Moses to put his hand into his chest, and it turned into a terrible disease called leprosy. When Moses put his hand into his chest again, his hand returned to normal.

Then Moses said, "I am not a good speaker, Lord. I speak too slowly."

God answered, "Who made man's mouth? Who makes the deaf and the blind? Don't I, saith God? Now go, and I will be with your mouth, and I will teach you what you shall say."

But Moses begged the Lord, "Please send me a helper, someone who will be next to me and speak to Pharaoh."

God became angry with Moses, but God gave Moses his request, and God let Aaron, Moses's brother, do the speaking.

Then Moses returned with the rod in his hand, said good-bye to his father-in-law, and took his wife and child, and off they went to Egypt. For God told Moses, "Go, return to Egypt, for all the men that wanted to kill you are dead. Go and do all the wonders I have told you. Pharaoh's heart will be hardened, and he will not let the Hebrew people go, but you tell Pharaoh, 'Israel is the Lord's firstborn son. Let my son go. If you don't, then the Lord will kill your firstborn son.'"

God had Aaron meet Moses in the wilderness as Moses and his family made their way to Egypt. There Moses explained everything to Aaron.

When they came to Egypt, Moses, and Aaron met with the wise men of Israel and explained to them all the words that God had spoken to them. Then they showed the people the wonders that God had showed them. And the people believed. When they heard how God visited them and saw their suffering and has now sent someone to save them from the Egyptians, they bowed their heads, and they worshipped God.

Then Moses and Aaron went to see Pharaoh. They stood before Pharaoh and said, "The Lord God saith, 'Let my people go that they may hold a feast in the wilderness.'"

Pharaoh answered, "Who is the Lord that I should obey his voice to let Israel go? I don't know the Lord, and I will not let Israel go."

With that, Pharaoh made it even harder for the Hebrew people. Now they were ordered to get the straw for themselves. Before Moses and Aaron came, they were given the straw to make bricks. Not only did they have to find their own straw now, they had to keep making the same amount of bricks as before when they were given the straw for the bricks.

Of course, this angered the Hebrews, and when they saw Moses and Aaron, they said to them, "You made it worse for us. The Lord judge you for this."

Moses said to the Lord, "Lord, why did you let this happen? Why did you treat them so badly? Why did you send me to Pharaoh? Ever since I went to Pharaoh, he has only done evil to these people, and you have not saved them from Pharaoh."

Then the Lord said to Moses, "Now you will see what I will do to Pharaoh. After I am done with Pharaoh, he will let them go, and he will drive them out of Egypt. Moses, I am the Lord, and I appeared to Abraham, Isaac, and Israel by the name of God Almighty.

"I have many names. And to you Moses, I will appear as Jehovah. I am Jehovah, the Deliverer. The Only One who can save Israel from Egypt.

"I have made my agreement with Israel, and I will give them the land that I promised to them, the land of Canaan. I have heard their cries and have seen their tears. I am the Lord, and I will bring them out of Egypt. I will set them free from their slavery. With my arm stretched out over them, I will free them. I will be their God, and they will be my people. They will know me. I am the Lord."

Moses went back to the Hebrew people, but they would not listen to him. They felt that if they listened to Moses, he would make it worse for them, not better.

But the Lord said to Moses, "Go to Pharaoh, king of Egypt, and tell him to let my people go. I have made you and Aaron to be very important people in the eyes of Pharaoh. You will say all that I command you. Pharaoh will not let my people go, but I will do many miracles and wonders in Egypt. And then Pharaoh and all of Egypt will know that I am the Lord."

Moses obeyed the Lord. Moses was eighty years old when he stood before Pharaoh. Aaron was eighty-three years old. He and Aaron stood before Pharaoh and said those words to him.

When they finished speaking to Pharaoh the Words of God, Pharaoh said, "Show me a miracle." Aaron threw down his rod (a large stick), and it turned into a snake.

Then Pharaoh called for his magicians and his "wisemen." (These "wisemen" were really evil men, and they did not know anything about the one true God.) They also turned their rods into snakes, but Aaron's rod swallowed up their rods.

When Pharaoh saw this, he made his heart harder and said, "I will not let the people go."

The following morning, Pharaoh went to the river. There Moses and Aaron met him, and Moses and Aaron said, "The Lord God of the Hebrews has sent us to you. Let my people go."

Then Moses and Aaron took the rod and hit the rivers of Egypt, and all the waters in all of Egypt—the ponds, the rivers, the streams, their pools—all of them turned into blood! Even in their houses, the water that was kept in pots turned into blood! This was all done right before the eyes of Pharaoh and his servants.

All the fish in the rivers died, and the rivers stank (smelled very badly). No Egyptian could drink the water. The magicians and "wisemen" of Egypt also did the very same thing. When Pharaoh saw that the magicians could do the same as Moses and Aaron had done, he said, "I will not let the people go."

For seven days, the rivers stank, and the Egyptians tried to dig around them, but it was no use. There was no water to drink anywhere. Then the Lord sent Moses and Aaron to Pharaoh, and they said to him, "Let my people go. Look, I will strike Egypt with frogs."

And Aaron stretched out the rod over all the rivers of Egypt, and out of all the rivers came so many frogs in large amounts! They went into all the houses of the Egyptians. The frogs went into all the rooms. Even the bedrooms were covered with frogs! The whole land of Egypt was covered with frogs!

Pharaoh called for his magicians, and again they did the same thing. Then Pharaoh said to Moses and Aaron, "Please tell the Lord to take away the frogs, and I will let the people go to sacrifice to the Lord."

Moses answered, "Tomorrow, the frogs shall leave the land of Egypt, and you will know there is only one God." The Lord did just as Moses said, and the dead frogs were all picked up and brought together and put into a large pile. The land smelt of dead frogs.

But when Pharaoh saw that the frogs were gone, his heart became even harder than last time, and he said, "I will not let the people go."

With that, Aaron stretched out his rod and struck the dust of the land with lice! There were lice everywhere—lice in the men and women, lice in every animal in the land of Egypt!

Pharaoh called for his magicians, but this time, they could not bring lice from the dust of the land. They could not bring something that is alive, like lice from something that is dead like dirt. Who is the only person we know of that can bring something dead back to life? God! And the magicians did not have the one true God in their heart.

The magicians said to Pharaoh, "This is the work of God." But Pharaoh's heart became harder and harder and he said, "I will not let the people go!"

The next morning, Moses and Aaron stood before Pharaoh, and God sent hundreds and hundreds of flies into the land of Egypt until all the land was covered with flies! There were so many flies you couldn't see a thing! The air was filled with them!

Pharaoh said to Moses, "Go and take the people and let them sacrifice in the land." Moses answered, "We can't sacrifice here. This is not the place that God wants us to worship him. You must let us go for three days into the wilderness."

Pharaoh said, "Take away all the flies, and I will let you go into the wilderness to sacrifice." Moses spoke to the Lord, and the Lord took away the flies from Pharaoh until not one little fly was found in all the land of Egypt.

After the flies were gone, Pharaoh said to Moses, "I will not let the people go. You will not take them anywhere."

Moses and Aaron came again to Pharaoh and said, "The Lord saith, 'Let my people go that they may serve me.' At a certain time tomorrow, the Lord's hand shall be upon your cattle in the fields, your horses, your donkeys, and your sheep. They will all have a terrible disease! But the Hebrews' cattle, horses, donkeys, and sheep shall not have this disease! Then you will know that he is Lord."

Sure enough, the next day, the Lord's word came to life. Every animal of the Egyptians was struck with this horrible disease, and many of them died. But when Pharaoh saw that not one of the Hebrew's animals died, his heart became harder than ever, and he said to Moses and Aaron, "I will not let the people go."

The Lord was not finished with Pharaoh. Moses and Aaron went again to Pharaoh, and Aaron took handfuls of ashes from the furnace (a very large oven), and Moses sprinkled it toward heaven in front of Pharaoh.

The ashes turned into boils with ulcers (a terrible skin disease). The boils came on every Egyptian man, woman, and child, and on every Egyptian animal that was living.

The magicians couldn't even stand before Moses and Aaron because they were covered from head to toe with boils! But Pharaoh had made his heart so hard against God that he no longer knew how to say yes to God. Instead, he said to Moses and Aaron, "I will not let the people go."

Early the next morning, Moses and Aaron stood before Pharaoh and said, "The Lord will now hold out his hand against all of Egypt. Will you, Pharaoh, build yourself up in pride against me, saith the Lord? I will show you my power, and you will know there is no one like me. Tomorrow you will see my power. I will cause it to rain in such a terrible way that ice and water in the shape of stones and little rocks shall fall upon the land of Egypt and all the Egyptians. You have never seen anything like this before! Go and get your cattle in from the fields before it is too late!"

Moses said, "All the servants of Pharaoh who fear the word of the Lord, get your cattle and yourselves into your houses and stay there! But whoever did not obey what God said, left their cattle in the fields."

The next day, as God promised, Moses stretched out his hand toward heaven, and the hail came down in tremendous amounts!

Every man and animal left in the fields died. Fire also came down with the hail. It was a terrible, terrible thing to see! The anger of God! But in the land where the Hebrews lived, not one piece of hail came down. God kept them safe.

Pharaoh called right away for Moses and said, "Please ask the Lord to take this away, and I will let you go." Moses answered, "As soon as I am out of the city, I will spread my hands out to the Lord, and the thunder shall stop, and the hail will be no more. Now you will know that the earth belongs to the Lord!

"As for your plants, your barley and flax are dead. But the wheat, and the rye plants are still in the ground and safe." But when Pharaoh saw that the hail, thunder, and fire stopped, he again set his heart against God and said, "I will not let the people go!"

Moses and Aaron appeared unto Pharaoh the next day and said, "Thus saith the Lord, 'How long will you refuse to let my people go? Tomorrow I will send locusts [they look a little like grasshoppers] to your land. They shall cover the face of the earth. There will be so many you will not be able to see the ground. Whatever plant or tree the hail did not kill, the locusts will eat. They will fill your houses and the houses of your servants and all the Egyptian houses as well. But the houses of my people they will not fill. Neither will they destroy their crops.'"

With that, Moses turned and left Pharaoh. Pharaoh's servants said to Pharaoh, "How long will we let this man do these things to us? Let the people go that they may serve the Lord, their God. Can't you see that Egypt is destroyed?"

Pharaoh called for Moses and said, "Who are all the people that you want to go with you?"

Moses answered, "We will go with our young and our old, our sons and our daughters, our flocks and our herds. We must hold a feast to the Lord."

Pharaoh said, "Only take the men with you. Leave the rest of the people here."

With that, Moses stretched out his hand over the land of Egypt, and the Lord caused a great east wind to blow on the land all day and all night. The east wind brought the locusts so that the next morning, just as God had said, the locusts came! They covered all the land of Egypt so that you could not even see the ground! They ate every tree and every plant that was left in Egypt from the hail. The land of Egypt was destroyed! Pharaoh called for Moses and Aaron and said, "I have sinned. Please beg the Lord for forgiveness for me. I have sinned against the Lord your God and against you."

Moses went out and asked the Lord for forgiveness for Pharaoh, and the Lord answered that prayer. He caused a great wind from the west to come, and it took away all the locusts from the land of Egypt and drove them into the Red Sea. Now there were no more locusts to be found.

But as usual, when Pharaoh saw that all the locusts were gone, he hardened his heart and said, "I will not let the people go."

The men of God, Moses and Aaron, stood before Pharaoh, and Moses held out his hand toward heaven, and suddenly, total darkness came upon the land of Egypt! For three days, there was blackness. There was a thick darkness in all the land of Egypt. You could not see another person. No one moved from their place for three days. But in the land where the Hebrews lived, there was bright sunshine during the day and light during the night.

Pharaoh said to Moses, "Go and serve the Lord. Only leave your flocks and herds here. You may take your little ones."

Moses answered, "We need our animals for the sacrifices. Our cattle shall come with us. We will not leave any behind."

When Pharaoh heard that, he said, "No! I will not let the people go. Watch out, Moses! I do not want to see you again. The next time I see your face, you will die!"

Moses answered, "You have spoken the truth, Pharaoh, for I will not see your face anymore."

The Lord said to Moses, "One more horrible thing will happen to Pharaoh and to all of Egypt. After that, he will let you go from here. He will push you out! Now go and tell my people to ask each of his Egyptian neighbors for gold and silver and clothing."

The Lord was feared greatly among the Egyptian people, and they came to respect the Hebrew people. The Egyptians also thought of Moses as a great man. They gave the Hebrews all that they had asked for. The Lord made sure the Hebrews would leave Egypt full and the Egyptians would have nothing.

Moses then said to Pharaoh and to his servants, "Thus saith the Lord, 'About midnight I will go out into the middle of Egypt and all the firstborn in the land of Egypt shall die—beginning with Pharaoh's firstborn son and all the way down to the last of the servants. Even the firstborn of the beasts shall die. No one shall escape this terrible thing that I will do. There shall be a great cry throughout all the land of Egypt. You will never see anything like this again! But unto all my people, not one shall die no, not even the animals. There will be a difference between the Egyptians and the Hebrews.'"

Moses said, "Then shall all your servants come down unto me, and they shall bow themselves unto me saying, 'Get thee out, and all the people that follow thee.' And then I will leave." With that, Moses went from Pharaoh in a great anger!

The Lord said to Moses, "Pharaoh shall not listen to you. But I will do my miracles in the land of Egypt." Moses and Aaron did all of these miracles in the sight of Pharaoh, and still Pharaoh kept his heart so hard and would not let the people go from his land!

Boys and girls, how are our hearts? Let us not let our hearts become so hard that we cannot hear what the Word of God wants to tell us. Ecclesiastes 12:1 says, "Remember now your Creator in the days of your youth, while the evil days come not, nor the years draw near, when you shall say, I have no pleasure in them."

The Lord said to Moses and Aaron, "Say to all of Israel, my people, 'This month shall be for you the beginning of months. It will be like the first month of the year. In the tenth day of this month, every home shall take a lamb. This lamb will not have any marks on it. It will be a male lamb.

" 'On the fourteenth day of this month, you will kill these lambs, and you will take the blood of these lambs and put it on the two sides of the door to your home and also on the top and bottom part of the door.'"

" 'You will eat this lamb in the night, roasted with fire. You will eat bread made without yeast and bitter herbs. You must eat this all during the night. There must be nothing left in the morning. If there is anything left over in the morning, you must burn it with fire.'"

" 'While you are eating, you must be dressed and ready to go! Have your shoes on and your walking stick in your hand. You will eat this dinner in a hurry. This is the Lord's Passover.'"

" 'For when I see the blood on the sides of the door and on the top and bottom, I will pass over your house. No one will die in your home. You will be saved. But I will pass through the land of Egypt and will kill all the firstborn in the land of Egypt, both man and animal, and against all the gods of Egypt, I will show my judgment. I am the Lord.'"

" 'You are to remember this day throughout all of history. You will keep this day as a holy time. Each year, you will have this Passover in remembrance of how I saved you from Pharaoh. You will teach your little ones so that they can pass it on from generation to generation, and so shall this be remembered.'"

And the children of Israel, the Hebrews, did as the Lord had commanded Moses and Aaron. God's Word came true that night. At midnight, the Lord passed over the land of Egypt, and he killed the firstborn son of Pharaoh and all the way down to the firstborn son of the prisoner who sat in the dungeon. Even the firstborn male of all the animals died.

Pharaoh rose up in the night and all his servants and all the Egyptians, and there was a great cry in all the land of Egypt. In every house of Egypt, a child was found dead.

Pharaoh called for Moses and Aaron in the night and said to them, "Leave! Get out from among my people. Go serve the Lord your God. Take all your people and all of your cattle, flocks, and herds, and leave this place! Only bless me."

The Egyptian people gave the Hebrews all that they wanted so that the Hebrews would hurry up and leave Egypt, for they said, "We are all like dead men!" The Hebrew people quickly got themselves ready, many of them taking their bread with them before it was done.

The Hebrew people left Egypt with silver, gold, and clothing just the way God said they would. The Egyptians were left with nothing.

Boys and girls, the Lord Jesus Christ came to earth as the Lamb of God. He died on a hard, wooden cross. He spilled his blood so that you would be saved. He is our Deliverer, our Savior.

He alone can save us from a terrible place called hell. If you receive his words and let him come into your heart and into your life, he will give you a beautiful home in heaven. You will live forever and ever. You will never die. You will share in God's riches just as the Hebrews left Egypt with all of the Egyptians' riches.

Just as God said, Moses is leading his people out of Egypt into the promised land. Do you remember the beginning of this story when God said to Moses, "I have chosen you to lead my people out of Egypt?" God never lies.

And the children of Israel (the Hebrew people) traveled on foot out of Egypt. There were so many of them! Just counting the men alone, there were around six hundred thousand! Just think of it, boys and girls, they were slaves in Egypt for exactly four hundred thirty years! On the last day of that four hundred thirtieth year, the Hebrew people left the land of Egypt as *free* men and women, boys and girls!

That day, they carried out the bones of Joseph. Remember Joseph? He was a Hebrew. He had eleven brothers. His brothers sold him into slavery, and God made him into a mighty man in Egypt! He ruled under Pharaoh. Joseph became second-in-command under Pharaoh. Only Pharaoh was greater. When Joseph died, he said, "God will surely visit you, and you shall carry my bones from this place." And Moses did just that! Even Joseph knew God would bring his people out of Egypt. That, boys and girls, is called faith. Believing God no matter what happens. We all need to ask God to give us faith to trust him.

What a happy day that must have been! In that day, the Lord went before them in a big cloud. In this way, he could lead them and show them the way. In the night, the Lord went before them in a big fire! That gave them light to see where they were going.

Boys and girls, the Bible tells us in Psalms 119:105, "Thy Word is a lamp unto my feet and a light unto my path."

The Lord was leading His people right to the Red Sea. In the meantime, when Pharaoh found out that the Hebrew people left the country, he became red hot and angry!

He called for his servants and said, "Why did you let them leave? They were our slaves! Get my chariot ready!"

Just as fast as he could, Pharaoh got into his chariot along with six hundred other chariots and they were out to get the Hebrew people. Pharaoh thought, *They will not escape that easily!* But God had other thoughts!

Many times, God's Thoughts are not our thoughts and God's Ways are not our ways. And this was one of those times!

Pharaoh and his men with their chariots and horses ran hard after the Hebrew people. When they came near to Moses and the Hebrew people, the people turned around and cried out to the Lord! They said to Moses, "Were there no graves in Egypt? Must we die here? It would have been better to be slaves in Egypt than to die in this wilderness!"

Boys and girls, what happened to their faith? Does that ever happen to us?

Moses said to the people, "Don't be afraid. Just stand still and see the salvation of the Lord! The Egyptians that you see today, you will see no more. The Lord shall fight for you. Just stand still, be quiet, and watch!"

Sometimes, the Lord God must put you in a place where you can't move so that you will call out to him. He is your Deliverer!

God said to Moses, "Tell the people to go forward! Lift up your rod and hold it out over the sea. The water will go to two sides like two gigantic walls. The children of Israel shall walk on dry ground across the sea."

Then the Lord took the big cloud from the front, where he was leading his people, to the back. To the Hebrews, the cloud gave light, but to the Egyptians, the cloud gave darkness. The Egyptians could not come near the Hebrews. It was too dark for them to see!

Then the Hebrews went right into the middle of the Red Sea on dry ground! What a miracle! The waters were like a wall to them: one wall of water on the left side and one wall of water on the right side. God held that water back until the very last of his people were safe on the other side.

Then came the Egyptians! They followed hard after the Hebrews, and they also began to cross the Red Sea on dry ground, but God had his eye on them. God began to take apart their chariots.

Their wheels became loose so that they were driving without wheels through the Red Sea. How scary!

The Egyptians cried out, "Let us run from the Hebrews. The Lord is fighting for them!"

The Lord said to Moses, "Stretch out your hand, Moses, over the sea."

As soon as Moses did that, God did another miracle! In the morning, the sea returned to its normal place. The waters came rushing back with a mighty force! None of the Egyptians escaped. They all died. The waters covered the Egyptians, their horses and their chariots.

Thus, the Lord saved Israel that day out of the hand of the Egyptians and the Hebrew people saw the Egyptians dead upon the seashore. When the Hebrew people saw what God had done for them, a great respect came upon them, and they believed the Lord and his servant, Moses.

Then sang Moses and all the people this song: "I will sing unto the Lord, for he has triumphed wonderfully: the horse and his rider hath he thrown into the sea. The Lord is my strength and song, and he is become my salvation. He is my God, and I will prepare for him a place to live, my father's God, and I will praise him...who is like you, O Lord? Who is like You so magnificent in holiness, fearful in praises, doing wonders? You shall bring your people in and plant them in the mountain of your inheritance in the place, O Lord, which you have made for yourself to live in, which your Hands have made. The Lord shall rule forever and ever. Sing to the Lord, for he hath triumphed wonderfully."

Do you remember before Moses became God's chosen leader, God said to Moses, "You will return with my people and worship me here on Mt. Horeb"? In time to come, they did worship God at Mt. Horeb just as God said! How truthful and faithful God is!

Boys and girls, if you have the Lord Jesus Christ in your heart and life, then you have the most powerful person living in you! He will help you, and he will fight your battles for you. You must turn to him and put all your trust in him. He will save you, and you will sing the song the Hebrew people sang.

> Truly, truly I say to you, whoever hears my word and believes him who sent me has eternal life. He does not come into judgment, but has passed from death to life.
>
> John 5:24 (ESV)

Who did God send to deliver the Hebrew people from slavery?
What was his brother's name?
How many years were the Hebrew people slaves in Egypt?
Can you name two miracles that God did to make Pharaoh let His people go?
What did the Egyptian people give to the Hebrew people before they left Egypt?

BALAAM

For many, many years the Hebrew people were held as prisoners of the Egyptian people in the land called Egypt. Day and night, they cried out to the living God. God heard the prayers of his people and he answered them.

He sent a Hebrew man named Moses to take his people out of the land of Egypt and away from the Egyptian people. God promised to take his people to the promised land. It was a land where they would no longer be slaves. It was a land which would belong to them. It was a land filled with many fruits and good food to eat. God promised them this land if they would trust and obey him.

While Moses was leading them to this promised land, they would often camp out overnight, for they walked many miles during the day.

One night, they camped out in the plains of Moab by the Jordan River. The country of Moab became afraid when they heard that the Hebrew people were staying near them. They became so afraid that the king of Moab sent his men to a false prophet (someone who make-believes he is a messenger of God). This false prophet's name was Balaam.

When the king's men arrived at Balaam's house they said to him, "There is a people that have come out of Egypt, a mighty people. There are many of them, and they are camping very near to us.

"Come now, I pray, and curse these people for me. Maybe then, I will be able to go against them and win. I know that whomever you bless, they are blessed, and whomever you curse, they are cursed."

The king's men then showed Balaam all the money and gifts the king would give to him if he would only come to Moab to curse the Hebrew people.

Balaam answered, "Stay here for the night. I will let you know my answer as soon as I speak with God."

Balaam should have said no right away. He knew the Hebrew people were God's people. But Balaam saw all the money and all the gifts and all the riches that the king of Moab had offered to him. The things of this world meant more to Balaam than the things of God.

God said to Balaam, "Who are these men that are with you?"

Balaam answered, "These men were sent by the king of Moab. He wants me to go to Moab so that I may curse the Hebrew people. If I curse the Hebrew people, then the king of Moab will be able to send them away from his land."

God said to Balaam, "You will not go with them. You will not curse these people, for they are blessed."

In the morning, Balaam said to the men, "Go back to your land. The Lord God will not let me leave with you."

The men went back and told the king of Moab all that Balaam had said to them.

The king of Moab had another plan to bring Balaam to Moab. He sent more men to Balaam, men with more power. When they came to Balaam's home, they said, "The king of Moab will give you a very high place in his kingdom, and he will do whatever you say, if only you will come with us and curse these Hebrew people. Let nothing, I pray, stop you from coming with us."

Balaam answered, "If the king of Moab would give me his house full of silver and gold, I would not go. The Lord God has told me not to go."

But Balaam could not stop thinking about all the riches and honor he would get if he would only curse the Hebrew people. Instead of saying no and turning away from them, he said unto them, "Please stay here tonight, and I will ask the Lord God for his answer."

God came to Balaam at night and said, "Even if the men beg you again and again to go with them back to Moab, remember my word that I said to you." ("You will not curse these Hebrew people for they are blessed.")

But Balaam *disobeyed* the Lord God. In the morning, he got his donkey ready for riding, got up on it, and rode back with the men to the land of Moab to curse the Hebrew people.

The Bible tells us that God became very angry, and the angel of the Lord stood in the way of Balaam and the donkey. The angel of the Lord had a sword in his hand ready to do battle with Balaam.

The donkey saw the angel of the Lord with his sword, and the donkey turned and went into the field. Balaam hit his donkey so that the donkey would go back on the path. But the angel of the Lord stood in the path where they grow grapes. There was a wall on one side of the path and another wall on the other side of the path. When the donkey saw the angel of the Lord standing there with his sword in his hand, she threw herself against the wall and crushed Balaam's foot. Balaam hit her very hard.

Again, the angel of the Lord stood in another narrow place where there was no way to turn, either to the right or the left. When the donkey saw the angel of the Lord standing there, she fell down to the ground. Balaam hit her with a stick.

The Lord God opened the mouth of the donkey so that she could speak, and she said to Balaam, "What have I done to you that you would hit me three times?"

Balaam said to the donkey, "You have made fun of me. I wish I had a sword in my hand so that I could kill you."

The donkey answered, "For many years I have been your donkey. Have I ever done anything like this before to you?"

Balaam said, "No."

Then the Lord God opened Balaam's eyes, and he saw the angel of the Lord standing there in the way with the sword in his hand—ready to kill him.

Balaam bowed his head and fell flat on the ground! The angel of the Lord spoke to Balaam and said, "Why did you hit your donkey three times? I stood before you three times with the sword in my hand ready to punish you for your disobedience against my word. The donkey saw me, and she turned three times from me. You could have been killed. She saved your life."

Balaam said to the angel of the Lord, "I have sinned. I didn't know you stood three times in my way. I will go back and return to my home."

Balaam's life turned out to be very sad. He did some evil things later on that angered the Lord God. Balaam heard God's words but did not obey them.

Boys and girls, if we obey the Lord Jesus Christ and let him into our hearts and our lives, we can do many good things for him. God is pleased when we obey what he tells us in his Word, the Bible.

> But be doers of the word, and not hearers only.
>
> James 1:22a (NKJV)

The king of _____ wanted to destroy the Hebrew people?
What did the king promise Balaam if he would curse the Hebrew people?
Did Balaam obey God?
Who was standing with a sword in his hand ready to kill Balaam?
Did Balaam's donkey save his life?

JOSHUA

After the death of Moses, who was Israel's leader for many, many years, the Lord spoke to Joshua and told Joshua that he was going to lead the people into the promised land. God told Joshua to be strong and always trust in God and that the Lord God would be with him wherever he went. God told Joshua that he would never leave him.

After God had finished speaking and strengthening Joshua, God told Joshua to bring the people together, for it was time to begin to enter into the promised land. Now there were many things to do upon entering into this new promised land.

One of the most important things to do was to begin to settle into the land, and that meant to search out the new area before going any farther.

Joshua knew there were many cities in the promised land, and the first city was called the city of Jericho. Joshua sent some spies to search the city and to see what type of people lived there.

This certain city was very wicked before the eyes of the Lord. In fact, all of the cities that were to be destroyed were very evil cities. They all had wicked kings. From these kings and all the way down to the people, they did many terrible things to anger the Lord God. God is a Holy God, and because he is holy, he hates sin. We know he loved the people, but if the people did not want to turn from their wickedness and turn to him, the sin would go on and on, becoming worse and worse.

After the spies had entered into the city of Jericho, some of the people from this city told the king. By this time, the spies were hiding on top of a house that belonged to a woman named Rahab. She hid them under some straw. The soldiers came to

Rahab's house to look for the spies but could not find them, and so they left.

Rahab believed that God was going to destroy Jericho after hearing about the wonderful things that God did for the Israelite people after they had left Egypt. Rahab was a prostitute but now had turned to God for mercy and forgiveness.

The spies were thankful Rahab hid them, and they told Rahab that when they come back to the city of Jericho to destroy it, they would remember her. She was to put a red scarf outside her house for her and her family. In doing this, she and her family would be saved.

We can see how the Lord God truly does save and forgive those who repent and turn to him. What does the red scarf remind you of? Isn't it something how the spies told Rahab to be sure the scarf was the color red? It speaks to us of the blood of Jesus Christ which was shed for us, and through his blood, we are saved.

The spies returned home and told Joshua that the people are afraid of us and that the Lord God had delivered them into our hands.

After five days had passed, they were going to cross the Jordan River in order to get to the city of Jericho. The priests' job was to carry the ark of the covenant, which contained the Ten Commandments, across the river. The Jordan River was a very large river, and the Lord said that the priests would go first, and as soon as their feet touched the waters, the waters would part just as it did when they crossed the Red Sea while escaping from the Egyptians.

This is exactly what happened. As long as the priests stood in the middle of the Jordan River holding the ark of the covenant, all the people passed through the river on dry ground. After all the people had passed, the priests passed. After the priests' feet touched the ground again, the waters came together and formed the Jordan River.

The Lord was going to help them fight the battle at Jericho, and this is how the Lord helped them: The Lord told Joshua that he and all the men and seven priests carrying seven trumpets were to walk around the whole city of Jericho once each day for six days. On the seventh day, they were to walk around the city seven times, and on the seventh time, the priests were to blow the trumpets and all the people will shout, and then the wall of the city will fall flat down and crumble!

Joshua and all the men and priests and people did exactly as they were told by the Lord God. Now Jericho was sealed shut. No one had left the city as Joshua and the people marched around the city. On the seventh day, they marched around six times, and on the seventh time, the priests blew the trumpets and the people shouted, and then God destroyed the City. The wall fell flat, and the soldiers then ran in and destroyed the city of Jericho. They did save Rahab. She was the woman who helped to hide the spies. (Do you remember her from the beginning of the story? Very good!)

God gave them their first victory in the promised land. They remembered to thank the Lord.

* * * * *

The Lord told Joshua not to be afraid to take all the people of war with you and go to the city of Ai. "You will also take that city," God told Joshua. Joshua obeyed God. Remember that word *Obey*. He took all the soldiers with him, and a war began between Joshua and his men and the king of Ai and his men. But something strange happened! The king of Ai and his men were winning the war! In fact, Joshua and his men had to begin to turn back and run away from them. When they finally got away from the enemy, Joshua fell down on the ground and asked God what happened. God answered Joshua and told him that a terrible sin took place in the Israelite camp.

This is what happened: When the Battle of Jericho was over and the Israelite people won, God said to take all the gold, silver, brass, and iron vessels, and put them into the treasury of the Lord to be used later on in the temple. God also told Joshua not to take anything for yourself. Because the people of Jericho were evil, God did not want the Israelites to use the things from the city of Jericho.

There just so happened to be a man named Achan who disobeyed God's orders and decided to take some clothes, silver, and gold and hide them in the ground outside his family's tent. In this way, no one would know or see what he stole. But someone did see. Who was that someone? God! God always sees everything we do.

God was very displeased, and that is the reason why the whole army and Joshua lost the war. God told Joshua to tell the people to clean themselves up and tomorrow God would tell them who disobeyed him. The people obeyed, and the next day, they stood before God, and God told Joshua that Achan must die for what he did, or else the sin will make the camp of Israel unclean. Only after Achan died was the sin gone.

Now the second time Joshua and the men went to fight against the city of Ai, God led them to victory. The city of Ai went up in smoke. Joshua kept his hand up until the battle was won and over with. After the battle was over, Joshua put his hand down. And this time, everyone obeyed the Lord God, and no one took or stole anything from the city of Ai.

* * * * *

One city that Joshua made peace with was the city of Gibeon. Let's first learn something about these cities. God told Joshua not to make peace with any of these cities because they were wicked, and not one, no not one city, obeyed or even worshipped God as the true God. We know that Joshua loved the Lord, so why did he disobey him and make friends with one of the cities that God said not to? We shall see.

The city of Gibeon was very much afraid of Joshua. They had heard all the stories of how Joshua won many battles and destroyed many cities. They knew they would be next. So some of the men dressed up in old clothes and carried old, moldy bread and old bottles and pretended they had come from a faraway country.

They found Joshua, and they told Joshua they were from faraway and they were such a little city and so helpless. Joshua felt so badly for them, and since they said they were from a faraway place, Joshua made peace with them and signed a peace agreement with them. That meant that as long as Joshua was the leader of the Israelite people, they would never go to war with Gibeon. Then the men from Gibeon went away.

Joshua's mistake was that he did not go to God. God would have told Joshua the truth. Joshua had to learn that he needed to go to God first before saying yes to anything. Is that a lesson we should learn also?

When Joshua found out how the men of Gibeon lied to him and that they were really their next door neighbors and that the city of Gibeon was a very large city and not a small city, he made all the people of Gibeon become slaves. He was very angry with the city of Gibeon, but the city of Gibeon told Joshua that they would be his servants and would help him fight in the battles.

And of course, no matter what we do wrong, God always loves and forgives us. He forgave Joshua.

There was one king who heard what the large city of Gibeon did and how they made friends with Joshua. This king was so afraid that he told four other kings about this matter, and they all decided to have a war with the city of Gibeon.

The people of Gibeon told this news to Joshua, and they asked Joshua to come and help them. This time, Joshua asked God first, and God said, "Yes, and you will win the battle."

The war began, and God did help Joshua. God sent down large stones from heaven, and these stones killed many of the kings' soldiers. God also did another miracle. God made the sun and moon stand still, and he gave Joshua bright sunshine until Joshua and his army won the battle.

Meanwhile, the five kings hid in a cave. When Joshua found out that they were hiding in a cave, he told his men to roll a stone across the front of the cave. When the war was over and Joshua won, they took the stone away and killed the five wicked kings who had planned and carried out this war.

These are just a few stories of how God began to deliver city after city in the promised land to Joshua.

There are many other cities that Joshua won for the Lord God. And in each story, when Joshua asked God first, God helped him. The Lord God will help us, too when we give our heart and life to him. He loves us very much.

> Have I not commanded you? Be strong and courageous. Do not be afraid; do not be discouraged, for the Lord your God will be with you wherever you go.
>
> Joshua 1:9 (NIV)

What was the name of the first city Joshua and the Israelite people won in the Promised Land?
What was the woman's name who hid the Israelite spies on top of her house?
When the Israelite men won the battle of Jericho, did they remember to save her and her family?
What was the name of the second city Joshua and the Israelite people had to fight?
Why didn't Joshua win the battle with the third city called Gibeon?

JUDGE DEBORAH

This story took place after the death of Joshua. Israel did not have a king to rule over them like the other countries. But the other countries did not have the one true God as their God. God sent judges to guide and teach the people of Israel the holy ways of the Lord God.

This story is about Deborah. Deborah was the fourth judge of Israel. And the children of Israel again did evil in the eyes of the Lord God after Ehud, the third judge of Israel, died.

Boys and girls, because of Israel's wickedness, the Lord God sold them as slaves into the hands of the king of Canaan. His name was King Jabin. The Canaanites were powerful! King Jabin of Canaan had nine hundred chariots made out of pure iron. King Jabin used these chariots of iron against Israel. Israel had no chariots. King Jabin had a commander of his army named Sisera. The Bible tells us, boys and girls, that King Jabin ruled over the children of Israel and treated them very meanly for twenty years.

The children of Israel could not take it any longer! They cried to the Lord God for help. They wanted the Lord God to help them even though they disobeyed the Lord God. The Lord God who is full of mercy, kindness, and love heard the Israelites' cry for help and helped them by sending the Israelite people a judge named Deborah. God used Judge Deborah in a mighty way to free the Israelite people from wicked King Jabin of Canaan.

Deborah's husband was named Labidoth. Deborah lived in a home under the palm tree called "Deborah." She lived between the two cities of Ramah and Bethel, which was in the mountain of Ephraim.

The children of Israel came to Deborah for judgment, answers, and wisdom for their problems in their lives. Deborah loved the Lord God of Israel. Deborah was a holy and godly woman. She used the wisdom of God to rule the Israelite people.

It was this Deborah that God sent to his people to save them from the king of Canaan, wicked King Jabin, and his commander of the army, Sisera.

When the children of Israel cried to Judge Deborah about wicked King Jabin of Canaan, Judge Deborah sent and called for Barak the son of Abinoam from the place called "Kedeshnaphtali." Barak was the fifth judge of Israel.

Deborah said to Barak, "Has not the Lord God of Israel commanded, saying, 'Go and draw near to the mountain of Tabor and take with you a thousand men of the Israelite tribe of Naptali and the Israelite tribe of Zebulun? I, the Lord God of Israel, will come near to you to the River Kishon. At the River Kishon, you will find Sisera, the commander of King Jabin's army, with all his chariots and all of his men of war. I, the Lord God of Israel, will deliver them into your hand?' Did not the Lord God say this Barak?"

And Judge Barak said to Judge Deborah, "If you, Deborah, will go with me, then I will go. But if you do not go with me, I will not go."

Deborah answered, "Barak, I will certainly go with you, but understand this: This journey of war which you will take against King Jabin and Sisera, his commander of the army, will bring no honor to you. The Lord shall sell Commander Sisera of the army of wicked King Jabin into the hand of a woman."

With that, Deborah arose and went with Barak to Kedesh just as the Lord God of Israel had commanded. Barak called the men from the two tribes of Israel which were Naptali and Zebulun to Kedesh.

There were ten thousand men under the command of Judge Barak who went with him to Kedesh, and Judge Deborah went with Barak.

The Bible tells us, boys and girls, that Heber the Kenite who was of the children of Hobad, the father-in-law of Moses, had separated himself from the Kenites and lived in the flatland called Zaanaim, which is right by Kedesh. They showed Captain Sisera that Barak, the son of Abinoam, had gone up to the mountain of Tabor.

Wicked Sisera gathered together all his chariots of pure iron, nine hundred in all, and all the people who were with him. He brought them all together beginning from Harosheth of the nations and all the way to the river of Kishon.

Deborah said to Barak, "Arise, for this is the day in which the Lord has delivered the evil commander Sisera into your hand. Is not the Lord with you?"

Barak listened to Judge Deborah and went down from the mountain of Tabor with his ten thousand men after him, and when Judge Barak and his army of Israelites met the evil commander Sisera and his army of Canaanites, the Lord God Almighty sent heavy cloudbursts, (which was a very gigantic amount of rain from heaven), into the Kishon River, overflowing the land.

Wicked Sisera's horses and his nine hundred chariots of pure iron were no match for God! The chariots and horses became stuck in the mud and could not move. This scared the evil commander Sisera, and he got out of his chariot and ran away on foot! Some Commander!

But the Bible tells us that Barak and his men chased after the chariots and after the enemy's army all the way to Harosheth, and there, Sisera's army of men were killed by the sword of the Israelites!

Not one man was left alive of the army of the evil commander Sisera! However, Commander Sisera ran away to the home of Jael, the wife of Heber the Kenite, for there was peace between

King Jabin of Hazor and the house of Heber, the Kenite. They were friends, and Commander Sisera thought he was in a very safe place and would be able to hide from Judge Deborah, Judge Barak, and the whole army of Israel.

Did you know, boys and girls, that the Bible tells us in Jeremiah 23:24, "Can anyone hide himself in secret places that I will not be able to see him, saith the Lord. Don't I fill heaven and earth, saith the Lord?"

Boys and girls, you can hide from people, but you cannot hide from God! God is everywhere. God sees everything. God knows all things. The Bible tells us in Numbers 32:23, "Be sure your sin will find you out."

Boys and girls, we will now see this Bible verse come to life. God cannot tell a lie!

Sisera, thinking he was safe, naturally went into Heber and Jael's home, which was a tent. When Sisera came into their tent, Jael covered him with a mantle.

Boys and girls, a mantle is a large overcoat. It is made of wool or goat's hair, and sometimes it is made of cotton. It serves as protection from the wind and rain and the hot sun. It can also be a blanket at night.

This is what Jael covered Commander Sisera with.

And Sisera said to Jael, "Give me, I pray thee, a little water to drink, for I am so thirsty." And Jael opened a bottle of milk and gave it to Sisera to drink, and then she covered him with the mantle.

Again, Sisera said to Jael, "Stand in the door of the tent, and if any man comes to the door and asks if there is a man here, you will answer no!"

After Commander Sisera spoke, he fell fast asleep, for he was very, very tired. When Sisera was in a deep sleep, Jael took a nail that is used to hold down the tent, and she took a hammer and walked softly over to Sisera while he was sleeping and put the nail on the temple of the side of his head and drove the nail through his head and fastened the nail to the ground with the hammer!

Can you believe that, boys and girls? Wow! The Bible then tells us that the wicked commander Sisera of King Jabin's army died. Right after Jael killed Sisera, Jael saw Barak and said to him, "Come and I will show you the man you are looking for." And when Barak came into the tent, behold, he saw Sisera dead—the nail in the temple of Sisera's head.

God stopped King Jabin, the king of the Canaanites, on that day before the children of Israel.

And the Israelites became great, and they fought and won against King Jabin of the Canaanites until the Israelites had destroyed Jabin, the king of Canaan. And the land of Israel had peace and rest for forty years! When everything was over and the battle was won, Judge Deborah and Judge Barak sang a song of praise to the Lord God, saying, "Praise ye the Lord for fighting for Israel when the people willingly offered themselves. Hear, O ye kings, give ear, O ye princes, I, even I, will sing unto the Lord. I will sing praise to the Lord God of Israel."

Boys and girls, these are only the first two verses of the song that Deborah and Barak sang. In Judges 5:1–31, you will find the whole song that Deborah and Barak sang.

Boys and girls, can you sing a song of praise to the Lord God for what he has done for you? Do you know what God has done for you? God has sent his only Son, the Lord Jesus Christ, into this world to die on a hard, wooden cross for your sins and my sins. The Lord Jesus Christ gave his all for us. He shed his blood for our sins. The Lord Jesus Christ did not deserve to die, for he did nothing wrong. He was perfect. We should have died on that cross for our sins for we are sinners. We are not perfect.

When you ask the Lord Jesus Christ into your heart and you tell him all your sins, he will come into your heart and into your life. He will give you much joy and a home in heaven. The choice is up to you, boys and girls.

> As many as received him, to them gave he power to become the sons of God, even to them that believe on his name.
>
> John 1:12 (KJV)

What was the name of the woman who was the fourth judge of Israel?
There was also a man judge. Do you remember his name?
What was the name of the wicked commander?
What was the woman's name who killed the wicked commander?
What did she use to kill the wicked commander with?

GIDEON

Many generations after the death of Joshua, the Lord sent judges to guide the people. This is a story about a young man named Gideon who was called by God to free the Israelite people from their enemies.

Israel had again become wicked in the eyes of the Lord, and the Lord sent prophets to speak to the people of Israel, but they would not listen. Instead, they had the prophets stoned to death. But this time, the Lord had warned Israel that their enemy, the Midianites, would takeover their land and destroy everything they owned.

It was because of their disobedience to God that God let their enemies attack them. He wanted to correct their sinful ways and have them turn to him and not to false idols made of stone and clay.

When the Midianites came to takeover Israel, they did destroy all of Israel's crops, cattle, sheep, goats, and land. They left Israel with nothing. Israel cried out to the Lord God for help, and the Lord answered their prayer. God never fails to answer prayer. Even when we do not stay true to God, God *always* stays true.

This is the story of how their prayer was answered: An angel of the Lord sat under an oak tree and watched a young man named Gideon working. Gideon was a farmer, and he was probably trying to plant some seeds and till the ground since the Midianites had destroyed all of the Israelites' crops and land.

The Bible tells us that the angel of the Lord appeared unto Gideon and spoke to him. The angel said to Gideon that he was going to save the people from the hands of the Midianites and their other enemies. At first, Gideon was very much afraid because he was just a farmer and knew nothing about leading an army against the Midianites—their dreaded enemy.

Gideon was unsure whether everything the angel of the Lord said was true or even if the angel of the Lord was really sent from God. Gideon asked the angel for a sign so that he might be sure. The angel of the Lord told Gideon to prepare an offering for the Lord God. Gideon went into his home and found a lamb and made some bread and set them upon an altar. Then the angel of the Lord took the end of the staff, which he was holding in his hand and touched the lamb and the bread, and the Bible tells us that fire came out and burnt up the offering.

Well, after Gideon saw what happened right before his eyes, he didn't ask any more questions. The Lord spoke to Gideon and encouraged and strengthened him for the job which lay ahead.

The next morning, Gideon took ten men (his servants), and during the night, went into the temple where they worshipped the idols and broke a certain idol named Baal.

When the people discovered what happened and found out how Gideon and his ten servants went into the temple at night and destroyed the idol of Baal, they came to Gideon's home looking for him.

Gideon's father, Joash, was standing outside the home as the men came to his house. The men told Joash that they wanted Gideon killed for what he had done to their most holy idol. Joash said to them, "If Baal is a god, let Baal take care of Gideon. Are you going to fight Baal's battles for him?" The men thought it through and left. But before leaving, they placed a curse upon Gideon. But the Bible tells us that the spirit of the living God came upon Gideon, and Gideon blew a trumpet so as to bring together all the men of Israel to form an army.

How many times do we do things believing with all of our hearts that what we are doing is right, but later on when we are alone, questions enter into our minds, and we wonder if it is the right thing? That is exactly what happened to Gideon. He was so unsure that he had to ask God directly for a sign to prove that he was to be the leader. Gideon took a piece of cloth, which came from the sheep. This is called fleece. He asked God to have the fleece become wet with dew and the ground to remain dry. The following morning, God had done what Gideon asked. Still not quite sure, Gideon asked God to have the fleece remain dry this time and the ground to become wet. The next morning, God had done what Gideon asked. Gideon was satisfied.

Gideon rose up early the next morning with his army and set up camp by a well so that the Midianite army was on the north side of them by a hill in the valley. The Lord spoke to Gideon and told him that the people that are with you now are just too many. Let the ones who are afraid and full of fear return home to their families. Twenty-two thousand men went back to their homes, and that left Gideon with ten thousand men.

Gideon brought the men down to the water. It was here that God told Gideon there were still too many men for the battle. God told Gideon to watch the way the men drank the water and to only choose those men who lapped up the water as a dog would do. There were three hundred men who drank this way. The other men drank on their knees keeping their heads down at all times.

Gideon sent them home. So with three hundred men and God's approval, they set off to win the battle. During the night, God told Gideon to take his servant and himself to the Midianite camp where God would show Gideon how he was going to let Israel win the war and free them from their enemies.

Gideon was going to hear for himself what the enemy was saying. The Midianites and the Amorites and the children of the East lay along the valley like grasshoppers, the Bible states. There were so many of them! Just at the time that Gideon came with his servant to the edge of the Midianite camp, a man was telling a dream he had where he saw a loaf of bread come tumbling into their camp turning over one of the tents till it laid flat. The other man listening to the story said, "This story can only mean that Gideon will win the war tomorrow and God has delivered us into their hands." After Gideon heard this, he went back to his camp worshipping God, thanking him for the victory and the freedom of his people.

He then told his men to arise for the Lord God had delivered the enemy into our hands. He divided the three hundred men into three companies, and he put a trumpet into each man's hand, along with a lamp in a pitcher so that the enemy would not discover them as they made their way to the Midianite camp.

Gideon said unto them, "Watch me, and when I go to the outside of the camp, follow me. When I blow the trumpet, you shall also blow your trumpets."

Gideon and one hundred men came to the outside of the enemy's camp and blew their trumpets and broke the pitchers and shouted, "The sword of the Lord and of Gideon." The other two hundred men did exactly the same thing. The Midianites saw this and fled before the army of Israel. Israel chased them and overtook them. God led them to victory that day, and Israel once more received freedom from their enemies. Now God would see whether or not, this time, they would remember the true God and learn to obey and look to him for all things.

When you allow God to work in your life, he will begin to show you just how much he loves and cares for you. He can fill the emptiness in your life and leave you totally satisfied, amazed and full of joy! There is no one like the one true God.

> For the Lord your God is the one who goes with you to fight for you against your enemies to give you victory.
>
> Deuteronomy 20:4 (NIV)

Who appeared to Gideon to ask him to free the Israelites from their enemies?

When Gideon wasn't sure that God spoke to him, what did he put down on the ground?

How many men did Gideon start with?

How many men did Gideon end up with?

Each man was given a _____ and a _____?

SAMSON

This is the exciting story of Samson, the strong man. You will find this story written in the Hebrew part of the Bible called Judges. Samson was a judge of Israel for twenty years. Israel did not have any kings yet to rule over them; instead, the Lord God sent judges to guide them. This is where the story of Samson begins.

Again, the children of Israel did evil in the eyes of the Lord God, and the Lord God had their enemy, the dreaded Philistines, come upon them and capture them and keep them as prisoners for forty years.

Now, there was a certain man from a place called Zorah who came from the tribe of Dan. His name was Manoah. The Bible does not tell us the name of his wife, but the Word of God does tell us that she could not have any children.

On a very special day, the angel of the Lord appeared unto the woman and said, "Behold, you are not able to have children, but now you will give birth, and you shall have a son. Be careful, I pray, and do not drink wine or any strong drink. Neither eat any unclean thing, for you shall give birth to a son. You will not cut his hair. This little boy child will be a Nazarite unto God from the moment he is formed in the womb. He will deliver Israel out of the hand of the Philistines."

The angel of the Lord then left the woman. The woman went to find her husband, and she told him, "A man of God appeared unto me, and his face was like the face of an angel of God, very awesome to look upon. I did not ask him where he came from, neither did he tell me his name. But he did say unto me, 'Behold, you will give birth to a son. Do not drink any wine or strong drink, neither eat any unclean thing for the child will be a Nazarite to

God from the moment he is formed in the womb until the day of his death.'"

The husband, Manoah, prayed, asking the Lord, "O my Lord, let the man of God whom you sent come again unto us and teach us what we shall do unto the child that shall be born."

God listened to the prayer of Manoah, and the angel of God appeared again to the woman as she sat in the field. But Manoah, her husband, was not there. The woman ran and told her husband, "Behold the man appeared unto me, the same man who appeared the other day before me."

Manoah quickly got up and followed his wife, and when they came to the man, Manoah said, "Are you the man who spoke unto the woman?"

He answered, "I am."

Manoah said, "Now let your words come to pass. How shall we instruct the child and how shall we train him?"

The angel of the Lord said to Manoah, "All that is said unto the woman, let her be aware of it and obey. She may not eat of anything that grows from the vine, neither let her drink wine or strong drink. Let her not eat any unclean thing. All that I command her, let her do."

Manoah said to the angel of the Lord, "Stay, I pray, until we have prepared a baby goat for you."

The angel of the Lord answered, "Though you will have me to stay, I will not eat any food, and if you offer a burnt offering, you must offer it unto the Lord God." (Manoah did not know that he was speaking to the angel of the Lord.)

Manoah said unto the angel of the Lord, "What is your name so that when all of this comes to pass, we will remember you and your words?"

The angel of the Lord replied, "Why do you ask me my name seeing it is *Wonderful?*"

So Manoah took a baby goat with the meal offering and put it on a rock and offered it up to the Lord God. While it was being offered up to the Lord God, the angel of the Lord performed a miracle. Manoah and his wife looked on.

As the flame went up to heaven from off the altar, the angel of the Lord went into the flame of the altar and went up into heaven. Manoah and his wife saw this miracle, and they fell on their faces to the ground.

The angel of the Lord did not appear anymore to Manoah and his wife. Manoah then realized who the angel of the Lord was, and he said to his wife, "We shall surely die because we have seen God."

But his wife answered, "If the Lord God wanted us to die, he would not have received our burnt and meal offering from our hands, neither would he have shown and told us all these things at this time."

The woman did give birth to a son and called his name Samson. The child grew, and the Lord blessed them. The Word of God tells us that the power of God began to work in Samson while he lived in the camp of Dan between the places of Zorah and Eshtaol.

One day, after Samson was grown, he went down to a place called Timnath, where the Philistines lived. When he arrived home, he told his father and mother, "I saw a woman in Timnath, a Philistine woman, who I want for a wife. I want you to get her for me so that I may have her as my wife."

His father and mother answered, "Isn't there a woman among your own people that you can have for a wife? Must you find a wife among a people who do not honor the Lord God?"

But Samson replied to his father, "I want her. Get her for me."

The father and mother did not know that the Lord God was going to use this as an opportunity to show the Philistines the power and strength of the man Samson. (Remember, the Israelite people were still under the rule of the Philistines.)

Again, Samson went down to Timnath. This time, he took his father and mother with him. When they came to the vineyards (a place where they grow ripe, juicy grapes), a young lion came out of the vineyards and roared against Samson. Samson stood there alone against this roaring young lion.

The Bible tells us that the the power of God came mightily upon Samson, and Samson grabbed that lion and tore him into pieces as if he were a baby goat. He fought and killed that lion with his bare hands. Samson did not tell his father or mother what he did.

They continued on to Timnath, and when they arrived at Timnath, Samson met and talked with the Philistine woman he wanted as his wife. He was very happy with her.

After a while, he returned to the woman so that he may take her as his wife. As he was walking, he saw the body of a dead lion, and he noticed that there was a huge group of bees and honey in this body of the lion.

With his hands, he took the honey from the body of the lion and ate it. When he came to his father and mother, he also gave them some of the honey, but he did not tell them where he got it from.

Samson's father then went to visit with the Philistine woman, the one his son wanted to marry. In the meantime, Samson had prepared a feast as the young men would do when marrying a woman. He had thirty men at his feast, and it lasted seven days.

Samson thought it would be a good time to ask them a riddle, and so he said, "If you can give me the answer to this riddle within seven days of this feast, I will give you thirty pieces of linen garments and thirty pieces of clothing. But if you cannot tell me the answer, then you will give me thirty pieces of linen garments and thirty pieces of clothing."

They answered, "Tell us the riddle so that we may hear it."

Samson said, "Here is the riddle: Out of the eater came forth food, and out of the strong came forth sweetness." For the next three days, they did not have an answer to Samson's riddle. In fact, they didn't have the answer on the fourth, fifth, or sixth day, either.

On the seventh day, they came to Samson's wife and said, "In some way or plan of yours, make your husband tell you the answer to this riddle. If you don't, we will burn you and your father's house with fire. Do you want him to take everything we have? Is this what you want?"

Samson's wife wept before him and said, "You don't love me. You tell my people a riddle, but you won't tell the answer to me, your wife."

Samson said, "I haven't even told my own father and mother the answer, and shall I tell you?"

But she kept crying and crying in front of him until he could no longer bear to see her this way. He finally said yes to her, and he told her the answer on the seventh day.

Once she knew the answer, she told it to her people. (Remember, her people were going to burn her and her father's house with fire if she did not find out the answer.)

The men of the city said to Samson on the seventh day before the sun went down, "This is the answer to the riddle: What is sweeter than honey and what is stronger than a lion?"

Samson answered, "If you would not have bothered my wife, you would not have had the answer."

The power of the Lord God came upon Samson, and he went down to Ashkelon (a place belonging to the Philistines), and he killed thirty men and took their clothing and linen garments and gave it to the men who answered the riddle.

His anger then went away, and he returned to his father's house. But in the meantime, Samson's wife was given to a Philistine friend of Samson's. Samson did not know they had done this.

After some time had passed, Samson visited his wife. It was during the wheat harvest, and he brought with him a present for her. It was a baby goat. When he arrived at Timnath, Samson said to his father-in-law, "I will go into the room to see my wife." But his father-in-law would not allow him to enter the room. Instead, he said to Samson, "I truly thought you hated her, and I gave her to your friend. She is now his wife. I have a younger daughter who is prettier. I pray, thee, marry her."

But Samson said, "Even though I will do evil to the Philistines, I shall be found more innocent than they because of what they have done to me."

Samson stormed out of the house, and he caught three hundred foxes. He tied the foxes together by their tails. He then took torches (long sticks) and put one in between each of the foxes' tails. Next, he lit each torch with fire, and he let the foxes go. They ran into the long, standing grain that was waiting to be picked by the farmers. Then the foxes burnt all the Philistines' grain, vineyards, and olive groves.

When the Philistines saw that all of their crops were destroyed, they became red hot and angry! (Their faces turned almost as red as the fire!)

The Philistines said, "Who did this?" The people answered, "Samson, the son-in-law of the Timnite. He became truly mad when his father-in-law told him that he had given his wife to his friend."

Then the Philistines got up and went to Samson's wife's home, and they burnt alive her and her father with fire. (What a horrible thing to do!)

Boys and girls, when someone has been very mean to you, you must remember what the Word of God teaches. And that is first, let God take care of it, for he is the true judge; and secondly, treat the person with kindness because the Lord Jesus Christ treated his enemies with kindness. That is an example for us to follow. The Lord God will help you, and he will give you the strength to be able to do this. He will also reward you for this.

When Samson found out, he said, "Now I will get even with them."

He killed them with a great slaughter. When he was done, he went to live on the top of the rock of Etam.

The Philistines had plans of their own for another attack of revenge on Samson. They gathered themselves together and went into Judah (part of the Israelite camp). The men of Judah said, "Why are you coming up against us?"

They answered, "To bind Samson and to do to him what he has done to us."

Three thousand of the Israelite men went to the top of the rock of Etam to visit Samson, and they said to him, "Don't you know that the Philistines rule over us? What did you do to them?"

Samson answered, "What they have done to me, I have done to them."

The three thousand men answered, "We have come to take you and to bind you so that we may deliver you into the hand of the Philistines."

Samson said, "Promise me that you will not kill me."

They said, "No, we will not kill you, but we will bind you tightly, and we will deliver you into their hand, but we will surely not kill you."

So they bound Samson with two new cords and brought him up from the rock. When Samson came unto Lehi (the place where the Philistines were staying), the Philistines shouted against him. They were armed and ready to kill him. But the power of the Lord God came mightily upon Samson, and the cords which were tightly bound around him became as string that was burnt with fire, and they fell loosely from his strong arms.

He found a jawbone of a donkey, and with that jawbone, he killed a thousand men! When he finished killing all the Philistine men that came up against him, he said, "With the jawbone of a donkey, heaps upon heaps, I have killed a thousand men."

He threw the jawbone away, and he called the place *Ramathlehi*, which means "The hill of the jawbone."

Of course, after killing all those men, Samson became very thirsty, and he called on the Lord God and said, "Into my hands you have given this great victory, and now shall I die because of thirst and fall into the hands of men who do not honor you?"

God heard his prayer and did a miracle to satisfy Samson's thirst. God split a hollow place that was in the jawbone of the donkey, and water gushed out for Samson to drink.

When Samson finished drinking, his strength came back to him, and he called that place *Enhakkore*, which means "The well of him who cried."

Yes, Samson was Israel's judge for twenty years while they were under the hand of the Philistines. But even a judge has weaknesses, and Samson was no different. He had one big weakness, and that was he loved foreign or strange women that did not worship the true and living God of Israel. This led to Samson's downfall.

After he had killed the thousand Philistine men and drank water from the jawbone of the donkey, he went to a foreign place called Gaza. There he met a prostitute (one who sells their body for money), and he stayed with her.

The Gazites found out that Samson was there, and they secretly circled around him and waited for him all night in the gate of the city. They said to each other, "In the morning, we shall kill him."

But Samson tricked them. He got up at midnight, and he took the doors of the gate of the city along with the two posts and the bar holding the gates. He put them on his shoulders and carried them up to the top of a hill where he threw them down and walked away as if nothing had happened. (The Gazites knew what happened, though.)

The Bible tells us that some time later, Samson loved a woman who lived in the valley of Sorek. Her name was Delilah. The Philistine rulers went to see Delilah one day and said to her, "Make him tell you the secret of his strength. What is it that makes Samson strong? We must find this out. We can then come up against him and win. We will bind him, and then we will torture him. If you can do this, we will all give you one thousand and one hundred pieces of silver."

When Samson arrived to see Delilah, she said to him, "Tell me, please, I pray you, where does your great strength lie? What can be done to you so that you will no longer be strong? Please tell me."

Samson answered, "If they bind me with seven green cords that were never dried, then I will become weak, and I will be as an ordinary man."

The Philistine rulers gave Delilah seven green cords (never dried), and she bound Samson with them. While she was tying Samson up, there were Philistine men hiding and waiting with her in the room. She cried out, "The Philistines are come against you, Samson."

Samson broke the cords as if they were a piece of rope when it has been torched by fire. Still, they did not know where his strength came from.

Delilah said to Samson, "You have made fun of me by telling me lies. Please tell me, I pray, what will take your strength away."

Samson responded, "If you bind me tightly with new ropes, ropes that were never used before, then I shall become weak, and I will be like an ordinary man."

Delilah did just that. She took brand new ropes, never used before, and tied Samson up with them. The Philistine men were hiding and waiting in the room with her. She said to Samson, "Samson, the Philistines are come against you."

The ropes fell off like a thread from Samson's strong arms. Delilah said, "Samson, again you have made fun of me. Please tell me what will make you weak."

He answered, "If you weave the seven locks of my hair with the web (strong material used to braid hair), then I will become weak."

Delilah weaved Samson's hair and fastened it with a pin and said, "The Philistines are upon you, Samson."

Samson awoke from his sleep, got up, and took the pin of the beam and the web with him.

Delilah said to Samson, "How can you say you love me when your heart is not with me? Three times you have made fun of me, and you still have not told me where your strength lies."

Each day, all day long, Delilah urged Samson to tell her where his strength came from. Samson, tortured by her words, finally said to her with all his heart: "No razor has ever come upon my head, for I am a Nazarite unto God from the day I was formed in the womb. If you shave my hair, I will become weak, and I will be like an ordinary man."

Delilah knew that Samson had finally told her the truth, for he said it with all his heart. Delilah did not care about Samson; instead, she sent for the Philistine rulers, saying, "Come quickly! Samson has told me the truth!"

The Philistine rulers came right away and gave Delilah her money. She made Samson fall asleep on her knees. Then she had a man come in, and he shaved all the seven locks of hair from Samson's head. She began to hurt Samson, and she saw that his strength was gone from him.

Then she said, "Samson, the Philistines are upon you." He arose from his sleep and said, "I will get up and loose myself."

Samson did not know that the Lord God departed from him. Samson chose to leave the Lord God out of this area of his life, and Samson suffered because of the choice he made.

The Philistines came, and they took Samson (once the strongest man that lived), and they took his eyes out. Then they took him down to Gaza and bound him with chains of bronze. They made him "grind the meal" (take seeds of grain and crush them into powder). It was done between two heavy stones called millstones. This was a job for a slave or beast to do. Poor, poor Samson!

Even though Samson forgot about God, God remembered Samson. The Bible tells us that Samson's hair began to grow again.

One day, shortly after the capture of Samson, the Philistine rulers came together to offer a great sacrifice to their god, Dagon. It was a time of happiness for them. They said, "Our god has delivered Samson, our enemy, into our hands. He was the destroyer of our country, and he killed many of our people."

Dagon was an idol made of stone. It was the national god of the Philistine people. The two most famous temples were at Gaza and Ashdod. The idol had the face and hands of a man and the tail of a fish. This idol could not hear, it could not see, it could not speak, and it had no feelings. It was a cold, dead piece of rock. It was to this "god" the Philistines worshipped.

While they were enjoying themselves, they said, "Bring Samson here so that we may make fun of him." When they had brought Samson to the party, they placed him between two pillars (pillars were tall towers made of stone to hold the building together). There they teased and made fun of Samson. And I am quite sure they also made fun of the living God of Israel.

Samson quietly said to the young boy who led him by the hand, "Let me feel the pillars that hold up the house. Allow me to lean upon them."

Now the house was full of men and women and all the rulers of the Philistines were there as well. On the roof of the house were about three thousand men and women. They were all making fun of Samson.

This time, Samson remembered the Lord God, and he called upon him, saying, "O Lord God, remember me, I pray and strengthen me one more time, O God, so that I may take revenge immediately upon the Philistines for taking away my eyes."

Samson took hold of the two middle pillars upon which the house stood. He held one pillar with his right hand and the other pillar with the left hand.

Samson continued his prayer to the Lord God, saying, "Let me die with the Philistines." He bowed himself with all his strength, and the house fell on the Philistine rulers and upon all the people who were in it. They all died.

Samson killed more people at his death than he killed when he was living. His brothers came along with the members of his father's household. They took Samson and buried him where they had buried Samson's father, Manoah.

Samson judged Israel for twenty years.

Samson, strongest man that ever lived, was strong when he stayed close to the Lord God. He became the weakest man when he left God out of his life. This story is in the Bible to teach each one of us that if you truly want to become a mighty servant for God, you must stay near the Lord God at all times during your life. It is God's strength that makes you strong, not your own.

> Draw near to God, and he will draw near to you.
>
> James 4:8a (AKJV)

What was Samson's father's name?
Who gave Samson his power and strength?
What was the name of the enemies of the Israelites?
Samson used a jawbone of a _____ to kill one thousand of his enemies?
What was the name of the woman who helped to destroy Samson?

RUTH

The story of Ruth is a beautiful love story of God's kindness and mercy shown through a young woman's love for her mother-in-law. God blessed this young woman for her obedience by returning to her the love she had given to others.

This story takes place during the time when judges ruled over Israel. There were no kings yet. There was also a famine in the land, which meant there was not enough food to eat.

A certain man named Elimelech and his wife, Naomi, and their two sons, Mahlon and Chilion, left their home in Bethlehem of Judah because of the famine and moved to a strange country called Moab where the people neither worshipped nor obeyed the living God.

It was in this country that Ruth was born. Out of this idol worshipping country did the lovely young woman come from which God would use. He was going to take her world and change it into something beautiful to be looked upon by others in amazement.

It was in this country of Moab that Elimelech, (Naomi's husband), died. Now only Naomi and her two sons were left.

After Naomi's husband passed away, her two sons married women who were Moabites. One was named Orpah, and the other was named Ruth. After ten years, Naomi's sons also died, and now only the three women remained.

Naomi decided it was time to return to her homeland of Judah (which is in Israel), for she heard that the famine was over.

Naomi said to her two daughters-in-law, "Go and return each to your mother's house, and may the Lord treat you with kindness as you have treated my sons and me. May the Lord give you rest in your new husbands' homes." Naomi kissed them and cried. Orpah and Ruth told Naomi, "We will return with you to your people." Naomi answered, "Why will you come with me? I have no other sons that I may give you for husbands, and if I did, would you wait for the sons to grow up? No, my daughters, for it makes me very sad for your sakes that the hand of the Lord is against me." All three women cried and were so very sad. Orpah then kissed her mother-in-law and left, but Ruth held on to her mother-in-law and would not go back.

Did you know that the name *Ruth* means "friendship" We shall now see how Ruth remains a loyal and true friend and servant to Naomi.

Naomi tried to make Ruth go back to her country and live with her people, but Ruth said to Naomi, "Please don't tell me to leave you or go back from following you. For where you go, I will follow and where your home is, I will stay with you. Your people shall be my people, and your God shall be my God. Where you die, I will die, and there I will be buried. I will not let anything come between us except death itself."

After hearing this and seeing that Ruth would not change her mind, Naomi stopped trying to talk her into staying. So on they went back to where Naomi began. When they had reached Bethlehem, they stopped, for it was at Bethlehem that Naomi would once again settle into.

The whole city heard of Naomi's return, and they all came out to meet her as she and Ruth entered the city. They asked, "Is this Naomi?" Naomi answered, "The Almighty has dealt very bitterly with me. I left Israel with everything, and now I have come back with nothing. Call me Mara." *Mara* means "bitter."

When we have the Lord in our hearts and leave him to go out into the world, we will always leave the best behind us. God sometimes lets this happen to teach us a lesson because, at times, we will not listen to him when he speaks to us. If we obey what it says in James 4:8, "Draw near to God, and he will draw near to you," we will never have to go through this sad lesson.

So Naomi returned with her daughter-in-law, Ruth, and settled down in Bethlehem at the beginning of the barley and wheat harvest.

Now, Naomi had a close relative named Boaz who was related to her husband. Boaz was a very rich and powerful man. One day, Ruth said to Naomi, "I will go to the field, and if I should find kindness in the eyes of the owner of the field, I shall pick up the ripened grain of wheat and barley that has fallen from the hands of the servants who are gleaning the field."

It so happened she came to a part of the field which belonged to Boaz. She heard Boaz ask one of his servants, "Who is that young lady?" The servant answered, "It is the Moabite woman who came back with Naomi from the country of Moab. She asked me if I would please let her gather barley and wheat after the reapers.

"She has come every day and has continued from the morning even until now gathering the barley and wheat. She has rested for only a little while in the house."

Boaz then walked over to Ruth and said unto her, "Do not go to glean in another field, neither go from here, but stay close by my women servants. I have told the young men not to bother you in any way, and when you are thirsty, you may go and drink the water that the men will draw for you from the well."

Ruth bowed to the ground and said to Boaz, "Why have I found kindness with you, and why is it that you should even notice me seeing that I am a stranger from another country?"

Boaz answered, "I know all you have done for your mother-in-law since the death of your husband and how you left your mother and father and the land of your birth and you are here now with a people that you have never known before. May the Lord God give back to you what you deserve and reward you because you have come to trust in him."

Ruth replied, "Let me find favor in your sight, my lord, for you have been very kind to me even though I am different from the other women."

Boaz answered, "At mealtime, I would like for you to have your lunch with the others working in the field."

Ruth ate with the servants of Boaz at mealtime until she was full and then went back into the city where she lived with her mother-in-law, Naomi. Ruth then showed Naomi all she had gleaned that day in the field, and Naomi said, "Blessed be the man who has shown this kindness unto you and has noticed you and helped you." Ruth pointed him out to Naomi, and Naomi shouted, "Blessed be the Lord who has not held back his kindness to us! Ruth, the man's name is Boaz, and he is a very close relative of ours."

Ruth said, "He told me I can stay close by the young men until the harvest is ended." Naomi said, "It is good that you are with his other women servants, and it is good that you are not going to another field to glean." So Ruth stayed close to the women servants of Boaz and gleaned until the end of the barley and wheat harvest and lived with her mother-in-law, dear Naomi.

Ruth remained obedient throughout the entire time she lived in Bethlehem, and she came to trust in the Lord God, the Almighty One. Because of her obedience to Naomi and to the Lord, we shall now see the reward which the Lord God will give to her.

Boys and girls, when we honor the Lord God and put him first in our lives, he will help us and reward us. In this way, he is showing us how pleased he is with our life. Others will see a difference in our life, and they will respect us for it.

Naomi decided it was now time to give her attention to Ruth and to see if she would be able to help Ruth find someone she could share her life with. She came to Ruth one day and said, "Isn't Boaz one of our near relatives? I want you to get dressed and go to Boaz's house. There you will wait until he has finished eating and drinking. When he lies down, you will go in and uncover his feet and lie there. He will tell you what to do next." Ruth did exactly as Naomi said and went to get ready.

What Naomi said might sound very strange to us, but in those days, this was a custom. It was done to let the near relative know that he must take care of unfinished responsibilities which Naomi had because her husband was dead.

That night, Ruth did everything Naomi said. She waited for Boaz to finish eating and drinking, and when he laid down, she uncovered his feet. At midnight, Boaz woke up surprised and said, "Who is there?"

Ruth answered, "I am Ruth, your handmaid. Spread your skirt over your handmaid for you are our near relative."

Boaz answered, "Blessed be the Lord, my daughter, for you have shown more kindness at the end than at the beginning. You have not gone after the men whether they were poor or rich. Do not fear. I will do everything you ask, for all the city of my people know that you are a pure woman. It is true, Ruth, that I am a near relative of Naomi's, but there is someone who is even closer than I am. Tomorrow I will meet with him, and we will talk about this matter. If he cannot do the things that need to be done for Naomi, then I will do them."

So Ruth laid at his feet until morning and then got up and left before anyone could see her. She went back to Naomi and told her all that happened that evening. Naomi said, "Have a little patience, dear, for Boaz will not rest until this matter is finished."

Boaz went up to the gate, and at the gate, he met with the other relative. He asked him to please sit down so that they may talk about this important matter. (In those days, the gate to the entrance of the city was where they held their very important meetings. It was a place of authority, and you would find the most important men called "elders" gathered there during the day.)

It was at this gate that Boaz and the relatives and the ten men or "elders" of the city met. They had to talk about the necessary steps they must take regarding Naomi's future because her husband had passed. Someone must carry on the responsibilities.

Boaz said to the relative, "Naomi has come back again from Moab to Bethlehem, and she is selling a piece of land which belongs to our brother Elimelech. I would like for you to buy this piece of land in front of the elders. In this way, the elders will see that you are willing to save and buy back Naomi's inheritance, and you will not let her future die." The other relative answered, "I will buy it." Boaz then said, "The day you buy this field, you must also marry Ruth, the Moabitess, because she was married to Naomi's son, who has also died." The relative answered, "This I cannot do, for if I marry Ruth, I will lose my inheritance, and my children will have no inheritance. No, I cannot save and buy back Naomi's inheritance, but you can. You buy the land."

The relative then took off his shoe and gave it to Boaz. (In those days, to make sure an agreement stayed true, a man would take off his shoe and give it to his neighbor in front of all the elders and people.)

Boaz turned to the elders and people and said, "You are witnesses this day that I have bought all that belongs to Elimelech and his two sons, Mahlon and Chilion. Moreover, Ruth the Moabitess will be my wife. I will give her children, and her husband's name will be remembered. You are my witnesses."

All the elders and people answered, "We are witnesses. The Lord bless Ruth and may the Lord give her children."

Boaz and Ruth did get married and became husband and wife. After a while, Ruth had a little baby boy named Obed. Naomi was so happy and often took care of little Obed while he was growing up.

The women of the city praised Ruth and told Naomi, "Blessed be the Lord who has not left you this day without a relative, and may little Obed's name become famous in Israel. May Obed bring you happiness in your older years, for Ruth who loves you has treated you better than seven sons."

Naomi's happiness once again came back into her life as she realized the Lord never left her but, in his great and loving way, made a way that blessing would once again enter into her life.

The Bible tells us, boys and girls, that Obed grew up to be the father of Jesse who grew up to be the father of David. David grew up to be a great king of Israel. Yes, David was loved so very much by God. Because David obeyed God, God called David, "A man after my own heart." From David's family line came the Lord Jesus Christ.

This beautiful story was allowed to happen in God's perfect time because a young woman chose to follow the ways of our loving God over the cares of the world. The cares of the world would have passed away with nothing worthwhile to show for them.

Let us allow the Lord God to work in our lives so that as we get older, we can look back and say from a pure and humble heart:

> I have fought a good fight, I have finished my course, I have kept the faith: henceforth there is laid up for me a crown of righteousness, which the Lord, the righteous judge, shall give me at that day: and not to me only, but unto all them also that love his appearing.
>
> 2 Timothy 4:7–8 (AKJV)

How many sons did Naomi have?
Who was Naomi's husband?
Can you name the daughter-in-law that did not stay with Naomi?
What was the name of the place Ruth and Naomi traveled back to?
Who fell in love with Ruth and married her?

HANNAH

This is a beautiful Bible story of how God heard and answered the prayer of a godly woman who honored both the Lord God of Israel and her husband. We will see that when she first came to God, she was empty, and when the Lord answered her prayer, he satisfied her fully. Hannah learned to put the Lord God first in her life, and God blessed her for this.

Hannah lived during the time when Israel did not follow in the steps of God. They wanted to do things in a different way than what God wanted. Because they chose their own way, they brought suffering and pain upon themselves.

One of the things that God had wanted was for all the husbands to have one wife. Even Hannah's husband, Elkanah, had two wives. One was named Penninah, and the other was named Hannah. The Bible does not say too much about Penninah, but the Word of God does tell us that Penninah had children and Hannah had none.

Many times, Penninah would tease Hannah because she had no children. She would make Hannah cry. It made Hannah very sad to know that she could not have children.

Once a year, Elkanah and his two wives would go to a place called Shiloh. At Shiloh, they would worship and offer sacrifices unto the Lord God of Hosts. God has many names, and in this story, we shall learn another one of his Names. We must remember that although God has many names, he never changes. The Bible tells us that, God *always* remains the same.

When it was time for Elkanah to offer the sacrifice, he gave to Penninah and to her sons and daughters their portions, but he gave to Hannah (whom he loved very much), a big portion even though she could not have any children. This would make Hannah very sad, and she would begin to cry so much that she would not eat any food. Elkanah would have to speak soft, loving words to her and try to make her feel better. He would remind Hannah about how much he loved her.

But again, Penninah teased Hannah about not having any children, and it made poor Hannah cry very much. This time, after they had offered their sacrifices and had eaten, Hannah got up and went to the place of worship, (which is called the temple), and there she poured out her soul to the Lord God and cried out with many tears, telling the Lord all about her sorrow, weeping while explaining to the Lord why she was so sad. She then made a promise to the Lord of Hosts, and the Bible states that Hannah said, "O Lord of Hosts, if you will surely look on the deep sadness of your handmaid and remember me and not forget your handmaid, but if you will give to your handmaid a little boy child, then I will give to you, O Lord, all the days of his life, and there shall no razor come upon his head." She prayed these words from her heart with only her lips moving.

In those days, when people made a promise unto the Lord concerning a child, they would not cut the child's hair so that they would keep their promise to God.

Now, in every temple, there is a priest. The priest's job was to make sure the people obeyed the rules of God, and he would help the people who would come to the temple looking for answers to their problems by reading and explaining the Word of God to them. The name of the priest who was at the temple at Shiloh was Eli. From the minute Hannah entered the temple crying, Eli watched her.

He watched her as she prayed. Her lips were moving, but no sound came from her mouth. She kept the words to her prayer deep within her heart. Only the sounds of her tears poured out. Eli the priest thought she was drunk.

When Hannah finished telling the Lord God her request, Eli walked over to Hannah and said, "How long will you be drunk? Put away your wine."

Hannah answered, "No, my lord. I am a woman that is very sad, and every part of me is hurting. I have not been drinking wine or strong drink, but I have poured out my heart and soul to the Lord. Do not see me as an evil woman, for out of my heart, there is a lot of sadness, and this is why I have been speaking to God."

Why couldn't Eli see this? He was a priest. He should have known after all the years of being a priest and helping people what a very sad person would do. Maybe his heart was not as pure as Hannah's heart?

Children, how are our hearts? We must tell the Lord Jesus everything at all times so that our hearts can remain pure and clean like Hannah's heart.

Then Eli answered Hannah and said, "Go in peace, and the God of Israel will give you the answer to your prayer that you have asked Him." Hannah answered, "Let your handmaid find kindness and mercy in your sight."

So Hannah left, not like when she came in, sad and crying, but instead, she was so happy and excited because she was able to tell the Lord everything! Hannah knew her prayer was going to be answered because she had something we all should have— faith. She believed with all her heart that God heard every word and would answer her prayer.

Hannah is a beautiful example of a woman, who, in her pain, went straight to God and told him everything and didn't worry about what the priest or anyone else thought. We should learn from Hannah that we also must run to God and tell him everything. Then we must believe that God will answer our prayer.

We should be happy, for the Lord God will answer our prayer.

The next morning, Elkanah and his family, including Hannah, rose up and worshipped the Lord and returned to their home in Ramah, which is a little town in Israel. There the Lord remembered Hannah's prayer, and after a time, Hannah had a little boy named Samuel. *Samuel's* name means "I have asked of the Lord."

The following year, Elkanah went up to the temple at Shiloh, and Hannah followed later on, for Samuel was still a little baby. When Hannah was at Shiloh, she went to the temple and said to Eli the priest, "I am the woman you saw praying to the Lord. I prayed for this child to be born, and the Lord answered my prayer. Therefore, I will also remember my promise that I made to the Lord, and I will give little Samuel to the Lord for as long as he lives."

Hannah was so happy! In the Bible, she praises the Lord and talks about how great our Lord God is. Hannah then gave little Samuel to Eli, the priest, as she promised God. Every year, Hannah would go up to the temple and visit Samuel and would bring him a new coat that she had made for him. Eli blessed Elkanah and Hannah, and the Lord gave Hannah more children. She had three more sons and two daughters.

Samuel grew strong in the Lord and was well-liked by both the people and especially God.

Yes, Hannah remembered her promise, and because the Lord answered her prayer, she also kept her promise and gave Samuel to the Lord. The Lord used Samuel in a great way. The Lord needed Samuel so much.

The Lord needs more men and women and boys and girls like Hannah who would live a life full of faith and would give back to the Lord what the Lord has given them. And yes, the Lord will greatly use that thing or person because you gave it to the Lord with a pure heart and lots of love. It can become a beautiful tool in the Lord's hand.

Boys and girls, let us pray to be like Hannah, who was a true servant of God.

The prayer of a righteous person is powerful and effective.

James 5:16 (NIV)

What was the name of Hannah's husband?
Why was Hannah so sad?
Did God answer Hannah's prayer?
What was the name of Hannah's little boy?
What did Hannah bring her son every year when she visited him?

KING SAUL

After Israel had entered the promised land, God sent Israel many judges and leaders to guide them. He sent them men such as Joshua, Gideon, and Samuel, to name a few.

But Israel was not satisfied with what God had done for them. They looked at the other countries around them and saw that they had kings to rule over them. They also wanted to have a king, especially now that Samuel was getting older and no longer able to judge them, and Samuel's sons were doing many wicked things in the eyes of Israel and God.

But instead of turning and looking to God for their needs, they went to Samuel with their complaints and told him of their strong wishes of wanting a king to rule over them. They wanted to be like everyone else.

It broke Samuel's heart when he heard this news. He prayed to the Lord God, and God spoke to Samuel and said, "Listen to the people of Israel, for they did not say no to you, Samuel, but they have said no to me that I should not rule over them.

"Despite everything that I have done for them and performed many, many miracles and great acts in their sight, they pushed me aside to worship a handmade piece of metal which they called an idol that can neither hear, smell, touch, feel, or see to become their god. Now they again come to me and tell me that they want to be like everyone else around them, and they want a man to rule over them. Samuel, let them have their king, but let them know what it will be like when a man rules over them instead of God."

Samuel went before the crowd of people and said, "Listen, unto the words of the Lord. This is what the king will demand of you: That you take your sons to be captains over thousands and hundreds and fifties, and they will leave your home never to return again but will work in the king's fields and will plow the king's ground and reap the king's harvest. They will make instruments of war and new chariots for fighting. He will take your daughters to cook and clean and bake in the king's palace.

"He will take your best fields, vineyards, olive yards for himself and his officers and servants. He will take your best servants to be his servants. He will demand one-tenth of your land and everything that is grown on that land. You will cry out to the Lord God because of the king you have chosen, and the Lord God will not hear you in that day."

Nevertheless, the people refused to listen to Samuel's warning. Instead they said, "Give us a king. We want a king. We want to be like the other countries so our king will judge us, and when we go to battle, our king will go before us."

Samuel told the Lord every word the people said, and the Lord said, "Make them a king."

When we give our life to the Lord God, let us not forget that we are different from the others around us. He rules in our hearts and lives. He is everything we need. He provides and cares for our every want.

Still God could not forget them. He loved them and wanted them to see what the difference would be between a man ruling over them and God ruling over them. The Bible states that there was a man of the Tribe of Benjamin. How many tribes are there? Twelve is correct. Benjamin was the smallest of the tribes. Out of the Tribe of Benjamin would come the new King of Israel. His name was Saul. Saul's father was named Kish. One day, Kish had Saul and a servant go looking for some lost donkeys. Saul and the servant had passed through four lands, and upon entering the fifth land called Zuph, Saul told the servant, "Let us return to my father's house, for we cannot find the donkeys."

Saul's servant answered, "I know there is an honorable man that lives in this city. A man of God can surely tell us where the donkeys are. I have some money we can give in exchange for the information."

The Lord knows the future, and he had told Samuel the day before that Saul and his servant were looking for him in search of finding their donkeys.

When Saul appeared before Samuel with his servant, the Lord told Samuel, "This will be the new King of Israel."

Samuel told Saul not to worry about the donkeys, for they were found three days ago, and then Samuel showed Saul what his new role in life would be.

That evening, after sending the servant away, Samuel anointed Saul with oil, proclaiming him king in a secret ceremony, which was soon to be made known to all the people. Saul returned home telling no one about being the first king of Israel.

Not too much later, at a place called Mizpah, Samuel brought all the people together and told them they would have a king today even though they had rejected God. He had the people line up by tribes, and from the tribes, he called out Benjamin's tribe. He called out Kish's family and then called out Saul's name. But Saul was nowhere to be seen. God told Samuel that Saul was hiding among the baggage. They ran and got him from behind the baggage. Now Saul was more handsome than any other man in Israel. He was also taller than any other man in Israel. God knew this is what the people wanted. He knew the outside appearance would please the people of Israel very much. God is so different from us in that the Bible tells us that God looks at our heart, not our outside appearance to see what we are really like.

The people did like Saul. They celebrated with their new king and gave him many gifts, and Saul ruled his kingdom from the city of Gibeath.

As usual, in the beginning, Saul was an obedient king both to God and to Israel—but only to build up pride. It is this pride in man that brings his downfall. Saul was no different. Here is one story that resulted in the end of his kingship and kingdom.

Samuel said to Saul, "You are going to fight the people of Amalek, and you must destroy them and everything they own, not sparing one thing. God has instructed me to tell you this."

The reason why God wanted Amalek destroyed was because when the people of Israel were called to flee Egypt and run for their lives from Pharaoh, the people of Amalek came up behind them and killed many of them. They killed a lot of the weak, the sick, the weary, and tired. The people of Israel could not fight back because they were not prepared to fight; instead, they were worn out and tired from escaping from Pharaoh of Egypt.

But now after taking the promised land and having rested from their enemies, God once again remembered Amalek and told Saul through Samuel, "I do not want you to take any of their things nor spare any person or animal. They are a wicked nation before my eyes."

Saul did kill the Amalekites, but he disobeyed God in that he kept alive Agag, the very king of the Amalekites, and he also took the very best of their sheep and lambs plus everything else that was good.

The Bible tells us that Samuel rose up the next morning to see Saul. Saul came out to greet Samuel, as he usually did, not thinking or not trying to show the sin which he was guilty of. But Samuel asked Saul, "What is it that I am hearing? The bleating of the sheep and the lowing of the bulls. Tell me what this means."

King Saul explained to Samuel that the people made him disobey the command of the Lord God. He told Samuel the people took the sheep and the bulls themselves to sacrifice to the Lord God.

God then told Saul, through Samuel, "It is better to obey than sacrifice. In this, you have greatly sinned."

Yes, what Samuel had to do next was very hard, but he knew it was the right thing to do. He told King Saul, "Your kingdom will be taken away from you, and it will be given to a neighbor that's better than you. I will give it to a man after my own heart."

As Samuel turned to leave, Saul caught hold of his robe and tore it in two. Samuel turned to Saul and said, "The Lord will tear the kingdom of Israel from you in the same way you have torn my robe."

Samuel never saw King Saul again until Saul's death.

This is a sad story. Not everything in life ends happy. This story is in the Bible for a reason. It is to show us what happens when we knowingly leave God out of our lives. Many people end up with lives like this—torn in two. Choosing to be away from God, they die without Christ in their hearts and lives. Had they only said yes to the Lord Jesus, he would have changed their sorrow into joy and their night into morning. No longer would they have to face this world alone—without Christ—for he promises to be with us wherever we go.

I hope you have made Christ the captain of your life, looking to him and not to yourself for the help you need in your life. You will have a perfect person watching your life, knowing fully what your future will be. He will make perfect everything that concerns you. What a lovely, personal touch to your life, he would be.

> And the blood of Jesus Christ, his Son, cleanseth us from all sin.
>
> 1 John 1:7b (AKJV)

Who was Samuel?
Who became the first King of Israel?
What tribe did he come from?
Why did the people like him?
How did the king disobey God?

DAVID AND GOLIATH

The story of David and Goliath is one of the most famous stories of the Bible. It is the story of a young shepherd boy by the name of David and a Philistine giant called Goliath. Let's first learn a little about each of them.

David came from a little town in Israel called Bethlehem. Who else do we know was born in that town one glorious star-filled night? It was the baby Lord Jesus who came to save each one of us from sin.

David's family was considered to be poor. Shepherds were one of the poorest people in that time. David's father was named Jesse. Jesse had many sons of which David was the youngest. One of David's chores was to take care of his father's sheep. He would take them to green pastures and see to it that they had enough grass to eat and water to drink. I'm sure it was during these quiet times, he shared many hours with the Lord—talking and singing songs to Him.

The Bible tells us that David was a handsome boy and very godly. David loved the Lord. He wanted to obey the Lord God. Do you want to obey the Lord God?

The Israelites had one major enemy during the young life of David and they were the dreaded Philistines. The Philistines and the Israelites often went to battle together. But one day something different happened.

A giant appeared to the Army of Israel. His name was Goliath. He came from a place called Gath. He was awesome and just one look at him would frighten you! He would come down from the mountain to the valley below each day, proclaiming to Israel, "Choose you a man for me to fight with. If he will kill me, then we will be your servants. Should I kill him, then you shall be our servants. I challenge the army of Israel this day. Give me a man to fight with."

When King Saul and all the men of war heard these words, they became very discouraged and lost hope. They were so terrified that no one, not even King Saul, would answer the challenge of Goliath. This went on day after day.

One day, along came the shepherd boy of Bethlehem. David was sent by his father to see how his brothers were doing since they were all in the King's army. As he was talking to his brothers, Goliath came down to the valley and made his challenge known again to the army of Israel. David heard the words of this giant. He became angry at Goliath. How dare he dishonor and curse the armies of Israel!!

The servants of King Saul heard the words of David and ran to tell King Saul. King Saul had David brought before him. David told the King, "Don't be discouraged and don't lose hope because of Goliath. I will go and fight this Philistine." Saul said, "You can't fight Goliath. You are too young and he's a man of war." David told King Saul about his experiences of being a shepherd and how he had killed a lion and a bear with his bare hands and if the Lord had protected him from those animals, then surely the Lord would protect him from being killed by a giant that curses the name of the Living God.

With this, Saul had David put on his very own armor and a helmet of brass was placed upon David's head. But David told Saul, "I can't wear this armor. I'm not used to it and I haven't learned how to fight with it on." So he removed the armor and with a staff and a sling in his hand, he chose five smooth stones from the brook and put them in his shepherd's bag and headed off to meet the awesome giant of Gath.

You can imagine how insulted and angry Goliath became when he saw this young shepherd boy in his shepherd's clothes armed and ready in his way to do battle with the Giant of Gath!!

The Philistine cursed David by his gods, the Bible states. Goliath told David, "Come to me and I will give your flesh to the birds of the air and to the beasts of the field."

But David, strong in the Lord, answered Goliath, "You come to me with a sword and a spear, but I come to you in the Name of the Lord of Hosts, the God of the armies of Israel. The very armies you dare to curse. This day the Lord will deliver you into my hand; and I will kill you and I will give your body to the birds of the air and to the beasts of the earth, that the whole earth may know that there is a God in Israel for the Lord doesn't need a sword and spear; for the battle is the Lord's and He will give you into our hands."

Then the Philistine giant arose and came near David and David ran toward Goliath, took hold of one of the five stones and with his sling aimed it right at Goliath and the stone sank into Goliath's forehead, which was not protected, causing Goliath to fall upon his face to the earth. David then ran over to Goliath, drew the giant's sword and killed him and cut off his head.

David did win over the Philistine and Goliath's body was fed to the birds of the air and the beasts of the earth.

Here is a perfect example of a young boy being brought up in the teachings and ways of the Lord Almighty—having fully trusted God in everything, never doubting. Because of his faith, God answered David's prayer and used David to show all of Israel and the Philistines the great things God can do in the life of a person who trusts in Him. God will use you despite your age, looks, background. He looks upon the heart.

Let us bow our heads and ask the Lord from a true heart, if He will help us to become more faithful to Him and use us as He did David to prove His mightiness to the people who do not have the love of our Lord Jesus Christ in their hearts and lives.

Have faith in God.

Mark 11:22 (KJV)

Lois M. Bitler

What little town was David born in?
What was David's job?
What was the name of the giant of Gath?
Who helped David fight the giant of Gath?
Did David win the battle or did the giant win the battle?

ELIJAH: CHALLENGE OF BAAL

Elijah the Prophet was a mighty man of God. He lived during the reign of King Ahab and Queen Jezebel. King Ahab and Queen Jezebel worshipped an idol named Baal. They made all of Israel worship this idol. In fact, they had just killed many of God's people who would not bow their knee to this idol called Baal. Together, King Ahab and Queen Jezebel were very wicked unto the Lord God. The Bible states King Ahab did more to anger the Lord God of Israel than all the kings of Israel who were before him.

Elijah was one man who would not worship Baal and, as a prophet of God, tried to stop the people of Israel from also worshipping Baal.

Baal was a false idol made of stone from man's hand. Many evil ceremonies, rituals, and feasts were held in this false idol's name. During these ceremonies, rituals, and feasts, the people and so-called "prophets" of Baal would often perform dances. While they were dancing, they would cut themselves with swords and knives believing that Baal would listen to them. They also sacrificed their children alive to Baal, again, believing that Baal would see them as being "good."

It is wonderful to see how in the midst of all this confusion and turning away from the one true God, Elijah came forth, shining brightly for the Lord God and untouched by their filthy and wicked deeds.

Elijah met with King Ahab one day and asked for a chance to challenge these so-called "prophets" of Baal. So King Ahab took all the prophets of Baal to Mount Carmel.

There Elijah spoke unto all the people and said, "How long will it take you to decide between two choices? If the Lord be God, follow him but if Baal, then follow him."

The people remained silent. Then Elijah said unto the people, "I am the only prophet of the Lord that remains, but there are four hundred fifty prophets of Baal. Give us two bulls one for them and one for me. We will each build an altar, put wood on the altar, cut up the bull in pieces, and lay it on the altar. We will put no fire under the bull. You call on your god, and I will call on mine. The God that answers with fire, let him be the true God."

All the people agreed.

Elijah told the prophets to go first. They took the bull, built their altar, put wood on the altar, and then laid the bull across the altar. They then cried out to Baal. The Bible states, "They called upon Baal from morning until noon saying, 'O Baal, hear us.' But there was no voice, neither any that answereth."

The prophets of Baal even jumped up on the altar that they had made—crying out to Baal for an answer.

Now it is noon, and they cried out to Baal for quite some time. Elijah said to the prophets, "Cry louder, for he is a god. Either he is talking or he is chasing someone or he is on a journey or perhaps he is sleeping, and you must wake him up."

They began to cry louder and even cut themselves with swords and knives until the blood flowed out on them, but there was no answer. They continued until evening. In fact, Elijah gave them most of the day to have their god answer them. There was no voice, neither any answer. Just empty silence.

Elijah then called to the people, "Come near unto me."

Jesus said, "Come unto me all ye that labor and are heavy laden, and I will give you rest." (Matthew 11:28)

Elijah then started to repair the altar of the Lord that the wicked King Ahab and Queen Jezebel of Israel (along with many of the people), had destroyed. He then took twelve stones (one stone for each tribe of Israel), and built the altar. He put the wood on the altar and cut up the bull in pieces, laying it evenly on the altar.

Elijah then did something very different. He dug a deep hole all around the altar and said, "Fill four barrels with water and pour it on the burnt sacrifice which was the bull."

Why would Elijah do something like that, knowing full well that water puts out fire? Not only did he ask the men to do this, but when they finished pouring four barrels of water on the sacrifice, Elijah again said, "Do it a second time." They did. And again, Elijah said, "Do it a third time." The water ran round about the altar, and he filled the deep hole also with water. Elijah was making it very hard for God to answer this prayer!

By this time, it was evening. Elijah the Prophet lifted up his eyes toward heaven and prayed, "Lord God of Abraham, Isaac, and Israel, let it be known this day that you are God in Israel and that I am your servant and that I have done all those things at your Word. Hear me, O Lord, hear me, that these people may know that you are the Lord God."

Do you know what happened next? The fire of the Lord fell and ate up the burnt sacrifice, all the wood, the twelve stones, and the dust and licked up the water that was in the deep hole! When all the people saw this great happening, they fell on their faces, and they said, "The Lord, he is God, the Lord, he is God." And God turned his heart toward his people. Isn't that a beautiful thought? Yes, even today, we can still say, "The Lord, he is God, and besides him, there is no one else." What a mighty God we serve when we give our hearts to him, and in return, he gives his heart to us. What a love he has for us! Let us each make this powerful and loving God first in our lives and give him the rightful place as captain of our lives and most importantly, captain of our hearts.

> God sent not his Son into the world to condemn the world; but that the world through him might be saved.
>
> John 3:17 (KJV)

_____the prophet was a mighty man of God?
What was the name of the wicked king?
What was the name of the wicked queen?
There were _____ false prophets of Baal?
Did the true and living God of Israel win the challenge?

WIDOW'S OIL

Elisha was a man of God, a prophet. The Lord God used prophets to teach his people about the living God. Elisha loved the Lord God of Israel, and he would go all over the country of Israel, helping people to follow and obey the one true God.

On one of his many journeys, he met a woman whose husband had just passed away. She is now a widow. The poor widow had just lost her husband, and now she had received some more terrible news. She went to find Elisha, and after she found him, she told the man of God, "Your servant, my husband, is dead, and you know how much he truly did love the Lord God. Now, the person we owe money to has come to my home to take away my only two sons. He will use them as slaves because I cannot pay the bills."

Elisha answered the widow, "Let me see how I can help you. What do you have in your house?"

She answered, "Your handmaid has nothing in the house except one pot of oil."

Elisha answered, "Go and borrow many empty pots from your neighbors. When you go back to your house, I want you to close the door to your house. Then you and your sons will take that one pot of oil, and you will pour it into all of the many empty pots until they are all filled with oil."

The widow did not ask Elisha any questions. She obeyed him. She borrowed many empty pots from her friends, and when she returned to her house, she closed the door, and she and her two sons filled each pot with oil.

When all the pots were filled, she asked her sons to bring her another pot, but they said, "There are no more." And the oil stopped flowing. What a miracle that must have been! From one pot of oil, she filled many pots of oil!

She found Elisha, the man of God, and she told him what happened. Elisha then told her, "Now go and sell all that oil, and with the money from the oil, you can pay all your bills. After you finish paying all your bills, then you and your children can live off the rest of the money."

How happy she must have been! Boys and girls, this poor widow had a big problem, but she knew who to go to—Elisha, the man of God.

Many people today have big problems, but instead of going to God, they go to others to find an answer. Instead of having a happy ending to their life, they end up with a very sad life. The woman in this story ended up with much joy.

Boys and girls, has the Lord Jesus Christ filled your life? Even when your problems are big, he will give you much joy.

> Neither be ye sad; for the joy of the LORD is your strength.
>
> Nehemiah 8:10b (Webster's Bible)

What was name of the prophet?
Why did the widow have to see the prophet?
How many sons did the widow have?
Where did they get all the pots from?
What did they do with the money they received from selling the oil?

THE KIND WOMAN

Boys and girls, do you remember the story we just finished reading? It was about a widow who had two sons and not enough money to pay her bills. Elisha, who was a prophet (a man of God), had done a mighty miracle and made it possible for the woman and her two sons to be able to live without being hungry again.

The Bible tells us that right after Elisha did this powerful miracle, on a certain day, Elisha went to a place called Shunem. At Shunem, there was a woman who was well-known among the people of Shunem. She was a Shunammite. She came from Shumen. She was a woman who loved and respected the Lord God.

The Bible tells us that whenever Elisha passed by Shunem, this certain woman asked him to come into her home and eat with her and her husband.

One day, the Shunammite woman said to her husband, "I truly believe that Elisha is a holy man of God. Because Elisha passes through our town many times, let us make him a little room. This way, he will have a place to stay.

"The room will have walls, and we will put a bed, a table, a lamp, and a chair in the room for him. Everytime he passes through Shunem, he can come here to his room and rest and eat with us."

The husband agreed with his wife, and they made a room just for Elisha. One day, when he came to this well-known woman's home, Elisha said to his servant, Gehazi, "Call the Shunammite woman."

Gehazi obeyed his master, Elisha, and called for the Shunammite woman. She came and stood before Elisha and his servant, Gehazi. Elisha, the prophet and the man of God, said to his servant, Gehazi, "Say to her, 'You have shown much kindness to us by doing all these wonderful things for us. What can we do for you? Would you like me to speak to the king about you? Would you like me to speak to the Captain of the Army about you?'"

Gehazi did exactly as Elisha said and asked these questions to the Shunammite woman. The woman answered, "No, I want to live among my own people. I will stay here."

Gehazi told Elisha the prophet what she had said.

Elisha then said to Gehazi, his servant, "What can we do for her?"

Gehazi answered, "Truly, she has no children, and her husband is old."

Elisha said to Gehazi, "Call her."

When Gehazi called for the Shunammite woman, she stood by the door. Elisha said to her, "About this time, next year, you will have a son."

She answered, "No, my lord, you are a man of God, do not lie to your handmaid."

The Bible tells us, boys and girls, just as Elisha had said, the woman gave birth to a son!

Everything happened exactly the way Elisha had said. What a miracle God had done!

When the child became older, he went with his father to see the servants working in the fields. He said to his father, "My head, my head."

The father said to a young man, "Carry my son to his mother."

When the young man had taken him and brought him to his mother, the boy sat on his mother's knees till noontime, and then the boy died.

Boys and girls, how sad! Her only son had died on her knees. She must have been so sad!

She found the strength to put her son in Elisha's room on Elisha's bed. Then she closed the door.

She said to her husband, "Please, I pray, give me one of the donkeys and a young man, and I will run to see the man of God, Elisha. I will come back again."

Her husband said, "Why do you want to see him today? It is not the holy day of rest nor is it a special day."

She answered her husband, "It shall be well."

Then she got the donkey ready and said to her servant, "Drive and go forward. Do not slow down for me unless I tell you!"

The servant obeyed, and they came to Elisha at Mount Carmel where he lived.

When Elisha saw her coming, he said to Gehazi, his servant, "Look over there! It is the Shunammite woman. Run to her now, and say to her, 'Is it well with you? Is it well with your husband? Is it well with your child?'"

The Shunammite woman said to Elisha's servant, Gehazi, "It is well."

When the Shunammite woman came to Elisha, she caught him by his feet. Gehazi was right there ready to push the woman away from Elisha.

But Elisha said to Gehazi, "Leave her alone, for her soul is torn up within her. The Lord has hidden something from me about her, and he has not told me."

Then the woman said to Elisha, "When you said to me, 'I will have a son,' did not I say to you, 'Do not trick me, for my husband is old?'"

Elisha said to Gehazi, "Go and take my staff in your hand. Do not stop to talk to anyone. If anyone talks to you, do not answer them. But go straight to the woman's house and put my staff upon the face of the child."

The mother of the child (the Shunammite woman) answered, "As the Lord lives, and as my soul lives, I will not leave you." And Elisha arose and followed her.

Gehazi went before them and put the staff of Elisha upon the face of the child. Nothing happened! The child did not speak. The child could not hear. Gehazi told Elisha and the boy's mother, "He did not wake up." He was still dead.

When Elisha, the man of God, came into the house, he saw that the child was dead and laying on his bed. Elisha went in alone and shut the door.

Boys and girls, the Bible tells us that Elisha first prayed to the Lord God! To pray to the Lord is a very important first step!

Then Elisha put himself on the dead child and put his mouth on the boy's mouth, and his eyes on the boy's eyes and his hands on the boy's hands. Elisha stretched himself upon the child.

Do you know what happened next? The child's skin became warm. Then Elisha returned and walked backed and forth in the house and went up to where the child was laying. Elisha stretched himself on the boy.

The Word of God tells us that the child sneezed seven times and the boy opened his eyes! What a powerful miracle God did that day!

Elisha called Gehazi and said, "Call the boy's mother." When she stood before Elisha, Elisha said, "You may now take up your son."

The woman went into the room and fell down at Elisha's feet and bowed herself down to the ground. She was so happy and so thankful! She took her son, who is now alive, into her arms, and they left the room.

This time, boys and girls, she left the room happy, for her son, who was once dead, was now alive!

Boys and girls, if you have not asked the Lord Jesus Christ into your heart, the Bible tells us you are dead in your sins.

And what exactly is sin? The Bible tells us that sin is dirty. Sin is wrong. Sin is everything that is against God.

God is holy. God is clean. God hates sin.

If you told a lie, that is Sin. You did not tell the truth. Sin is what keeps a person from going to heaven, for heaven is a perfect place. There is no sin in heaven!

That is why, boys and girls, God sent his only Son, the Lord Jesus Christ, to come to earth. He died on a cross to take your sin and my sin away so that you and I can go to heaven.

You must ask the Lord Jesus Christ into your heart to take away all your sins—and he will! He will come into your heart and into your life. He will take away your old, dirty sin, and he will give you a clean heart. He will become your best friend and captain of your life. Boys and girls, the choice is up to you. What will you do with the Lord Jesus Christ?

> Behold the Lamb of God, which taketh away the sin of the world.
>
> John 1:29 (AKJV)

What did the Shunammite woman and her husband build for Elisha, the man of God?
Did this Shunammite woman love and respect the Lord God?
What did Elisha do for her for all her kindness to him?
Why was the Shunammite woman in a hurry to see Elisha?
Did this story have a happy and thankful ending?

NAAMAN

This is a true story of how God used a little girl (who was taken prisoner to live in a strange country), to tell about the one true God to a very great man.

This well-known man's name was Naaman. Naaman was captain of the army of Syria. Naaman was a Syrian. Syrians were one of the many enemies of the Israelite people. The Bible says because he was the captain of the whole army of Syria, he was a very powerful man. But Naaman, no matter how great he was, had a terrible disease called leprosy. Yes, Naaman was a leper, and he was becoming sicker each day. He needed help!

Leprosy is a disease which eats away at your skin and body. In those days, they had no cure for this disease. They did not know how to make leprosy go away.

There is another disease which can eat away at your life—little by little—and that disease is called sin.

We shall now see how God showed himself to a country called Syria. The Syrians, including Naaman, did not truly know about God but instead worshipped idols made of wood and stone.

Because Syria and Israel did not like each other, they often went to war. This time, when they went to war, Syria won the battle. When the Syrians returned from Israel, they brought back with them a little Israelite girl. The Bible does not tell us her name, but she did work for Naaman's wife. She was her little helper. This little girl loved God very much and knew all about God.

We need to be like this little girl and be God's little helper. God needs little workers.

This little servant knew that Naaman was a leper and was very sick. One day, she said to her mistress (Naaman's wife), "I wish my master could see the prophet that lives in Samaria. This prophet would make my master well again."

Someone heard the little girl say this to her mistress, and this someone told Naaman what she said. Then they told the king of Syria what this little girl had said about the prophet healing Naaman of leprosy.

The king of Syria had a plan to help his captain, Naaman. He wrote a letter to the king of Israel. He also sent the king of Israel a lot of silver, gold, and clothes along with the important letter, telling about the prophet who would heal Naaman.

When the king of Israel received this letter and read it, he tore his clothes and said, "Am I God that I can heal this man of leprosy? See how this king of Syria wants to start a fight with me?" (In Israel, when the king tore his clothes, that was a very, very serious matter.)

The prophet who could heal Naaman's disease had heard of how the king of Israel tore his clothes. The prophet's name was Elisha. Elisha sent a messenger to the king, asking the king why he had torn his clothes. When Elisha found out that the reason had to do with Naaman being a leper, he told the king of Israel to send Naaman to him.

So Naaman came with his horses and his chariot and stood at the door of Elisha's house. Elisha never came out of his house but instead, sent a messenger to Naaman, saying, "Go and wash in the Jordan River seven times, and you will be well again."

This made Naaman very angry! He was mad! And he was mad for several reasons. It all had to do with pride. Naaman said, "I thought Elisha would come out of his house and stand before me and call on the name of the Lord his God and put his hand on my leprosy and heal me. But instead, he tells me to wash myself seven times in that Jordan River."

First of all, the Jordan River was in Israel, and we know Naaman was from Syria. Secondly, the Jordan River was one of the dirtiest rivers in Israel, and Naaman knew this.

Naaman said, "Aren't our rivers the Abana and Pharpar Rivers better than the rivers of Israel? Why can't I wash in those rivers and become clean?" He walked away red hot and angry!

It's a good thing the servants of Naaman were not full of pride. They said to Naaman, "If the prophet Elisha told you to do some great thing, you would do it without one complaint. All he said was a very simple thing, and that was to go to the Jordan River and wash yourself seven times and you will be cleaned."

All our evilness was taken away when the Lord Jesus Christ died on the cross. All we have to do is one very simple thing, and that is to ask him into our hearts and lives. He will come in and take away our sin and make us clean. It is as simple as that.

Fortunately, Naaman had the good sense to listen to his servants, and he and his servants traveled to the Jordan River.

When they arrived at the river, Naaman got out of his chariot, walked away from his servants, and went down into the Jordan River with all his leprosy clinging to him. When he got into the Jordan River, he began to go under that dirty water. One, two, three, four, five, six, and finally for the seventh and last time, Naaman went under the water.

Do you wonder what Naaman was thinking as he went under the water for the last time? The Bible does not tell us what he was thinking, but the Bible does tell us that when he came up after the seventh time, just as Elisha said, Naaman's skin became new. It was just like a little child's skin, and he was clean!

Naaman returned to Elisha and told the prophet, "Now I know that he is the one true God, and I will only worship him from now on."

The little Israelite maid did a big job for the Lord God Almighty. A little girl with faith in the Lord was not afraid to talk about God in a strange country in order to save her master.

Boys and girls, let's live for the Lord Jesus. It will be worth it all.

> Well done, thou good and faithful servant: enter thou into the joy of thy lord.
>
> (Matthew 25:21) (AKJV)

Where did the little girl in this story come from?
What was wrong with Naaman, Captain of the Syrian Army?
What river did Elisha the prophet tell Naaman to wash in?
How many times did Naaman have to wash himself in the river?
Was the little girl right when she said she knew Elisha could help Naaman?

ELISHA: GOD'S ARMY PROTECTS

Elisha was a prophet of God. His job was to help the Israelite people follow after the Lord God. In this story, Elisha (God's man), saved Israel from being attacked and destroyed three times from their enemy, the Syrians.

The king of Syria had made plans with his men to attack Israel. They were going to make a surprise attack upon the Israelite people.

Elisha found out about this evil plan, and he sent a message to the king of Israel, saying, "Beware! Do not go to that place, for the Syrians are hiding there."

Many times, the Syrians and their king made plans to kill the king of Israel and his men, but each time, Elisha rescued them from destruction.

This really worried the king of Syria! He called for all his men, and he said to them, "Which one of you are against me and for the king of Israel, our enemy?"

One of the servants answered, "It is not us, O King. It is Elisha, the prophet who lives in Israel. He is telling the king of Israel all the plans you make in secret while in your room."

The king of Syria said, "Go and find out where Elisha is living. When you find him, bring him here at once!"

The soldiers obeyed their king's orders. They did find out where Elisha was living. He was living in a place called Dothan. The king of Syria then sent his horses and chariots and his great big army of soldiers to Dothan. They came to Dothan at night, and they circled the whole city of Dothan so Elisha could not escape.

When Elisha's servant woke up in the morning, he stepped outside for a little while, and he couldn't believe his eyes! There were horses and chariots and so many hundreds of soldiers surrounding the city! He ran inside and told his master, Elisha, "Master, what are we going to do?"

Elisha answered, "Don't be afraid. For those that are with us are more than those that are with them."

Elisha then prayed, "O Lord, I pray, open his eyes so that he may see."

The Lord heard and answered Elisha's prayer. The Lord opened the eyes of Elisha's servant, the young man, and he looked, and he saw God's army!

The mountain was full of horses and chariots of fire! They were all around Elisha protecting him from the king of Syria.

When the king of Syria's army came to Elisha, Elisha prayed to the Lord and said, "Strike these people with blindness. Make them blind."

The Lord heard and answered Elisha's prayer, and he sent blindness upon the whole army of Syria. They couldn't see a thing!

Elisha then said unto the army of Syria, "You are in the wrong city. You are travelling on the wrong road. Follow me, and I will bring you to the man you are looking for."

Elisha led the whole army of Syria to a place called Samaria. When they arrived at Samaria, Elisha prayed, "Lord, open their eyes so that they may see." The Lord heard and answered Elisha's prayer. He opened their eyes, and they looked, and they saw that they were right in the middle of Samaria! They were now prisoners!

The king of Israel said to Elisha, "Should I kill them? Should I kill them?"

Elisha answered, "You will not kill them. Instead, you are to give them bread to eat and water to drink. After they have eaten and are full, you will send them back to their master."

That is exactly what the king of Israel did. He fed them with bread and gave them water to drink until they could not eat or drink anymore. He then sent them back to their master, the king of Syria.

Do you know what happened next? The king of Syria saw that the king of Israel had treated his men with kindness, and he never attacked the king of Israel again.

When you accept the Lord Jesus Christ into your heart and life, he becomes captain of your life. You are then in God's army. It is a powerful army! God tells us in Luke 6:27, "Love your enemies, do good to them who hate you." Let us try to remember to obey these important commands. When we do, we are obeying the Lord God.

> Be ye kind one to another, tenderhearted, forgiving one another, even as God for Christ's sake, hath forgiven you.
>
> Ephesians 4:32 (AKJV)

The king of _____ made plans to attack the king of Israel?
How many times did Elisha rescue Israel from being attacked?
Was God's army bigger than the enemy's army?
Where did Elisha bring the enemy to?
What did the king of Israel show to his enemies?

JEHOSHAPHAT

There was a time when Israel had two kings. One king ruled over the part of Israel called "Israel," and another king ruled over the part of Israel called "Judah." This is a story of how King Jehoshaphat (who ruled over Judah), was in serious danger and went to the Lord God, the true God, for help in his time of great need.

There was going to be a terrible battle. The wicked countries of Moab, Ammon and Mount Seir were planning to attack Judah. In fact, the Moabites and the Ammonites were already dressed for battle. They had their uniforms on, their spears by their sides, everyone was lined up, and they began to march toward Judah.

Someone saw them coming and ran to King Jehoshaphat and said, "There is a great number of people coming against you on the other side of the sea."

What could King Jehoshaphat do? He wasn't ready. His men were not prepared for battle. No one knew the enemy was coming until the last moment. King Jehosphaphat did what was best. He went to pray with God. He asked the Lord for help.

King Jehoshaphat proclaimed a fast, which meant no eating was allowed and everyone was to dress in rags while he went to pray to the Lord. This was a very frightful time. The people could be killed; King Jehosphaphat could be killed. Of course, all the people listened to their King. (I guess many of them were also praying.)

King Jehoshaphat stood in the temple of the Lord and said, "O Lord, God of our fathers, aren't you the God in heaven? Don't you rule over all the kingdoms of the nations? Isn't there power in your hand so that no one is able to come against you? Didn't you give us this promised land and made your friend, Abraham, an agreement to give it to Abraham's children forever? They lived in this promised land, and they built a temple for you in this promised land. When evil comes upon us such as no food, war, disease, poverty, or judgment, we stand before this house, your house, and in your presence and cry to you in our pain. You will then hear us and help us.

"Lord, now the children of Moab and Ammon and Mount Seir are coming to fight against us. We did them no harm while we were traveling to the promised land. How can they come and take away our land that you promised us? O, our God, won't you judge them for what they will do to us, for we do not have the strength nor the army of men to fight against all of them? We don't know what to do except to keep our eyes on you, Lord."

And all the people belonging to the kingdom of Judah and all their little children and their wives stood before the Lord God while King Jehoshaphat prayed this prayer to God.

The Lord God spoke to the people through a man named Jahaziel, a Levite (a priest of God in the temple), and Jahaziel answered, "Listen, all of Judah and all peoples of Jerusalem, thus saith the Lord to you, 'Be not afraid. Do not give up because of this great number of people coming toward you, for the battle is not yours, but God's. Tomorrow, I want you to go down to the cliff of Ziz, and there you will see the enemy by the end of the valley before you get to the wilderness of Jeruel. You will not fight in this battle. You will not do anything! All I want you to do is prepare yourselves and stand still and see the salvation of the Lord with you, O Judah and Jerusalem. Fear not and don't give up. Tomorrow, go out against them, for the Lord will be with you.'"

King Jehoshaphat bowed his head with his face to the ground and worshipped the Lord God. All the people also bowed their heads with their faces to the ground and worshipped the Lord God.

All the children of the Levites (the priests), stood up to praise the Lord God of Israel with a loud voice on high.

The next morning, after the king and all the people rose up early, they marched into the wilderness of Tekoa, and as they marched, King Jehoshaphat stood and said, "Hear me, O Judah and Jerusalem. Believe in the Lord your God, and he shall set your life straight. Believe in his prophets, and you will live a successful life according to God."

Do you believe what God says is true? Do you believe he sent his only Son, the Perfect One, to die for you so that you may enter into heaven? John 14:6 tells us that the Lord Jesus Christ said, "I am the Way, the Truth and the Life. No man comes unto the Father except by me." This is believing in the Lord your God. Your reward is everlasting life with him.

King Jehosphaphat chose singers to sing to the Lord while they were marching to meet the enemy. He told them to sing this while they were marching, "Praise the Lord, for his mercy lasts forever."

When the people began to sing, the Lord God set up a surprise attack, which was waiting for the enemy. He had the enemies totally confused! Moab and Ammon thought the people of Mount Seir were going to turn around and attack them, so they all started fighting each other! They destroyed each other. When the King and all the people of Judah and Jerusalem came to where God told them to go, they looked at the great number of people and were amazed to see that all the people that were going to fight against them were already dead!

The Lord God kept his promise and won that battle for Israel! When King Jehoshaphat and the people of Judah and Jerusalem went up to their enemies, they took all their gold, silver, jewelry, expensive clothes, and anything they wanted. It took three whole days to carry away all the silver, gold, jewelry, expensive clothes, and everything they wanted. That is a true victory!

On the fourth day, they gathered together in the valley of Beracah. In that valley, they blessed the Lord. They truly thanked the Lord for the victory he gave them.

They all returned home with much joy and celebration! When they came to Jerusalem, they were happy, playing on string instruments and singing while entering into the house of the Lord, his temple.

The respect of God was on all the kingdoms and countries when those people in those kingdoms and countries heard how the Lord fought against the enemies of Israel. God blessed King Jehoshaphat and gave him rest from all his enemies. God will bless you too as you look to him to win your battles for you.

> Seek the Lord while he may be found; call upon him while he is near.
>
> Isaiah 55:6 (ESV)

What was the name of the King of Judah?
_____, _____ and _____ were planning to attack Judah?
What did the King of Judah tell the people to do while he was praying?
What was the name of the prophet who told the people not to be afraid?
Who won the battle for the king of Judah and all the people?

JOSIAH

There was a time when Israel was ruled by two kings. One king ruled over a part of Israel called "Judah", and another king ruled over a part of Israel called "Israel."

This is a story of how a boy—only eight years old—became king and ruled over the part of Israel called "Judah."

His name was Josiah. His father was King Amon, and his mother was Queen Jedidah. He ruled his kingdom from a city in Israel called "Jerusalem". The Bible tells us that some of the kings did evil in the eyes of the Lord and some of the kings did good in the eyes of the Lord.

King Josiah did that which was good in the eyes of the Lord God. He followed the ways of King David. (Remember the story of David and Goliath? This is the same David who later on became king of Israel. God called David, "A man after my own heart.")

At eight years of age, King Josiah began to search after the God of King David. When he became twenty years old, he took away all of the idols. He didn't care if the idols were made out of wood or out of melted gold. He destroyed them all. He cleansed Judah and Jerusalem from all these images that the people were worshipping.

Then he broke down all the altars that the images stood on. He had them all broken into pieces and had them pounded into dust and scattered over the graves of those people who sacrificed to them.

The priests who performed the ceremonies and who made the people join in by giving worship to these man-made pieces of rock and wood were killed by order of King Josiah. He burnt the priests' bones upon the very same altars they made for the idols!

King Josiah, at the age of twenty, destroyed everything that kept the people from worshipping the one true living God. He went throughout his kingdom, cleansing it. When he finished, he returned to Jerusalem.

When he turned twenty-six years old, he called for Shaphan, the scribe (one who writes all the king's books), Maaseiah (the governor of the city), and Joah, the recorder (one who keeps important information for the King). King Josiah told them, "Go to Hilkiah, the high priest. He will tell you the amount of silver which has been brought into the house of the Lord. The keepers of the house of the Lord have gathered this silver from the people. Let them then deliver the silver into the hands of the men who will do the work, such as carpenters, builders, and stonecutters. With the silver, they will buy timber and stone to repair the house of the Lord, his temple."

They obeyed the words of the king and went at once to visit Hilkiah, the high priest, about this important matter.

When they arrived, everything was already taken care of, and everything was done honestly and faithfully before the eyes of the Lord God.

As they were repairing the house of the Lord, Hilkiah, (the high priest), said to Shaphan, the scribe (one of the men sent by King Josiah), "I have found the book of the law in the house of the Lord."

Hilkiah then gave it to Shaphan so that he may read it.

When Shaphan returned to Jerusalem, he went to see King Josiah. He reported to the king on how the work was going. He then said to King Josiah, "Hilkiah, the high priest, has given me a book." Shaphan then read the book to the king.

As the king was listening to the words of the book of the law, he tore his clothing. (It was considered a very serious matter when a king of Israel tore his clothes.)

The king commanded Hilkiah, the priest, Ahikam (the son of Shaphan), Achbor, and Asaiah (the king's servant), to be brought before him. When they stood before the king, King Josiah said, "Go, ask the Lord God for me and for all the people and for all of Judah exactly what do the words of this book mean, for great is the anger of God against us because our fathers did not listen and do the words of this book. This book has to do with us and our lives, and we have disobeyed it."

So Hilkiah, the priest, Ahikam, Achbor, Shaphan, and Asaiah went to see Huldah, the wife of Shallum. She was a prophetess of God. (A prophetess was one who knew and could speak the Word of God.)

She lived in Jerusalem. They went to her home, entered it, sat down, and talked with her.

She said to them, "Tell King Josiah that the Lord said, 'I will bring evil upon this place. The people have thrown me aside and they have burned perfume unto other gods. In doing this, they have angered me with the wickedness they have done with their hands. Now my anger shall be set on fire against this place and it shall not be put out with water.'"

But tell King Josiah that the Lord has said, "Because your heart was tender and you humbled yourself before me, you, King Josiah, will not see all the evil that I will bring upon this place. I will bless your kingdom with peace in your lifetime."

The king's men then left and returned to King Josiah. They told the king all that the prophetess, Huldah, had spoken by the mouth of the living God.

After hearing these words, the king commanded that all the elders of Judah and Jerusalem be brought together. The king went up into the house of the Lord along with all the people, elders, and priests of Judah and Jerusalem.

It did not matter whether you were rich or poor, powerful or an everyday, hardworking person. Everyone entered into the house of the Lord, his temple.

King Josiah stood by a pillar (one of the stone towers which held up the temple), and he read the book of the law before all the people, elders, and priests. After he finished reading from the book, the king made a promise before the Lord God to follow after the Lord God and to keep God's commandments, written truths, and laws with all his heart and with all his soul. He promised to do exactly what was written in God's book, and all the people agreed to do the same.

The king then commanded Hilkiah, the high priest, and the other priests and keepers of the house of the Lord to bring out of the temple of the Lord all the vessels (such as cups and bowls) that were made for the idol Baal. King Josiah then burned the vessels outside of Jerusalem in the fields of Kidron. He carried the ashes to Bethel.

He then took away all the priests who made the people worship and bow down to these images made from man's hand. He broke in pieces the idols which were made for these gods: Baal (chief male god), Molech (god made of stone used in human sacrifice by having children pass through the fire alive), the sun god, the moon god, and gods made for the stars and planets.

He had the altars destroyed and the priests killed because it was a horrible thing before the eyes of the Lord God to have the people bow their knees and do these ceremonies and rituals.

He went through every area of his kingdom destroying anything that was worshipped in place of the true and living God. He also had all the witches and fortune-tellers killed because they did not want to obey the Lord God of Israel.

Next, King Josiah taught his people the Passover which God taught Moses to do, but through the years, most of the Israelite people had forgotten to keep it.

But King Josiah remembered the Passover, and he and all the people came together at Jerusalem and prepared themselves for the Passover. (Passover was the remembrance of the time when the Israelite people, under the leadership of Moses, fled out of Egypt from under the hand of Pharaoh.)

To help prepare for this special Passover, King Josiah gave to all the people thirty thousand lambs and baby goats. He told the people to cleanse themselves, for on the fourteenth day of the first month, they were to remember the Passover.

He said to the priests (Levites), "Set the holy ark, which holds the Ten Commandments, in the temple." The people gave willingly from their hearts.

So the service was prepared according to the king's commandment, and they killed the Passover lamb, and the priests sprinkled the blood, and the priestly tribe of the Levites stripped off the skin from the Passover lambs and goats.

Then they removed all the burnt offerings and divided it according to the families in order that they may offer it unto the Lord as was written by Moses.

They roasted the Passover with fire, but the holy offerings were boiled as Moses had commanded. Then the singers sang according to the commandment of King David. That day, everyone kept the Passover. The Bible tells us, "There was no Passover that was kept like this one in all of Israel from the days of Samuel the Prophet." None of the kings of Israel had a Passover like King Josiah had.

All of this took place while King Josiah was twenty-six years of age. King Josiah was a mighty servant of the living God. He was not afraid to take a stand for God. Because of his faithfulness to God, God blessed King Josiah and his kingdom all the days of his life.

The Bible tells us, "There was no king like King Josiah who turned to the Lord with all his heart and with all his soul and with all his strength according to the law of Moses."

When King Josiah died, Jeremiah (the prophet), cried for him. All the singing men and women sang songs about King Josiah. These songs were made into law so that the people would remember King Josiah.

The Lord God was very pleased with King Josiah's life. Would you like to please the Lord God? You can by accepting his only Son, the Lord Jesus Christ, the Lamb of God, into your heart and life. That is the most pleasing thing you can do for the Lord God and for yourself.

> You shall love the LORD your God with all your heart and with all your soul and with all your might.
>
> Deuteronomy 6:5 (ESV)

How old was King Josiah when he became the King of Judah?
Was he a good king or a bad king?
What was the name of the woman prophetess?
What was the name of the feast that King Josiah had all the people prepare for?
Did God bless King Josiah?

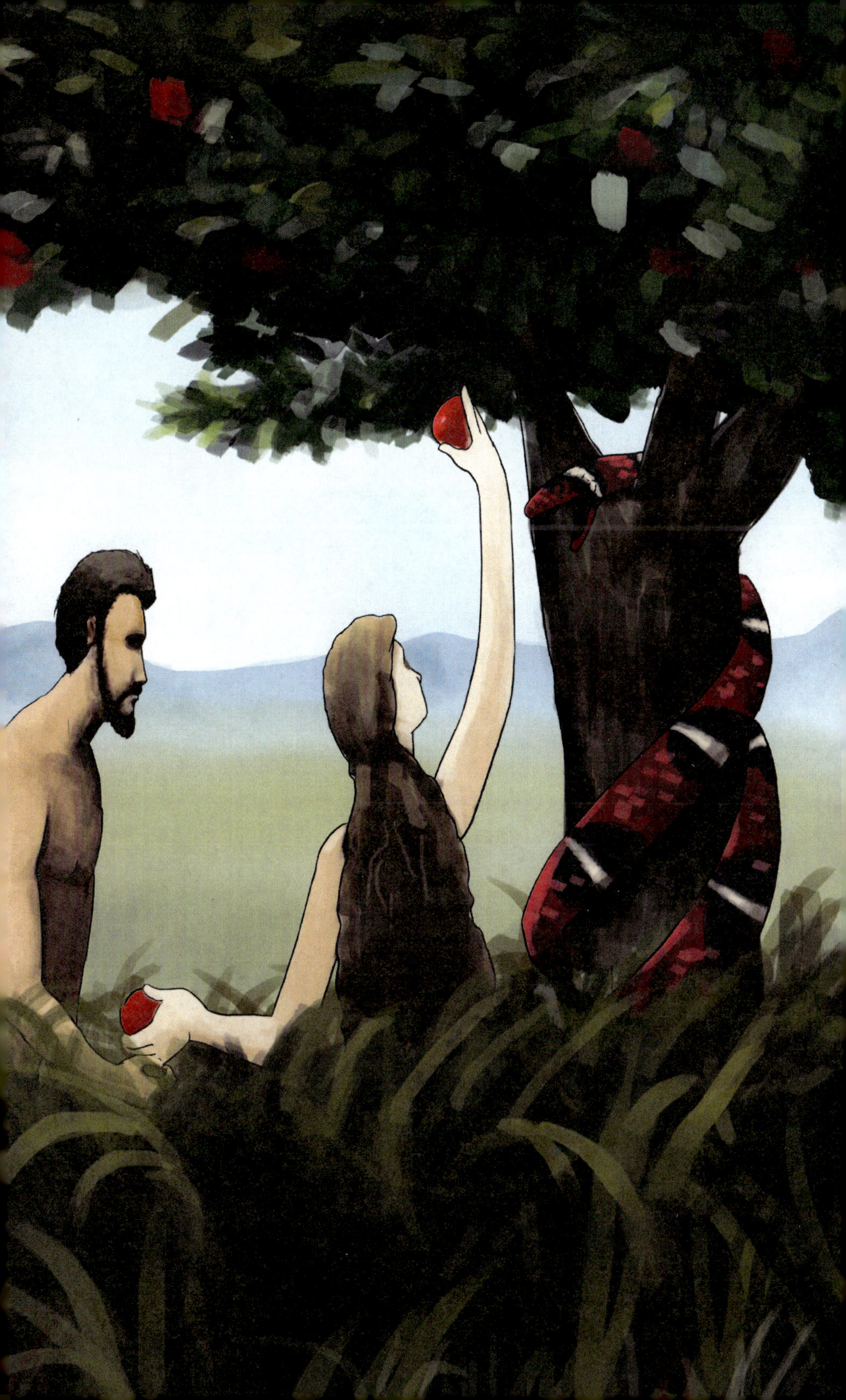

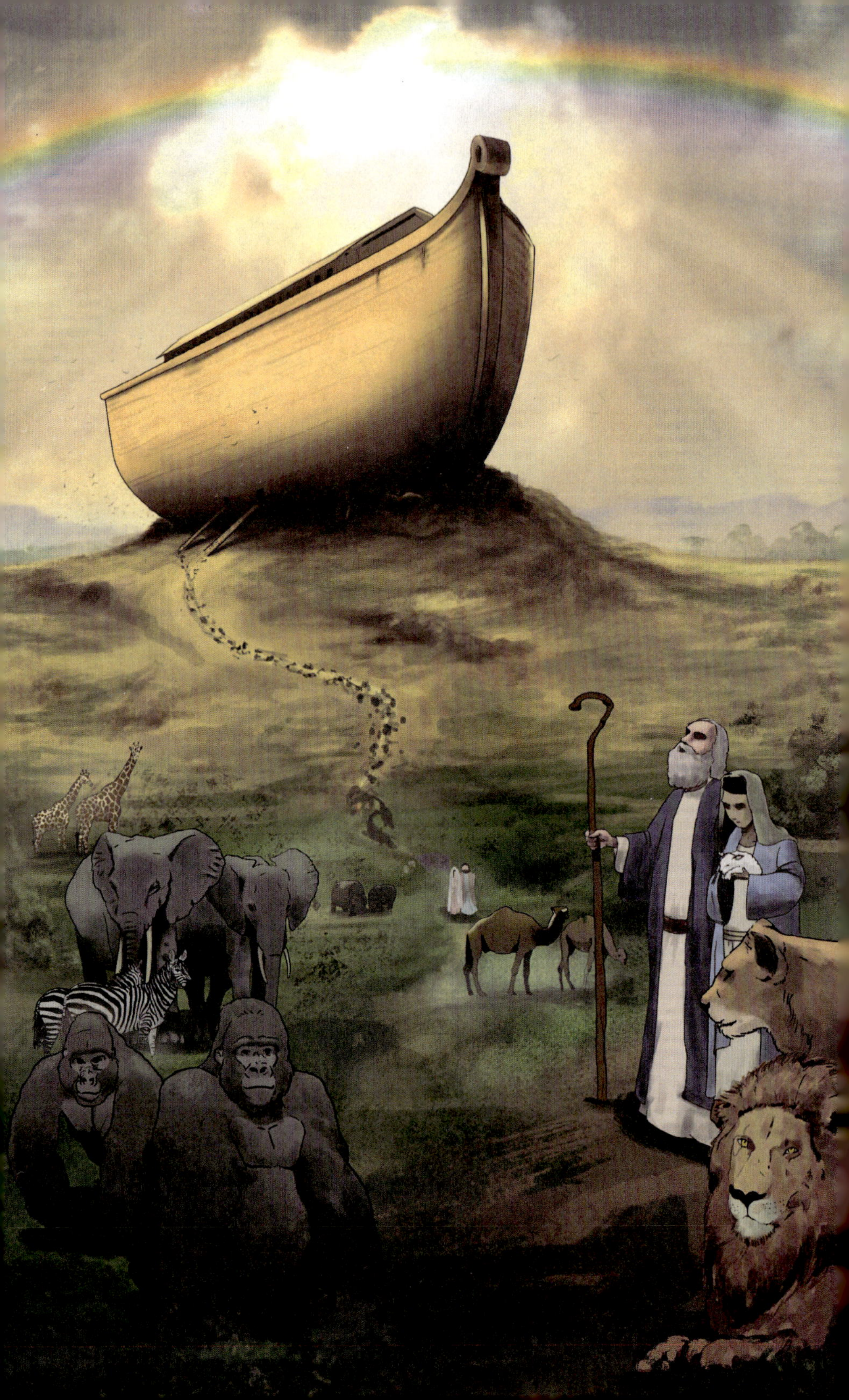

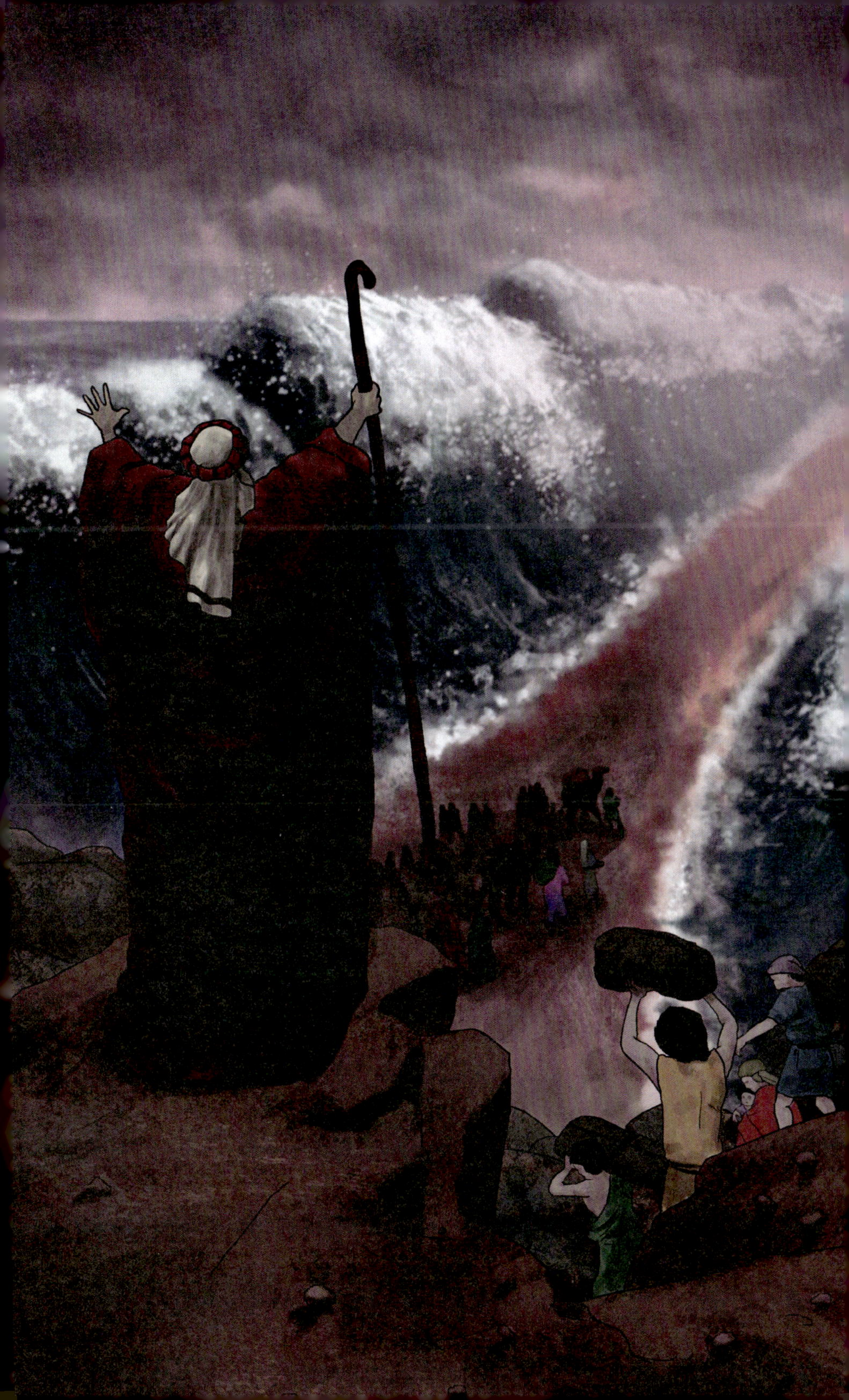

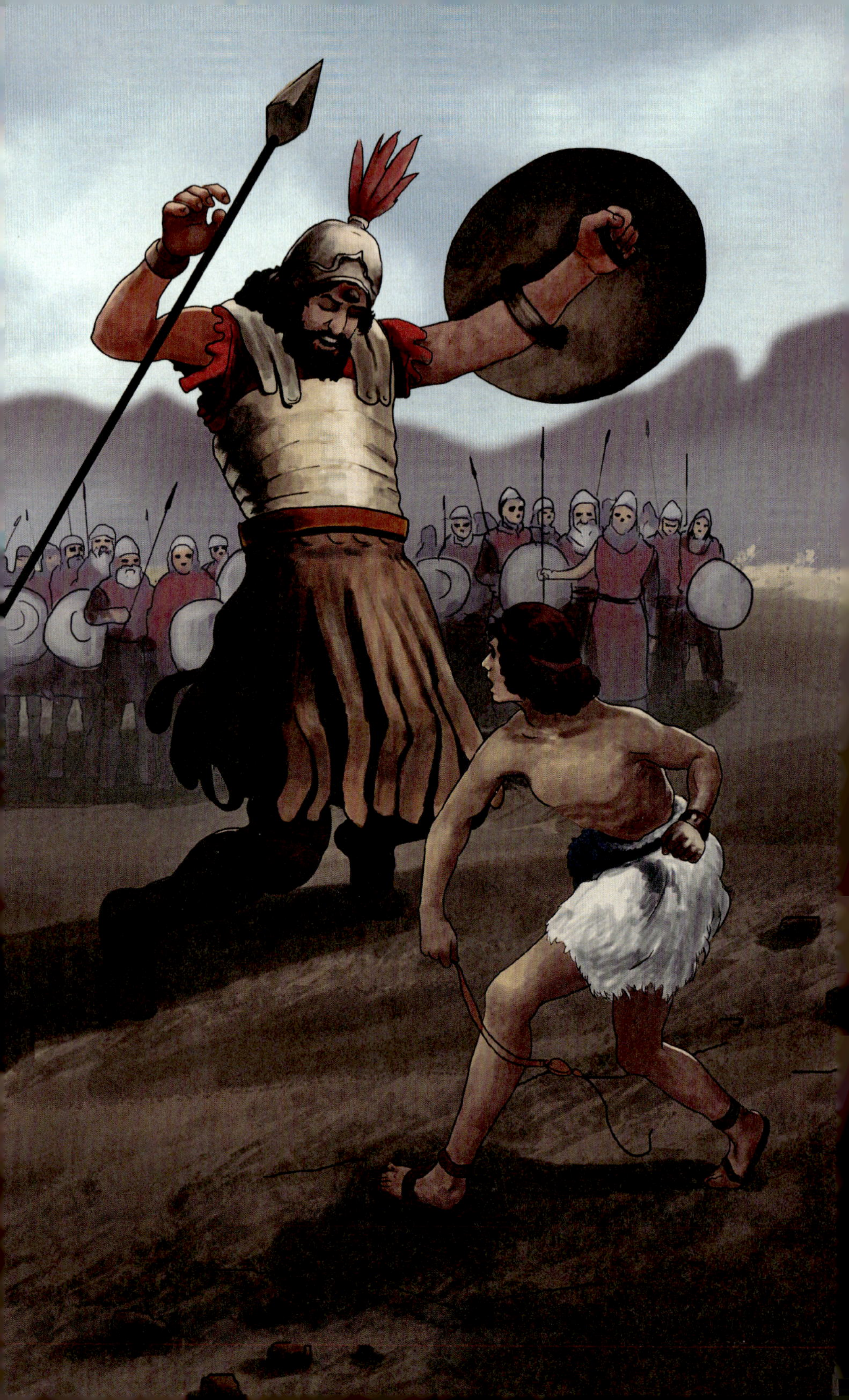

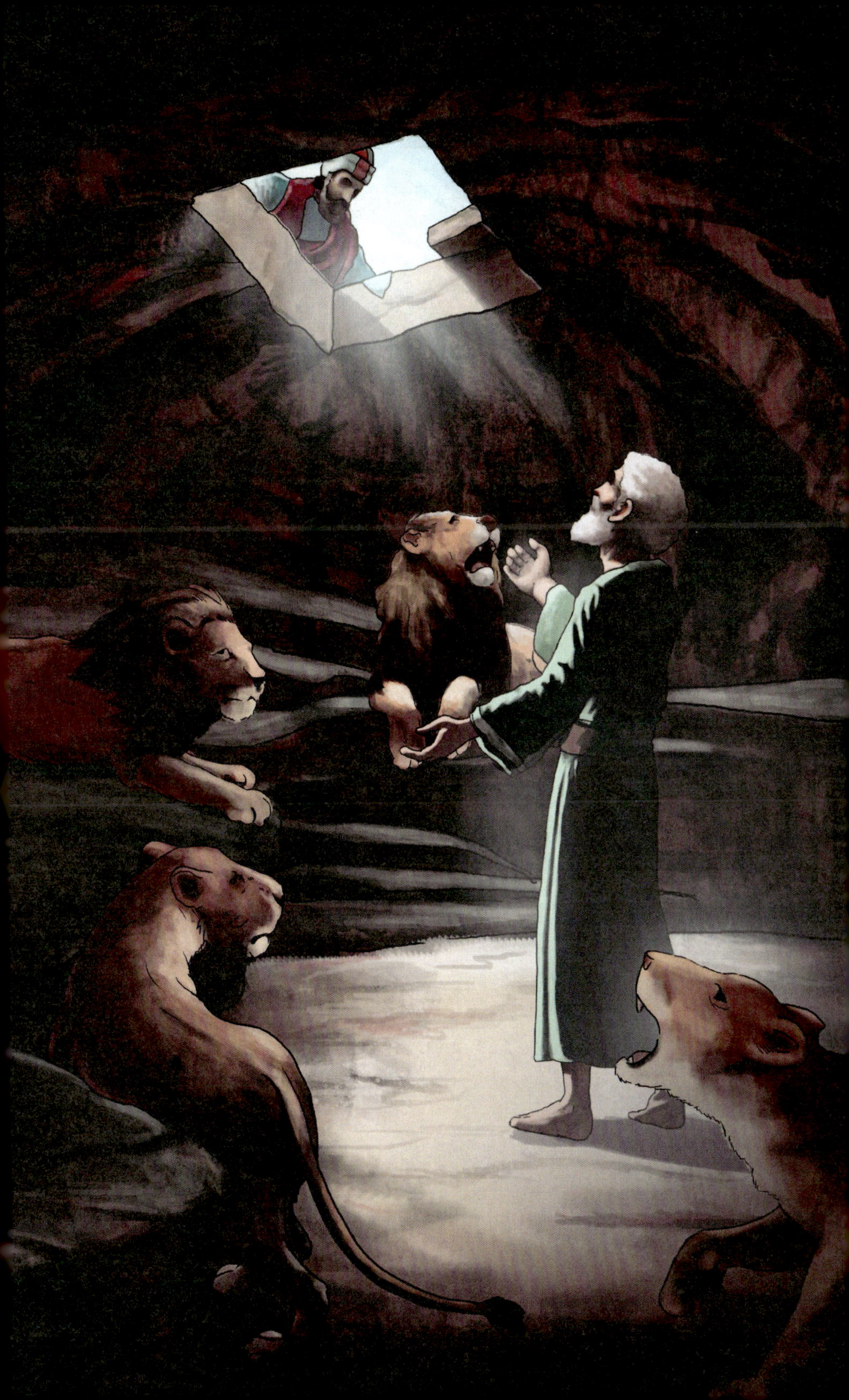

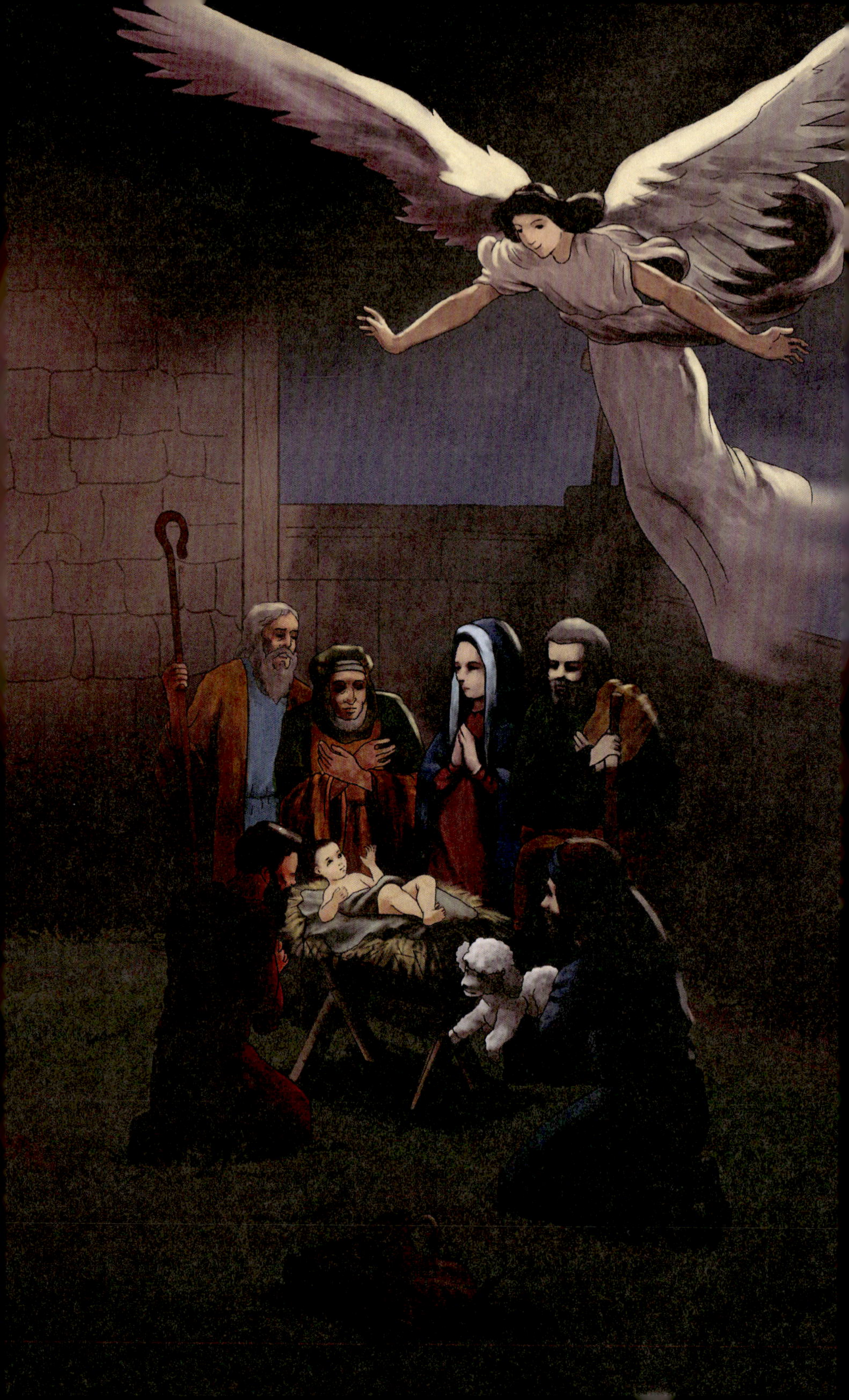

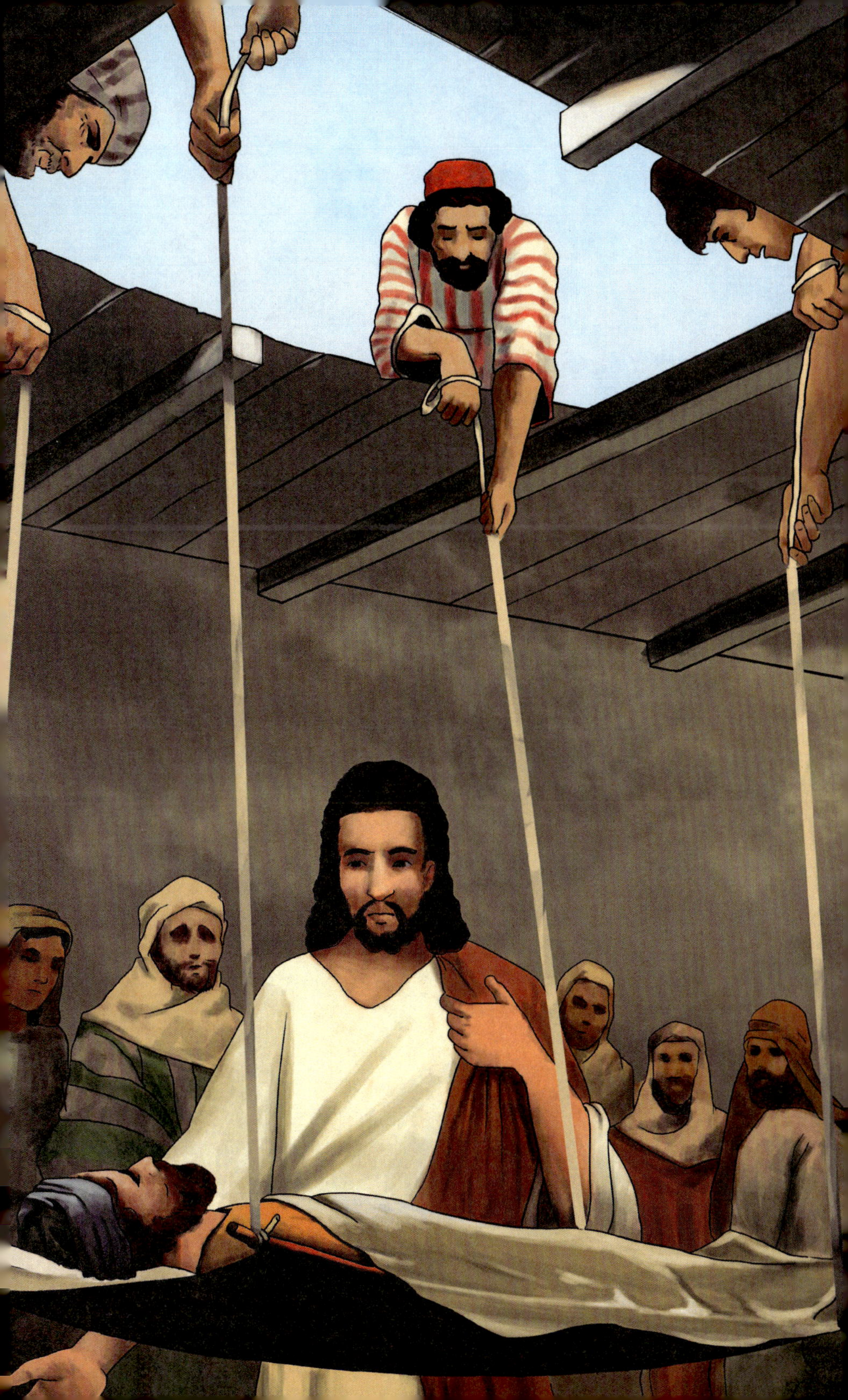

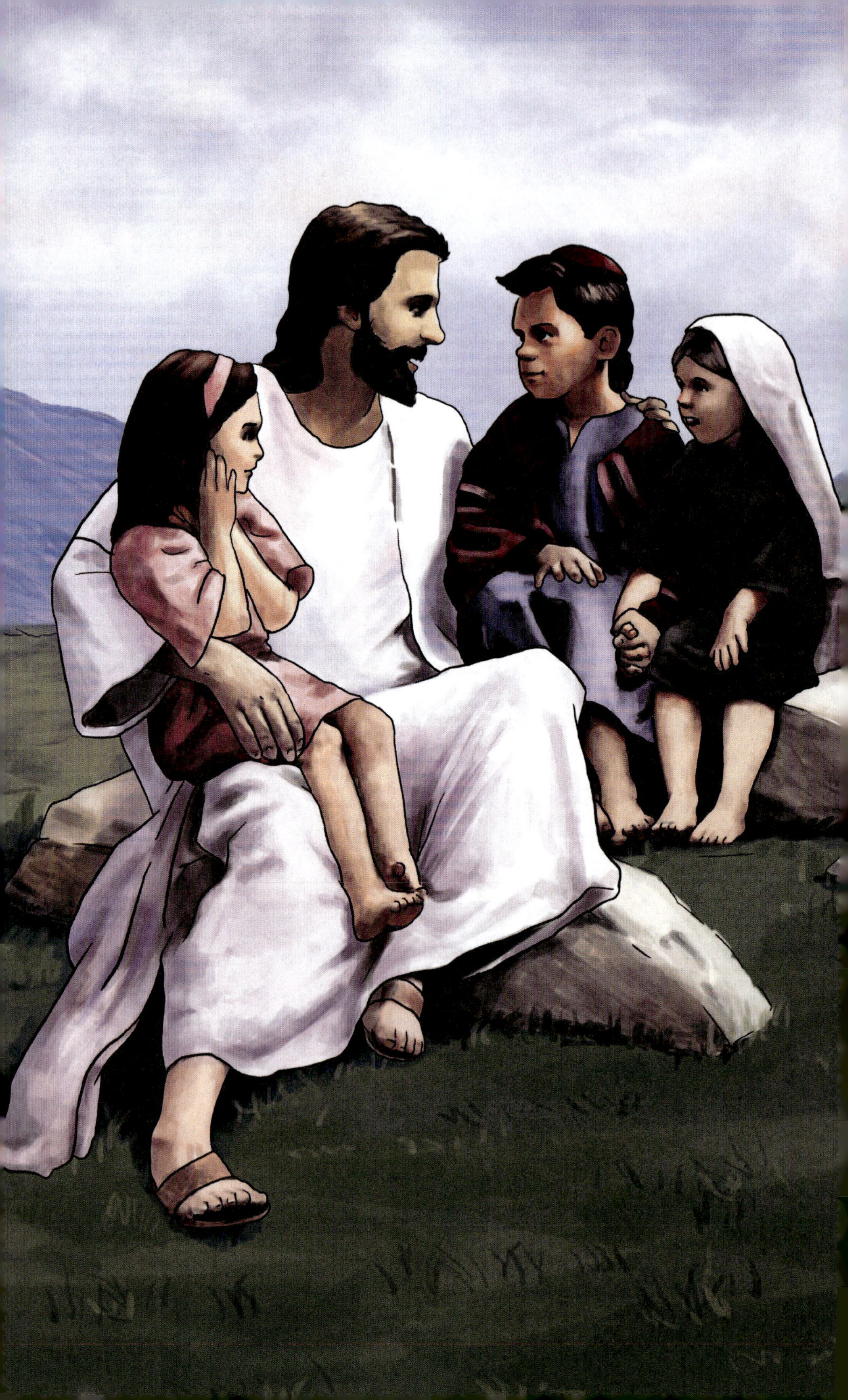

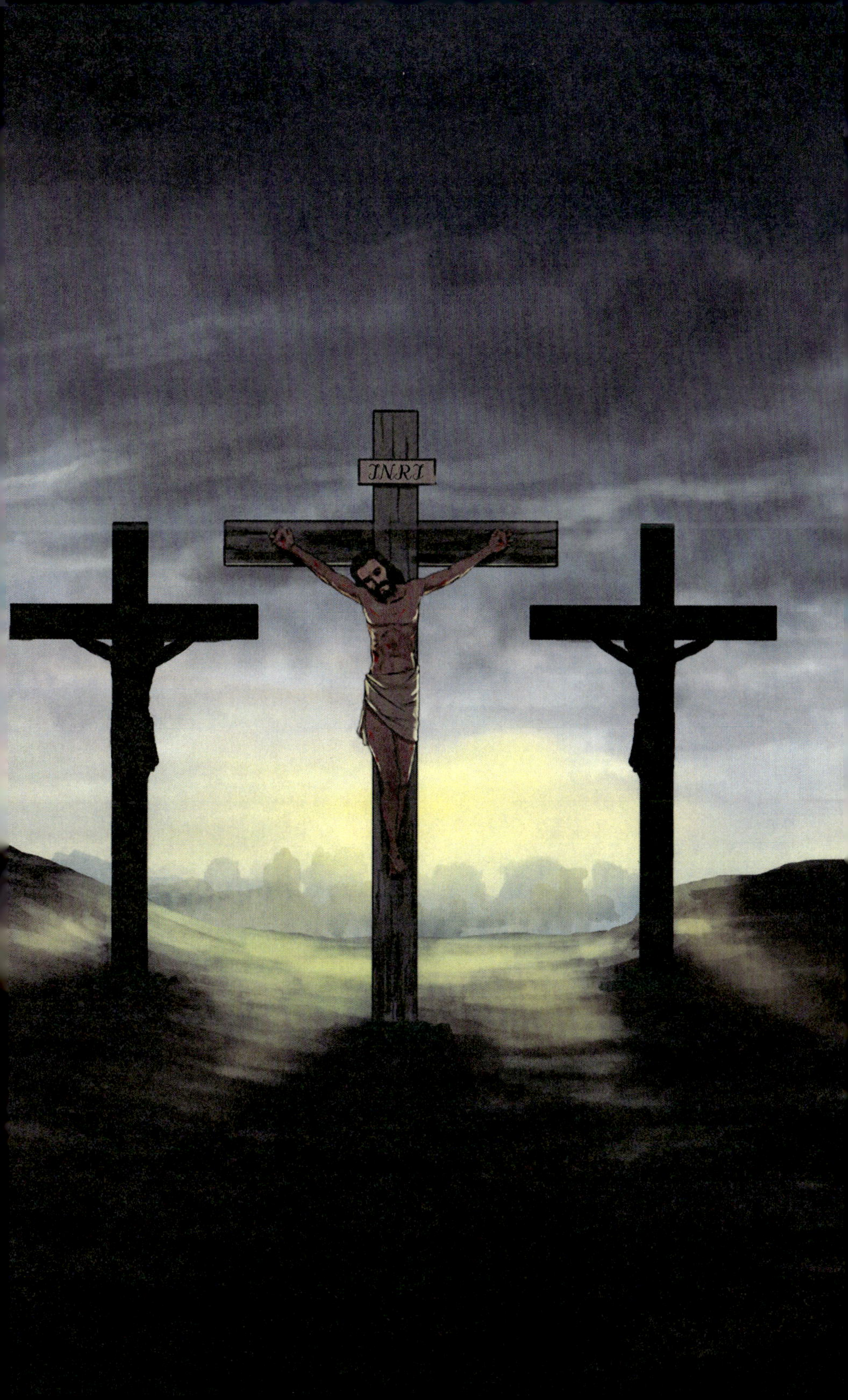
INRI

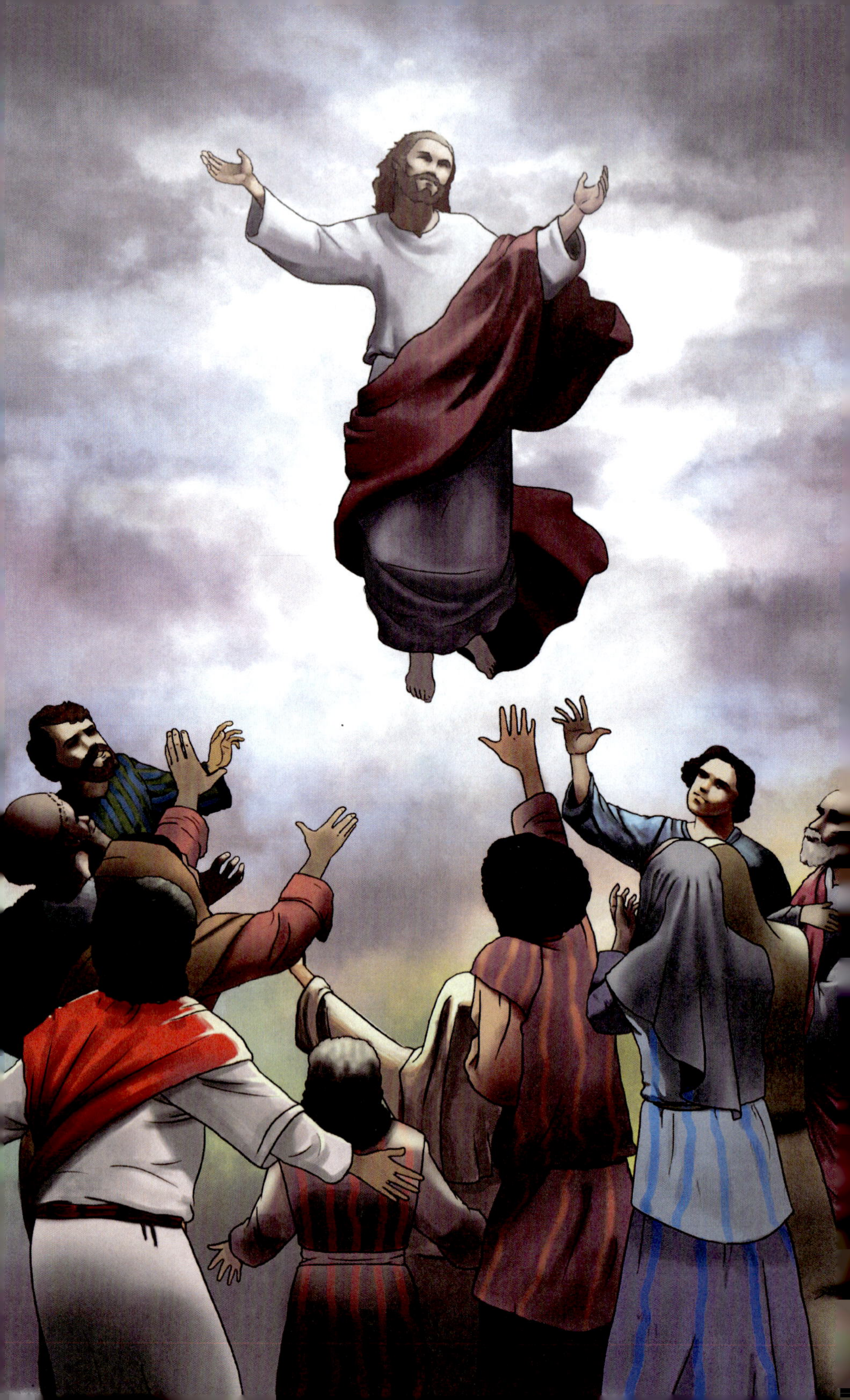

HEROES OF GOD

This is a biblical story of three men who refused to worship an image made of pure gold. This was no ordinary image, and these three men were no ordinary people. Their names were Shadrach, Meshach, and Abednego. They were three Jewish men who, along with many other Jewish people, were taken captive out of Jerusalem (which is in Israel), to Babylon. There they served under the king of Babylon whose name was Nebuchadnezzar. The king chose these three men to help rule the province of Babylon.

King Nebuchadnezzar was a proud king. One day, he decided to have an idol of himself built. It was to be made of pure gold, nothing less. The Bible states he placed this very tall idol of himself in the plain of Dura in the province of Babylon. Dura had very even land, and the king couldn't think of a better place to have all the people come together and worship this idol.

Oh, King Nebuchadnezzar just couldn't wait for the day when this idol, this grand monument of himself, would be finished. And that day finally came! The king had everyone gather together.

He had the princes, the governors, the captains, the judges, the treasurers, the counselors, the sheriffs, and all the rulers of the provinces come to the dedication of the image, which the King had set up. And they all came. They dared not miss this dedication! Their very lives were at stake!

As they gathered around the grand monument, an announcer cried out, "To you, it is commanded, O people, nations, and languages, that at the time you hear the sound of the horn, the pipe, the harp, the string instruments, the bagpipe, and all kinds of music, you are to fall down and worship this magnificent idol that your king has set up. Whoever does not fall down and worship this idol, in that same hour, he shall be cast into the middle of a burning, fiery furnace."

Well, that was enough to make anyone tremble! You had to be crazy not to obey that order! I am very sure that the king had a great big smile on his face and was standing tall and proud as the announcer read that command to all the people.

This was just a practice. Now came the real test. The Bible states that "Therefore at that time when all the people heard the sound of the horn, the pipe, the harp, the stringed instruments, the bagpipe, and all kinds of music, all the people, nations, and languages fell down and worshipped the golden idol that Nebuchadnezzar the king of Babylon had set up."

All but three, that is. And it was plain to see, that after everyone fell down, who was left standing smack in the middle of all the people! No sooner did this happen that certain Chaldeans couldn't wait to run and tell the king about the three Jewish men who wouldn't bend their knees to this image of gold. They made sure they told the king everything! They said, "Thou, O King, has made a law that every man that shall hear the sound of the horn, the pipe, the string instruments, the bagpipe, and all kinds of music shall fall down and worship the golden image, and whoever does not fall down and worship this golden image, he shall be thrown into the midst of a burning, fiery furnace.

"There are certain Jews whom you have placed over the important things of the province of Babylon whose names are Shadrach, Meshach, and Abednego. These men, O King, have not listened to your orders. They do not serve your gods, neither do they worship the golden idol which you have set up."

How do you think the king felt when he heard these words? He was furious!! While he was burning with anger, he commanded these three men to be brought before him to answer for themselves.

They did come before the king. The King said to them, "If this is true, then who is your God that shall deliver you out of my hands?"

The three men answered, "O, Nebuchadnezzar, we have no need to answer you in this matter. If it be so, our God, whom we serve, will be able to deliver us from the burning, fiery furnace, and he will deliver us out of your hand, O King. But if not, let it be known unto you, O King, that we will not serve your gods, neither will we worship the golden idol which you have set up."

That was all the king needed to hear! He was very mad, and he became as red as the fiery furnace. In fact, he was so furious he commanded his soldiers to heat the furnace seven times more than usual. He then commanded his most mighty men that were in his army to tie up Shadrach, Meshach, and Abednego and throw them right into that terrible burning furnace. Of course, the soldiers had to obey, and they tied up Shadrach, Meshach, and Abednego with cords and with all their clothes on, including their turbans (hats on their heads), they threw them into the middle of that fire.

Because the king's commandment was so urgent and the furnace exceedingly hot, the flame killed the soldiers—the mighty men—who threw the three men of God into the furnace.

And the three men fell down, bound into the midst of the burning inferno. At this point, the king thought he got rid of all the troublemakers, but was he in for a shock! Was he surprised at what he saw next! He got up and ran to his counselors and said, "Didn't we throw three men bound into the middle of the fire?"

They answered, "Yes, King."

Then the King said, "Look, I see four men loose and walking in the middle of the fire. They are not hurt, and the fourth man is like a son of the gods." The King went to the opening of the furnace and cried out, "Shadrach, Meshach, and Abednego, you servants of the most high God, come out from the midst of the fire."

Everyone from the king on down to his priests, his governors, his captains, and his counselors saw that none of these three men were burnt or harmed by the fire, neither was their hair burnt. Their clothes stayed nice, and there was no smell of fire on them. King Nebuchadnezzar realized that they had been with God, and he gave glory to their God. He made a law that no one was to hurt or bother these three men. He also gave each one of these three men a promotion in the province of Babylon.

Who was that fourth person who was in the furnace with the three men? Can this person keep us today as he kept the three men? He is still the most high God.

The most high God has sent us his only Son, Jesus, to come and save us from a burning place and has given us a chance to spend forever with him in heaven.

> Pray to me when you are in trouble! I will deliver you, and you will honor me!
>
> Psalms 50:15 (NET)

What are the names of the three men who would not worship the golden idol?
What is the name of the king?
What happened to the three men who did not worship the idol?
Who was the fourth person the king saw?
Can God still save us today?

WANTED BY GOD

There was a king who ruled over Babylon. His name was King Belshazzar. This king did not love the Lord God, and neither did his people, the people of Babylon.

The Jewish people were being held prisoners in the land of Babylon while King Belshazzar reigned.

One day, King Belshazzar gave a great feast. He invited a thousand of his highest servants to his big party.

While King Belshazzar tasted the wine, he commanded that they bring out the gold and silver cups which his father, King Nebuchadnezzar, had taken from the Jewish temple in Jerusalem.

These silver and gold cups were special because the Jewish people used them when sacrificing to the living God in their temple in Jerusalem (Jerusalem is in the country of Israel).

King Belshazzar took these cups, and he and his princes, his wives, and his girlfriends drank from these gold and silver cups. While everyone was drinking from these cups, they began to praise their gods made out of gold, silver, bronze, iron, wood, and stone. How do you think the living God felt?

In that very same hour that they were praising their gods which were made from a man's hand, there upon the plaster of the wall of the king's palace against the lampstand were fingers of a man's hand writing words!

The king saw with his very own eyes a part of the hand that was writing! Did his expression change! Not only did the look on the king's face change, but his mind began to trouble him, and he couldn't stop his knees from shaking together. He was falling apart!

The king cried out for his fortune-tellers and his wisemen of Babylon. The king said to them, "Whoever can read this writing and can tell me what it means, I shall clothe him in beautiful scarlet (a very bright red color), I will put a gold chain around his neck, and he shall be the third ruler in this kingdom." (They had two rulers already.)

In came all of the king's wisemen and fortune-tellers, but they could not read the writing on the king's palace wall, neither could they tell the king what the writing meant.

The king was very troubled, and his face had a very worried look on it. Everyone looked totally confused. They were shocked! No one could read the writing, no one could explain the writing, and no one even knew how the writing got on the wall of the king's palace!

Now, the queen, after listening to the king and his lords came in to see the king. She said, "O King, live forever. Don't let your thoughts trouble you. Don't worry. There is a man in this kingdom who is very holy. He helped your father, the king. The king gave him a high position because of his excellent spirit. He understands, and he tells the meaning of dreams. He knows a lot. He shows the meaning of hard sentences. He will take your doubts away. His Jewish name is Daniel; his Babylonian name is Belteshazzar."

Remember Daniel in the den of lions? This is the same Daniel. They brought Daniel to the King. The King said, "Are you Daniel, the same Daniel that was taken prisoner with the other Jewish people? Are you the same Daniel that my father, the king, took out of Israel? I have heard of you. I have heard that the spirit of the gods are in you, that light and understanding and excellent wisdom is found in you. My wisemen and fortune-tellers cannot tell the meaning of this handwriting on the wall. I have heard of how you can tell the meaning of dreams and take away doubts.

"If you can read this writing and tell me what it means, I will clothe you with scarlet, put a gold chain around your neck, and you will be the third ruler in all the land of Babylon."

Daniel answered the King, "Keep all your gifts. Keep all your rewards. I will read the writing to the king, and I will tell you the meaning. O King, the most high God gave Nebuchadnezzar, your father, a kingdom with majesty, glory, and honor. All people, nations, and languages trembled before him. They feared him. Whoever he wanted to be killed, would be killed. Whoever he wanted to live, would live. Whoever he wanted to give a promotion to, he would promote. Whoever he wanted to bring down, he did.

"But he became full of pride, and his heart became hard. He would not listen to the living God. God took away his kingly throne and all his glory. He was driven away from his kingdom. He lived like an animal. He ate grass like the bulls. His body was wet with the dew that fell from heaven, and his hair and nails grew long like the wild birds. He stayed this way until he knew that the most high God ruled over all kingdoms and men. It is God who could do whatever he wants and not man. But you, his son, O Belshazzar, you have not humbled your heart although you knew this happened to your father. Instead, you became more proud against the Lord of heaven. You drank from the cups that belonged to the temple at Jerusalem. You drank from them, your lords drank from them, and your wives and girlfriends also drank from them. You gave honor and praise to gods made of silver, gold, bronze, iron, wood, and stone. These gods can't see, these gods can't hear, and they know nothing. The God that is living, who holds your very breath in his Hand and knows all about you—to this God, the true God, you have given no honor or praise to. You have not glorified the only true God.

This is the writing on the wall: Mene, Mene, Tekel, Upharsin. This is the meaning of the writing on the wall: Mene—God has numbered your kingdom and finished it. Tekel—you are weighed in the balances and you are found guilty before God. Peres—your kingdom is divided and given to the Medes and Persians."

The king commanded that Daniel be clothed in scarlet clothing, and a gold chain be put around his neck. The king then made an announcement that Daniel be made the third ruler in the kingdom.

But poor King Belshazzar, after all of this, still could not humble himself and ask God for forgiveness. That night, King Belshazzar was killed. The kingdom was divided into two. This story did not have a happy ending for King Belshazzar. He chose to die full of pride and sin. There are many people today who are full of pride. Won't you ask the Lord Jesus Christ to come into your life and give you a clean heart? You can then tell others, as Daniel did, about your great and loving God.

> For the Son of man is come to seek and to save that which was lost.
>
> Luke 19:10 (AKJV)

What country did King Belshazzar rule over?
Who did King Belshazzar take as prisoners?
What did the handwriting on the wall say?
What man of God told the king what the handwriting on the wall said?
Did King Belshazzar humble himself and ask the true God for forgiveness?

DANIEL

The biblical story of Daniel in the den of lions took place at a time when the Jewish people were taken captive out of Jerusalem (which is in Israel), to the land of Babylon. They spent many years in Babylon and had many kings. They now served under the king of Babylon named Darius.

In the meantime, there was a Jewish man named Daniel who stayed faithful to the God of Israel during all the years he and his people were prisoners in Babylon. Daniel was an honorable, just, and godly man.

King Darius liked Daniel so much he made Daniel the first president over all the kingdom. (There were one hundred twenty princes and three presidents.) Daniel was the first president. All the other presidents and princes had to report to Daniel.

This made the other presidents and princes very, very jealous. They became so jealous they started thinking of a way to get rid of Daniel, but they could not think of anything nor could they find anything wrong with Daniel. Daniel stayed true to God and was a very holy man. He lived his life for God; therefore, they could not find one thing wrong with Daniel.

The presidents and princes came together for a meeting one day and said, "Since we cannot find anything wrong with Daniel, we must find something wrong with the way he serves his God."

After they finished their meeting, they went to see the king and said, "O King Darius, live forever. All the presidents of the kingdom, the governors, the princes, the counselors, and the captains have spoken together to make a royal law that whoever asks for something from his god or man for the next thirty days shall be thrown into the den of lions. The only one here that can ask their god or man for something is you, King Darius. Please sign this paper and make it a law according to the Medes and Persians."

That made the king feel so good that he signed the paper right away, and it became a law. The king thought that the presidents and princes were trying to make him feel important, but what the presidents and princes really wanted was to see Daniel thrown into the den of lions and die.

We see three sins here: pride, jealousy, and lying. These three sins can destroy your life. Daniel was a completely different person than those presidents and princes. He had in his life humbleness, love, and truth. He had these three beautiful qualities because he had God. The others did not have God. They did not want God.

James 4:7–8 tells us: "Give yourselves to God. Fight against the devil, and he will run from you. Come near to God, and he will come near to you."

After the king signed the new law, the presidents and princes were so happy and excited. They thought they really could get Daniel now.

When Daniel saw that the writing was now a law, he went to his house. His windows were opened toward Jerusalem. He kneeled down on his knees three times a day and prayed and gave thanks unto God as he always did. The law did not make him change his way of praying three times a day to God. He stayed faithful to God. The presidents and princes saw Daniel praying to God. They went to see the king and said, "Didn't you sign a law that said no one was to ask their god or man anything for the next thirty days except you, O King? If they did do this, they would be thrown into the den of lions? Didn't you sign that law?"

The king said, "Yes, I did sign that law. It has not changed."

Then they said, "Daniel, who is of the Jewish people taken prisoner, doesn't care about your law, O King, but every day, three times a day, he prays to his God."

When the king heard these words, he was very, very upset with himself because he loved Daniel. He tried all day until the sun went down to think of a way to deliver Daniel from going to the den of lions. But the presidents and princes said, "According to the law of the Medes and Persians, once the king signed a law, he could not change it."

The king commanded Daniel to be brought to him. They took Daniel, and they threw him into the den of lions. (Imagine being thrown into a den of lions, *hungry* lions!) The king said to Daniel, "The God whom you serve, he will deliver you."

They took a big rock and put it over the opening of the den so Daniel had no way of getting out. He was trapped in there. The king sealed the rock with his signature, and the lords (who served the king), also sealed the rock with their signatures. This meant no one could go against the orders of the king and try to rescue Daniel from the den of lions.

The king went to his palace. He did not eat the whole night. He did not want to listen to music. He could not sleep. It seemed as if morning would never come. Morning did come, and the king rose up very early and ran to the den of lions. Why do you think he ran?

When he came to the den of lions, he cried out to Daniel with a sad, weeping voice and said, "Daniel, O Daniel, servant of the living God. Did your God, whom you serve, did he deliver you from the lions?"

Daniel answered, "O King, live forever. My God sent his angel and shut the lions' mouths. They have not hurt me. My God found me innocent, and before you, O King, I have done nothing wrong."

The king was so happy! He commanded that they take Daniel out of the den of lions. When Daniel came out, they all saw that he was not hurt in any way, because he believed in God.

The king wrote a new law which stated, "Peace be multiplied to all people, nations, and languages in all the earth. I make a law that in every area of my kingdom, men will tremble and fear before the living God of Daniel; for he is the living God and he stays faithful forever. His kingdom will never be destroyed, and his power will be forever and ever. The living God, who delivered Daniel, delivers and rescues and works signs and wonders in heaven and earth."

God blessed Daniel in everything he did. God will bless you too when you give your heart and life to him. When you live your life for God, he will help you through the many hard times. He will then bless you because you stayed true to him.

Jesus Christ is the same yesterday and today and forever.

Hebrews 13:8 (ESV)

Where did this story take place?
What was the name of the king?
What three excellent qualities did Daniel have?
They threw Daniel into a den of _____?
Did God rescue Daniel?

JONAH

The fascinating story of Jonah's face-to-face meeting with God and nature took place in the eighth century before the Lord Jesus Christ was born. *Jonah* means "dove."

He was a prophet sent by God to go to Nineveh to tell the people there they must turn from their wicked ways. Nineveh was a great city in Jonah's time, but it was also one of the most sinful cities, and Jonah knew this.

Jonah also knew that if Nineveh would not ask God for forgiveness, then God would destroy the city. Jonah liked that idea. He wanted those people to pay for living their lives so wickedly. So instead of following God's orders, he thought he had a better idea. He caught the next ship to Tarshish, which did not go near Nineveh at all. He got a nice place on the ship and made himself cozy. He thought he had escaped from God, and he also knew that now Nineveh had an excellent chance of being destroyed. Who was going to preach repentance to the people there?

He thought he was running away from God, but the Bible tells us in Jeremiah 23:24, "Can anyone hide in secret places that I shall not see him, says the Lord; don't I fill heaven and earth, says the Lord?"

We know God had a watchful eye on Jonah, and God sent a great wind upon the sea.

Out of the wind, a storm exploded ripping across the waves, and all the men in the ship, which Jonah was on, became afraid. They each cried to their little god, but it was just no use. God wanted Jonah.

Now, while this tremendous storm was growing over the sea, Jonah was sound asleep in the ship. He was taking life easy until the captain of the ship came up to him and said, "Why are you sleeping? Wake up! Call to your God so that we will not die!"

When Jonah got up from his bed, all the men of the ship got together, and they gambled to see whose fault it was that had caused this storm to come in the first place. They gambled by drawing straws of all different sizes, and whoever had the smallest straw was in deep trouble with God. Who do you think drew the smallest straw? You guessed it! Jonah, of course. The men were scared! They asked him, "What do you for a living, where do you come from, and what nationality or race are you?"

Jonah answered, "I am a Hebrew. I respect the Lord, the God who made heaven and earth."

The men answered, "What can we do for you so that the sea will be calm again?"

Jonah told them, "Take me now and throw me into the water, and the sea will be calm once again, for I now know that I am the reason the Lord sent the storm."

But the men would not listen to Jonah; instead, they began to row harder and harder to try to bring the ship to land. But it was useless. The storm was too powerful, and they were going nowhere. In fact, the harder they rowed, the angrier the storm became. Frightful, isn't it?

Then they all cried to the Lord God and asked the Lord not to take their lives. It seemed they had no other choice than to throw Jonah overboard. They all picked Jonah up and threw him into the dark, deep ocean, and as soon as Jonah hit the water, the storm stopped. The sea, once again, became very calm. The men on the ship had earned a respect for the Lord God after they saw what happened, and they worshipped the Lord God.

The Lord did not forget about Jonah but had made a great big fish appear to come up to Jonah and swallow him. Jonah stayed in the belly of this great fish for three days and three nights. Quite a difference from his cozy place on the ship!

I am sure Jonah spent a lot of time thinking about all that happened. The Bible tells us that Jonah prayed to the Lord and cried out to him. He told the Lord about his sin of disobedience. He knew he should have listened to God. He also described to the Lord how it felt about being in the belly of the fish. He said he was in the deepest part of the waters and in the bottom of the mountains of the earth. He could feel the waters rushing over him while he was wrapped up in seaweed. Yes, God had to bring Jonah to his lowest point. This was the only way God could get Jonah's attention, for Jonah had a mighty work to perform for God, and no one else would be able to do it. God chose Jonah as his special ambassador.

You and I are also God's ambassadors if you know the Lord Jesus Christ as your personal Savior. Each one of us has a special place in the kingdom of God and a special job to do for him.

Jonah then asked the Lord for forgiveness, and he thanked God for hearing his prayer and for forgiving him of his sin of disobedience. He also thanked the Lord for bringing him out from the belly of the great fish.

How did Jonah know that God would forgive him and let him out of the fish's belly? Even Jonah, yes, even poor Jonah had a certain amount of faith in God. He knew God was merciful and slow to anger, but that faith was not put to use until Jonah was brought to the point where he could only depend on God. Let us trust in the Lord now so that when we go through hard times in our life, we will be able with joy to look up to the Lord Jesus. Jonah had to look up to God with sadness in his heart.

Yes, the Lord forgave Jonah, and then he spoke to him and told Jonah to go to Nineveh and preach to the people about their sins and how they needed forgiveness.

This time, Jonah got up and went straight to Nineveh. Now it took three whole days just to walk through that city. It was a very big place! On the first day, as Jonah entered the city, he cried out, "In forty days, this city will be destroyed because of your wickedness. Repent!"

When all the people of Nineveh (including the king) heard this, they believed what God told Jonah to say, and they made a fast. This means that they ate no food and dressed in rags and sat in ashes. The king of Nineveh left his throne, took his royal robe off, put on rags, and sat in ashes and ate no food. Everyone (including the animals) sat in rags and ashes and ate no food. They all cried out with a loud voice to the Lord God, asking for forgiveness.

The Lord God saw this and looked on them. He knew they were truly sorry for all the bad things they had done. God forgave them and did not destroy Ninevah.

God was pleased that all the people of Nineveh were truly sorry for their sins, but Jonah was very, very angry! He told the Lord, "The reason I did not go to Nineveh when you first asked me to go was because I knew that you, being a kind and forgiving God, would not destroy them if they repented. I did not want you to spare Nineveh because they deserve to die. Now, Lord, please take my life because it is better for me to die than to live."

God had to teach Jonah a little object lesson on how precious a life is. A soul is very important because once you die, you either go to heaven or to hell. There are no *second* chances after death. That is why God gave Ninevah a second chance while the people were still living.

God answered Jonah, "Do you have a right to be angry?" So Jonah left Nineveh, and he sat on the east side of the city. He wanted to see if there still may be a chance that God would destroy the city.

In the meantime, God had prepared a gourd (which is a fruit from the calabash tree. It is a common tree in that part of the world). God made the gourd to come over Jonah's head to protect him from the hot sun. This made Jonah very happy. But the next morning, God prepared a worm to kill the gourd, and the gourd died. Then God sent a furious east wind, and after the wind passed, God had the sun beating down on the head of Jonah. Jonah fainted from all of this and he said to himself, "I wish I were dead."

God spoke to Jonah and said, "Do you a right to be mad because of the gourd?" Jonah answered, "Yes, I do. I even have a right to wish I could die."

The Lord answered Jonah and said, "You feel sorry for the gourd, but you didn't plant the gourd, you didn't water the gourd, neither did you make it to grow. The plant was there for one day, and then it died, and here you are crying over it. What about Nineveh? There are over one hundred twenty thousand people and many cattle in that great city. These people cannot tell their right hand from their left hand because they don't know anything about me. Don't you think I should spare those poor, lost people who have asked for forgiveness?"

Oh yes, Jonah had many more lessons to learn from God, but Jonah did learn from this lesson how precious a soul is to the Lord God.

> Come to me, all you who are weary and burdened, and I will give you rest.
> And you will find rest for your souls.
>
> Matthew 11:28-29b (NIV)

Who told Jonah to go to Nineveh?
Where did Jonah go instead?
Why did the men on the ship throw Jonah overboard?
_____ days and _____ nights Jonah spent in the great fish's belly?
Did the people and the king of Nineveh ask God to forgive them of their sins?

QUEEN ESTHER

The biblical story of Esther took place at a time when the Jewish people were held prisoners in Persia. God never forgot about his people although they often forgot about him. In his great care for his own, he planned for Esther (a Jewish maiden) to become the queen of Persia and deliver her people from being killed.

In the darkest hour of our life, as we put our trust in the Lord, God stays faithful. Psalms 121:3 says, "He who watches over you will not sleep." Let us now see how God will put his loving plan to work.

During Esther's time, there was a king named Ahasuerus who reigned over Persia. During his third year of ruling the people, he made a feast for all his princes and servants. All the important people came to his banquet. While they were all enjoying his delicious food and never-ending wines, he showed them all the riches of his kingdom. This feast lasted one hundred eighty days. After that feast, the king made another feast. This time, he invited all the men whether they were rich or poor, important or unimportant. It took place in the king's garden, and it was beautifully decorated. It had colors of white and green and blue curtains, which were fastened with cords of fine linen and purple with silver rings around the curtains. It was attached to pillars of marble. The couches were gold and silver. The floor was made of red, blue, white, and black pavement. Every cup the men drank from was made of pure gold, and each cup was different. It lasted one week.

But one thing they had too much of at the banquet was wine and more wine. Every man was allowed to drink as much wine as he wanted, and no one could stop him or even tell him he was drinking too much. It was because of this, a very sad thing happened.

The queen's name was Vashti. During King Ahasuerus's feast, Queen Vashti also made a feast for all the women in the royal house.

Her feast lasted seven days also. On the seventh day of the feast, King Ahasuerus commanded his seven eunuchs to bring Queen Vashti before the king to show everyone how beautiful she was. She was only to wear her royal crown on her head. The king on this day of the feast was very drunk. When the queen heard what the king wanted, she refused to come. She said, "No!"

The king was mad! The Bible states, "His anger burned inside him."

Then the king said to his counselors, "How shall I punish the queen?"

One of his advisers, Memucan, answered, "Vashti, the queen has not only brought shame to the king but all the people too. Now, all the women will disobey their husbands because the queen disobeyed you. The women will rise up against their husbands if we don't punish the queen. I believe, O King, we should make a royal commandment and have it put into the law books that Queen Vashti will never again see the king. We shall choose another queen for you. This law will be written, read and sent all over your empire so that all wives will honor their husbands."

The king liked this idea very much, and it became a law and was read all over his kingdom. Queen Vashti was sent away to an unknown place and never saw the king or the palace again.

After some time had passed and when the king's anger went away, he remembered what he had done to the queen. The king's servants, knowing the king felt lonely, said, "Let's have all the young, single women from all over the area where the king reigns come to stay at the palace. We will have Hegai watch over them. We will let them go through beauty treatments and whichever maiden pleases the king, she will become the new queen." The king liked this plan, and it was soon made known throughout the area where the king reigned. All the single, young women came to the palace and stayed in a special part of the palace. One of the women was named Esther. Esther's mother and father had passed away when she was a little girl, but a close relative, named Mordecai, brought up Esther as if she was his own daughter. Esther was Jewish, and her name in the Hebrew language is Hadassah. The Bible states she was beautiful, and as soon as she was brought to the palace, Hegai liked her. He was very kind to Esther and wanted very much for the king to see her. He quickly gave her the beauty ointments and gave her seven maidens to help her. He put her in the best part of the palace where the women were staying.

Now Esther did not tell anyone she was Jewish. Mordecai told her not to tell it to anyone. Every day, Mordecai walked past where Esther was staying to see how she was doing. After a year had passed, Esther was to see the king. When Esther appeared before the king, everyone liked her. In fact, the king loved Esther above all the women, and he placed the royal crown on her head. Esther became the new queen. Then the king made a feast just for Esther. To celebrate his love for her, he told all the people there would be no more taxes and gave all the different places where he reigned presents.

Still, Esther did not tell anyone she was Jewish. She kept it a secret. She obeyed Mordecai. Mordecai had a position in the king's palace, and one day, he sat at the king's gate. While he was sitting, he overheard two of the king's servants, Bigthan and Teresh, planning to kill the king. Quickly, Mordecai told Queen Esther, and Esther told the king, "Mordecai overheard two of your servants planning to kill you."

The king had this matter checked out at once, and it was true. The king then had the two servants, Bigthan and Teresh, hanged on a tree, and this incident was recorded in the king's books.

King Ahasuerus never rewarded Mordecai for finding out about the plot to have him killed. Instead, the king gave a man named Haman a promotion. He made Haman higher than all the princes.

All the king's servants bowed before Haman as King Ahasuerus commanded—all except Mordecai. Mordecai would not bow before Haman. The king's servants told him to, but he would not listen. When Haman saw that Mordecai wouldn't bow in front of him, he became very angry. He wanted to grab Mordecai and harm him. Haman found out that Mordecai was Jewish (through the king's servants), and he began to think of a way to not only destroy Mordecai but all the Jewish people as well.

The Bible tells us that Haman "cast lots" or gambled to pick a month and a day that the Jewish people would be killed. In Hebrew, to gamble or to cast a lot is called Pur. Haman chose a superstitious way to pick the month and date, and it turned out to be the thirteenth of March. That was only eleven months away!

Haman began to put his plan into action. He went before the king and said, "There is a certain people living among us in every area where you reign and whose laws are different from our laws. They don't keep your laws, O King. What good does it do you, King Ahasuerus, to have these people living with us when they don't obey our rules? But I have an idea, O King, which would solve this problem. We should make a law to have these people destroyed, and I will put three hundred seventy-five tons of silver into the royal treasury for the men who carry out this business of having the Jews destroyed."

The king then took his ring off and gave it to Haman, saying, "You keep the silver and the people, and you do whatever you want with both the money and the people."

So on the thirteenth day of April (eleven months before the Jews would be destroyed), a law was written, passed, and sent to the governors and deputies over all the areas where King Ahasuerus reigned.

This law said that the Jews were to be destroyed and killed whether they were young or old, men, women, or children. All their property was to be taken. This would happen on March thirteen.

After reading this law to everyone, the king and Haman sat down to drink, but the people of the city of Shusan, (the capital where the king lived), were very upset about this news.

Haman wanted to see Mordecai killed because Mordecai would not bow down to him. Haman also knew Mordecai was Jewish and wanted to kill both Mordecai and the Jewish race. In order to do this, he lied about the Jewish people to the king, and the king believed him. But we know someone who is more powerful than Haman and the king put together, and since the Jewish people were his chosen people, we will now see God's plan put into action. We will also see what happens when man fights against God.

When Mordecai heard this news, he was very sad and went to the middle of the city and cried with a loud voice—weeping bitterly. Mordecai stood at the king's gate with his clothes torn and ashes all over him crying. In every place where the Jewish people lived, there was great sorrow. The people weren't eating. They were fasting (going without food) and crying loudly. Their clothes were torn, and they all sat in ashes. They felt their lives meant nothing. But God says in Psalms 121:4, "Behold, he that takes care of Israel will not sleep. The Lord will take care of you."

Esther's maids ran and told Esther that Mordecai was sad and sat in ashes with his clothes torn. Esther became very sad. She sent clothing to Mordecai, but he would not accept the new clothing. Esther then sent Hathach, (one of the king's servants), to find out why Mordecai was so sad. Mordecai told Hathach everything, and Hathach went back to the queen and explained the story of how Haman planned to kill all the Jewish people.

Hathach also showed Esther a copy of the law signed by the king, allowing the Jews to be destroyed on March thirteen. Esther then sent Hathach to Mordecai with this message, "All the people know that if you go into the king's inner court without being called by the king, you shall be put to death—unless he holds out the golden scepter, and then you will live. I have not been called by the king for thirty days." Hathach gave this message to Mordecai.

Mordecai answered, "You are also a Jew, and you will also be killed unless you go to the king now whether he calls you or not. If you tell him at this time, there is a chance we will be delivered. I believe, Esther, this is why the Lord God has made you queen. You can help us and deliver us all from this death sentence." Esther answered, "Gather all the Jewish people together and fast for three days and nights. I will also fast, and on the third day, I will go and see the king. If I die, I die." Mordecai listened to Esther and went to do what Esther asked.

On the third day, as Esther promised, she put on her royal clothing and stood in the king's inner court even though the king had not called her. The king was sitting on his throne in the inner court when he saw Esther standing before him. This could mean death to Esther, but instead, the king held out his golden scepter that was in his hand. Esther came close and touched the top of the scepter. The king asked Esther, "What would you like? I'll give you half the kingdom."

Queen Esther answered, "If it is all right with you, would you and Haman please come to a banquet today that I have made?"

Later during the banquet, the king asked Esther, "What is it that you would like? I will give you half the kingdom." Esther answered, "My request is, if it pleases you, O King, let Haman and yourself come again to a big dinner I shall make for the both of you tomorrow. At tomorrow's fancy dinner, I will tell you my request."

It took a lot of courage for Esther to see the king without his permission, but she knew she must take a stand for her people.

So the queen invited the king and Haman to another fancy dinner the following day. Haman was so excited that the queen was having a feast just for him and the king. Haman went home and told his wife and friends about this. He also told his wife about his big promotion and all the riches the king gave him. But no matter how happy Haman looked, he still became very angry when Mordecai would not bow down to him.

Haman's wife, Zeresh, and all his friends suggested to him, "Why not build a gallows and make it eighty-six feet high? Ask the king tomorrow if Mordecai could be hanged on the gallows. Then join the king at the fancy dinner and have a good time drinking and eating." Haman really liked this idea, and during the night, he had the gallows built just for Mordecai.

But that night while Haman was building the gallows, the king could not sleep, and he commanded that the king's books be read to him. The king discovered that Mordecai was the man who had told the king about the plot to have the king killed by his two servants. The king asked his servants, "Did we ever reward Mordecai for what he did? Did we honor him for learning about this plot?" The king's servants answered, "Nothing has been done for Mordecai. He was never rewarded."

The next morning, Haman came to see the king. He wanted to ask the king about having Mordecai be put to death on the gallows. But before he could say anything, the king asked Haman, "What should we do for a man that has shown me honor?"

Now Haman thought the king was talking about him, and so he answered, "Let this man wear your royal clothes and ride your horse and let him wear your royal crown. Let one of the king's princes take this man all through the city and let all the people know that you are having a parade for him by honoring him for all he has done for you."

Then the king said to Haman, "Hurry up and take my royal clothes, my horse, and my crown to Mordecai's house. Get him all ready, and I want you to lead him through the city, telling everyone that the king is honoring Mordecai."

Haman hated doing this, but he had no choice. When it was over, Haman ran to his home with his head covered in shame. Haman told his wife and his friends what happened that day, and they all said, "Now that the king has honored Mordecai, your plan will never work."

But it was too late. The king's servants came to Haman's house to bring him to the big dinner that the queen made for Haman and the king. So the king and Haman came to the feast that Esther made, and again the king asked the queen, "What is it that you want? I will give you half the kingdom."

Then the queen answered, "If I have found favor with the king, please hear my request. I and my people will be destroyed. We cannot even defend ourselves, for we were given no weapons. Instead, we will be killed. We have nothing to live for."

King Ahasuerus said to Esther, "Who is doing this to you and your people? Who would do this to my queen?"

Esther said, "It is your enemy, this wicked Haman!"

Then Haman became afraid, and the king rose up in anger from the dinner table and went to the palace garden. While he was there, Haman pleaded with Esther for his life.

Now, Esther was sitting on the couch, and Haman threw himself on the couch, and when the king saw this, he said, "Now you want to also harm my wife in front of me?"

One of the king's servants told the king that Haman had built a gallows to hang Mordecai on. The king said, "Instead of hanging Mordecai on the gallows, we shall hang Haman on it."

So the death sentence was passed, and Haman had to die.

All of this happened because Haman from the first day he met Mordecai thought evil thoughts of him. Haman's plan backfired.

Esther then had Mordecai brought before the king. Esther told the king how Mordecai was related to her and how he brought her up as a little child. The king took off his ring (which he had given to Haman), and gave it to Mordecai. Mordecai was given Haman's job.

Esther came before the king again (without his permission), crying and asking him if there was anything he could do to stop the Jewish people from being killed. The king held out his golden scepter, and Esther stood in front of the king. Esther said, "Is there a way we can have the law changed so that I and my people will not die on March thirteen?"

The king answered, "Yes." On this twenty-third day of the month of Sivan (nine months before March thirteen), the king passed a law that all the Jews in every place where the king reigned would be given everything they needed to defend themselves against anyone who would try to kill them.

This law was read in every city and area. Mordecai, who was now dressed in royal clothes instead of ashes, and all the Jewish people were filled with great joy and happiness. They knew they now had a chance to live.

Every city had a feast, and many people who were not Jews became Jews because they knew the king had shown kindness to the Jewish people.

Finally, that day came! All the Jewish people gathered themselves together in seven cities throughout all the area where King Ahasuerus reigned. Mordecai had become very respectful with all the people and was honored everywhere.

Because of Mordecai, all the princes, governors, deputies, and officers of the king helped the Jewish people.

On this day, the Jewish people won the battle over their enemies. In the capital city of Shusan, the Jews killed over five hundred men who had planned to destroy them. Also, the ten sons of Haman had joined in the war against the Jews, and they were also killed during battle. But the Jewish people did not take their land.

The king called Esther and said unto her, "Is there anything else I can do for you?"

Esther answered, "Yes, please have Haman's sons hanged on the gallows tomorrow." The king granted Esther's request, and the ten sons of Haman were hung on the gallows the following day.

Esther also requested to let the Jewish people defend themselves again tomorrow. Esther knew there still might be some men who would want to try tomorrow to go to battle with her people. The king granted this request also.

Outside of the capital city, the Jewish people held a feast to celebrate their victory, and the Jews living in the capital city held their feast on the fifteenth day of March.

Some of the Jewish people even sent presents to each other because they were so happy to be living. Mordecai passed a law that each year on the thirteenth and fourteenth of March, they would celebrate and remember that they could have been killed, but because of God's loving care, they are now living. They called these two days Purim after the name Pur (*Pur* is to cast lots which wicked Haman did in order to destroy all the Jews).

Mordecai was given many promotions over the years and became the next one to reign in power to King Ahasuerus. The Word of God tells us all of this is written down in the great books of the kings of Media and Persia. And to this date, the Jewish people all over the world still celebrate this victory.

Yes, the Word of God, the Bible is *living* today. The same way God helped his people overcome and live a victorious life, is still the same way that God will help each one of us to live a happy and victorious life today. Let us look to him with the rest of our life. Let us give the Lord Jesus Christ first place in our heart and life.

> I can do all things through Christ, who strengtheneth me.
> Philippians 4:13 (Webster's Bible)

What is the name of the king?
What is the name of the queen that the king sent away?
What is the new queen's name?
What is the name of the man that wanted to kill Mordecai and all the Jewish people?
What happened to this man?

BABY LORD JESUS

Do you know how the Lord Jesus Christ came into the world? Would you like to learn how God himself visited us many years ago? In this Bible story, we will learn about how much God loves us and how God sent us a "little love present" from heaven. Let's begin.

In the sixth month of the Jewish year, an angel named Gabriel was sent by God from heaven to earth with a very important message. You might think that because of this important message, the angel Gabriel would go to see the most important people on earth such as kings and queens. But God, in his wisdom, sent the angel Gabriel to visit a special young Jewish woman named Mary who lived in a town called Nazareth which is in Israel. At that time, Nazareth was a very poor and simple little town. No kings or queens ever lived there, just daily hardworking people. (So far in our story, we can begin to see how God is interested in common everyday people such as you and me today.)

Now Mary was engaged to a young man named Joseph who was a carpenter. Do you know what a carpenter does? That's right.

He makes and fixes things such as chairs and tables with his special tools such as a hammer and nails. In those days, a carpenter did not make a lot of money, but he did spend long hours working very hard. It was to this young woman and this young man that God sent the angel Gabriel. God was going to use them to do something great and mighty that would change the rest of the world forever.

Boys and girls, we should try to be little workers for God. God is very pleased when he sees you helping and obeying your father and mother. By obeying your parents, God knows that one day, you will be able to help him to do something wonderful also.

One day while Mary was alone, Gabriel appeared to her. You could imagine how frightened Mary must have been to look up and suddenly see an angel from God standing near her, but the angel spoke kindly to Mary and said, "You have been chosen by God because of your faith. The Lord is with you. Do not be afraid, Mary, for the Lord God is very pleased with your life. You will have a little boy, and you will call his name Jesus. He will be great, and he will be called the Son of the Highest. He shall be king, and he will rule forever and forever. His kingdom will never end."

Mary asked the angel, "How can I have a child when I am not married? I never had a baby before."

The angel answered, "The Holy Spirit will come to you, and the power of God will cover you, and the holy thing that will take place when God covers you will be called the Son of God. Nothing will be impossible with God."

There are times when you may think that God cannot help you with your problems. You may have forgotten how great God is, but the Bible tells us in Philippians 4:13, "I can do all things through Christ who gives me strength." Let us try to remember this important fact.

Mary answered the Lord, "I am the Lord's servant. I will obey the Lord."

Gabriel then left Mary. The Bible said Mary went away for a while to visit her cousin Elisabeth. While she was there, Mary gave God all the praise and all the glory for choosing her to be the mother of the Savior of the whole world. Mary spoke about all the magnificent things God did for the Jewish people and how God really does care about the poor and needy people. The Bible tells us in 1 Peter 5:7, "Casting all your care upon God; for he cares for you."

Mary stayed three months with her cousin, Elisabeth, and then went back to her home. In the meantime, Joseph was upset that Mary was going to have a baby because they weren't married yet. He thought a lot about what would happen if everyone found out.

While he was thinking about this, he fell into a deep sleep and began to dream. In his dream, an angel of the Lord appeared to him and said, "Do not be afraid to marry Mary, for God has chosen her to give birth to a son, and you, Joseph, will call his name Jesus, for he shall save his people from their sins."

When Joseph woke up, he believed and obeyed the Lord, and he married Mary. After they were married, the ruler of the land, named Caesar Augustus, passed a law which said that everyone in the world must be registered so that they can begin to pay taxes. In order to be registered, you must go back to where your family came from. Since Joseph was the husband, he and Mary went to his family's birthplace, which was a little town among the hills called Bethlehem.

God planned all along that Joseph and Mary would return to Bethlehem before the baby Jesus would be born, for Joseph was from the same family as King David. Remember him?

The Bible tells us that the Lord Jesus Christ would be born from the same family as King David. King David was also born in Bethlehem. God never lies.

After registering, Mary was ready to give birth to God's only Son, the Lord Jesus Christ. Because of all the people in Bethlehem, they could not find a place to sleep in the inn, so they had to go sleep in the manger. A manger is where they keep all the animals such as sheep, goats, and donkeys. In a manger, you will find straw for the animals. This is where, on that beautiful star-filled night that God created, the baby Jesus came into the world. Mary wrapped her newborn little boy in rags, for that is all she had. She laid him in the crib where the animals ate their food.

Can you begin to understand how the almighty God loves you so much he humbled himself so that you and I might one day go to heaven to live with him?

On that special, glorious night, shepherds came and visited the baby Jesus. A very great number of angels appeared suddenly in the sky and began to praise God, saying, "Glory to God in the highest, and on earth peace, good will to men." The wisemen came from faraway bringing the baby Jesus three precious gifts: Gold tells us of the Lord Jesus Christ being king forever; Frankincense is a very sweet perfume, and it tells us that the Lord Jesus's life was like a sweet perfume to God. (Luke 3:22 tells us that God said, "You are my beloved Son whom I love. With you, I am well pleased.") Myrrh is a bitter plant, which means the plant tastes terrible, and you wouldn't want to eat it. That gift tells us how the Lord Jesus Christ died on the cross for our sins. He took your place and my place so that we can go to heaven with him.

The most wonderful thing you can do in the whole wide world for God is to let the Lord Jesus Christ come into your heart and live your whole life for him. "For God so loved the world that he gave his only begotten Son that whosoever believeth in him should not perish but have everlasting life." (John 3:16)

Let us remember to thank the Lord God for caring and loving us so very, very much.

> Christ Jesus came into the world to save sinners.
> 1 Timothy 1:15b (AKJV)

Who told Mary she was going to have a baby?
What was the name of the man who married Mary?
Where was baby Jesus born since there was no room in the inn?
Why was this baby special?
What two different types of people visited the baby Lord Jesus after he was born?

JESUS IN THE TEMPLE

Boys and girls, this is a true story about the Lord Jesus Christ. The Passover took place once a year in Jerusalem. It was the time to remember when Moses, God's servant, led the Jewish people out of Egypt to the promised land as God commanded.

In this true story, this was the first time the Lord Jesus went with his parents to the Passover in Jerusalem. The Lord Jesus was twelve years old according to the Bible when he went.

The Passover lasted for seven days. When it was over, Joseph and Mary left Jerusalem with many other people to return to their home in a town called Nazareth.

In the meantime, while they were on their way home, the Lord Jesus stayed behind in Jerusalem. Joseph and Mary did not know this. They thought the Lord Jesus was with them and that he was somewhere, someplace with the big crowd of people that they were traveling with on their way back home to Nazareth.

Joseph and Mary traveled a whole day's journey before they asked about the Lord Jesus. When they could not find the Lord Jesus, Joseph and Mary went looking for him in the crowd. They thought, perhaps, he was with relatives and friends. But the Bible tells us, boys and girls, that when Joseph and Mary could not find the Lord Jesus with relatives and friends, Joseph and Mary went back to Jerusalem to look for him there.

I am sure they were very worried about the Lord Jesus. Where could the Lord Jesus be?

Finally, Joseph and Mary came to Jerusalem. They looked everywhere for the Lord Jesus. It took them three days to find him in Jerusalem! On the third day, they found the Lord Jesus Christ. And where did they find him? They found the Lord Jesus in the temple, which is the place of worshipping God. There was the Lord Jesus Christ, only twelve years old, in the temple, sitting in the middle of all the Jewish teachers! Imagine that, boys and girls!

Boys and girls, these Jewish teachers studied everything that was written in the Holy Scriptures about God! Here was the Lord Jesus listening to them and asking questions to these wise Jewish teachers. The Bible tells us that all of them who heard the Lord Jesus speaking were amazed at the Lord Jesus's understanding and his answers of the things belonging to God! These Jewish teachers could not believe the wisdom of God that was in the Lord Jesus at the age of twelve!

The Bible tells us, boys and girls, that the Lord Jesus Christ is God. The Jewish teachers did not know that God himself was sitting among them and talking to them!

Now when Joseph and Mary saw the Lord Jesus with the Jewish teachers in the temple at Jerusalem, they were shocked! They said to the Lord Jesus, "Son, why did you do this to us? Look, your father and I have been searching for you, wondering where you were. We were so sad!"

The Lord Jesus Christ said to Joseph and Mary, "Why did you have to search for me? Didn't you know that I must be doing my Father's work?" Boys and girls, the Lord Jesus Christ is speaking about his true Father in heaven.

His name is God. But Joseph and Mary did not understand what the Lord Jesus Christ said to them. The Lord Jesus went back with them to Nazareth, his hometown in Israel.

The Bible tells us that the Lord Jesus Christ was obedient and honored Joseph and Mary, his earthly parents.

The Bible tells us that the Lord Jesus grew more and more in wisdom and in good morals obeying the law and in grace, joy, and love with God and with man. The Bible tells us that God said to the Lord Jesus Christ, "You are my beloved Son. In you, I am well pleased." (Luke 3:22)

How about us, boys and girls? Can God say those same words to us? Would we like to hear God say those words to us? He can say, "I am well pleased with you," if you allow his Son, the Lord Jesus Christ, to come into your heart and into your life. What beautiful words coming from the mouth of God!

> And ye shall seek me, and find me, when ye shall search for me with all your heart. And I will be found by you, saith the Lord.
>
> Jeremiah 29:13–14a (AKJV)

What took place once a year in Jerusalem?
How old was Jesus in this story?
Why did Joseph and Mary go back to Jerusalem?
It took ____days before Joseph and Mary found Jesus in Jerusalem?
Who was Jesus talking to when Joseph and Mary finally found Jesus?

FOLLOW ME: FISHERS OF MEN

When the Lord Jesus Christ walked on this earth, he spent his last three years preaching and healing people. The Lord Jesus Christ went about doing good. The Lord Jesus Christ told the people he is God and that he is come down, in the form of a man, to save them from their sins.

The Lord Jesus Christ also did many powerful and wonderful miracles! The Lord Jesus Christ made the blind to see, the deaf to hear and the lame to walk. The Lord Jesus Christ made the dead to rise!

Boys and girls, who could do all those miracles? Only *God* could do all those miracles! The Bible tells us that the Lord Jesus Christ *is* God. This story, boys and girls, took place in the beginning of the Lord Jesus's work on earth.

Let us begin the true story according to the Word of God: Right after the Lord Jesus Christ had healed many people of many different kinds of sicknesses, he went to a lake called Lake Gennesaret. Lots of people followed the Lord Jesus Christ. They wanted to hear him speak and teach the Word of God to them!

At the lake of Gennesaret, the Lord Jesus saw two boats. The boats were standing by the lake, but the fishermen were not in the boats. The fishermen were standing in the water washing their fishing nets.

The Lord Jesus went into one of the boats which belonged to a man named Simon Peter.

The Lord Jesus sat down in the boat and asked someone to please push the boat out a little into the water. The Lord Jesus Christ then began to preach and to teach the people.

How thirsty the people were to hear the Lord Jesus Christ preach to them and to speak to them about things in heaven and earth!

Boys and girls, have you ever felt thirsty for God? Have you ever felt you wanted to see God and get to know God and to tell God everything? That's feeling thirsty for God. You are longing for God.

Boys and girls, the Bible tells us in John 4:14, The Lord Jesus Christ said, "Whosoever drinks of the water that I will give him, will *never* thirst again."

When the Lord Jesus stopped speaking to the people, he said to Simon Peter, who was the owner of the boat, "Go out into the deep part of the water and let down your fishing nets for a gigantic number of fishes."

Simon Peter said, "Master, we have worked all night, and we have caught nothing. There are no fishes in this lake, but because you said to let down our nets into the water, we will do it."

So the fishermen did as the Lord Jesus told them, and they let down their nets into the water and wow! What a surprise!

Into the fishing net came a huge amount of fishes! There were so many fishes their fishing net broke! They called other people who were in other fishing boats to please help them. And the other people came. Together they filled the two boats with fishes. The boats were so heavy with the fishes the boats began to sink!

Wow! What a miracle. Boys and girls, right before their eyes, the Lord Jesus Christ (who is God), created tons of fishes! When Simon Peter saw this miracle, he fell down at the Lord Jesus's feet and said, "Depart from me, for I am a sinner, O Lord."

Everyone was amazed at the great number of fishes that they caught the day the Lord Jesus Christ spoke to them!

The Bible tells us, boys and girls, that Simon Peter had two other friends who were also fishermen. Their names were James and John. These three men were surprised at what the Lord Jesus did just for them!

The Lord Jesus Christ said to them, "Do not be afraid. From now on, you will catch men."

When the three of them had brought the boats back to land, the three men left their boats, left their fishing nets, left all the fishes behind, and followed the Lord Jesus Christ from that day on.

Simon Peter, James, and John became the first followers of the Lord Jesus Christ. From that moment on, they caught men for God and for the kingdom of heaven!

Boys and girls, would you like to "catch" other boys and girls for God? First, you must be cleansed from your sin by asking the Lord Jesus Christ into your heart and into your life.

You see, boys and girls, sin is bad. Sin is evil. Sin is an enemy of God. Sin is of the devil.

God is holy. God is good. God is pure. Boys and girls, the Bible tells us in Romans 5:8: "But God showed his love toward us in that while we were still sinners, Christ died for us."

God loves you so much that he sent his only Son, the Lord Jesus Christ, to die for your sins. If you ask the Lord Jesus Christ to come into your heart and take away your sins, He will do just that! He will come in, and he will give you a clean heart. He will take all your sins away. Now, you can go to heaven!

He will give you a beautiful home in heaven where you will live with him forever and ever. Isn't that wonderful? Only God could do that! Then you will be able to "catch" other boys and girls for God. You will be God's little fisher of men!

> Follow me, and I will make you fishers of men.
>
> Matthew 4:19 (AKJV)

Lois M. Bitler

What are some of the miracles that the Lord Jesus did?
Do you remember the name of the lake that Jesus went to?
Who owned the boat that Jesus sat down in?
What miracle did the Lord Jesus do for the fishermen?
Who were the first three followers of the Lord Jesus Christ?

YOU MUST BE BORN AGAIN!

NICODEMUS

Boys and girls, this is a true story about a Pharisee named Nicodemus. A Pharisee was a religious ruler in Israel. He taught the Jewish people the rules of the Bible. This story begins when a Pharisee named Nicodemus came to see the Lord Jesus Christ at night. Nicodemus wanted to find out more about the Lord Jesus Christ.

When Nicodemus found the Lord Jesus, he said to him, "Rabbi, we know that you are a teacher that has come from God, for no one can do the miracles that you do unless God is with you."

The Lord Jesus Christ looked at Nicodemus, and with all the love the Lord Jesus had, he said to him, "Truly I say to you, unless a man is born again, he will not see the kingdom of heaven."

Nicodemus didn't understand that the Lord Jesus Christ was talking about Nicodemus's own precious soul. Nicodemus thought he was talking about being born again on earth the way a baby is born.

Nicodemus said, "How can a man be born when he is old? Can he go back into his mother's womb and be born?"

Lovingly, the Lord Jesus answered, "Truly, truly, I say to you, unless a man is born of water and of Spirit, he cannot enter into the kingdom of heaven. That which is born of the flesh is flesh, and that which is born of the Spirit is spirit."

Boys and girls, the Lord Jesus Christ was saying to Nicodemus that with the help of the Holy Spirit, you can ask the Lord Jesus

Christ to come into your heart. Nicodemus was amazed that the Lord Jesus said, "You must be born again."

Nicodemus thought that because he was a religious ruler of the Jewish people and that he obeyed the rules of the Bible, he was already going to Heaven.

But that is not true. You must be born again. You must be born from above. You must ask the Lord Jesus Christ into your heart. The Lord Jesus saw that Nicodemus was surprised and amazed at that answer, and so the Lord Jesus Christ said to Nicodemus, "Don't be shocked that I have said to you, 'You must be born again.'"

To help Nicodemus understand the things of God, things you cannot see with your eyes or touch with your hands, the Lord Jesus Christ used the wind as an example. He said, "Nicodemus, the wind blows where it wants. You hear the sound of the wind, but you cannot see it. You cannot tell where the wind came from and where the wind is going. When you are born again, the Holy Spirit comes into your life and stays there. You cannot see him, but he is there."

Nicodemus said to the Lord Jesus, "How can this happen? I don't understand." Nicodemus was spiritually blind and needed the Lord Jesus Christ to come into his heart.

The Lord Jesus said, "Nicodemus, how can you be a teacher of the Jewish people and yet you don't know these things?" Poor Nicodemus was lost without the Lord Jesus, just like so many of us today.

The Lord Jesus said, "Truly, truly, I say to you, 'We speak about what we know.'"

Boys and girls, the Lord Jesus Christ was talking about God the Father, God the Son and God the Holy Spirit. The Bible tells us that they have been here since the beginning, even before the earth was made. The Lord Jesus continued, saying, "We know what it means to be born again, but you, Nicodemus, don't accept what we are saying. Now, Nicodemus, if I told you about the things of earth, things that you can see with your eyes and touch with your hands, and you don't believe me, how then will you believe me if I tell you of things in heaven which you cannot see with your eyes or touch with your hands? Nicodemus, for God so loved the world that he gave his only begotten Son that whosoever believes in Him shall not perish but have everlasting life."

Boys and girls, Nicodemus did become born again. He asked the Lord Jesus Christ to come into his heart. He began to understand the deep things of God.

How about you? Do you know that your soul is very precious to God? Do you know that when you die, your soul will keep on living forever? It will either live in heaven or in hell. The most important thing you can do in your life is to ask the Lord Jesus Christ in your heart and in your life. If you ask him to come into your heart, he will give you a new heart, a new life, and a beautiful home in heaven. You will live with him forever. Won't you ask him into your heart today? He is waiting to come in. He loves you so very much!

You must be born again.

John 3:7 (ESV)

When did Nicodemus come to see the Lord Jesus?
Nicodemus was a religious ruler called a _____?
What did the Lord Jesus tell Nicodemus he needed to do in order to enter into the kingdom of heaven?
Did Nicodemus ask the Lord Jesus to come into his heart?
Did the Lord Jesus love Nicodemus?

THE PERSISTENT FOUR

This is a true story of how the persistent four brought a paralyzed man to the all-powerful Savior. The Lord Jesus Christ was in a town called Capernaum (a fishing town in Israel), for several days. He was at a certain home in Capernaum, and in no time at all, everyone knew where the Lord Jesus Christ was staying. Suddenly, there were a lot of people in the house, outside the house, and around the house where the Lord Jesus was staying! The Bible says, "The Lord Jesus Christ preached the Good News to all the people." Everyone had a chance to hear what the Lord Jesus was saying.

As the Lord Jesus was speaking, along came four men carrying a bed with a paralyzed man on the bed. (This paralyzed man could not move any part of his body. He could not feel. He was crippled.)

As they were walking toward the house where the Lord Jesus was preaching, the persistent four realized they could not come near to him because of all the people pushing to get closer to the Lord Jesus. That did not stop them from figuring out a way on how to get right up and close to the Lord Jesus Christ.

They were persistent, which means they were not going to give up! Why, why was it so important to bring this paralyzed man to the Lord Jesus Christ? We shall see.

They had a great idea! They thought if they could go up to the roof and remove some of the tiles, they could then lower their friend right down to where the Lord Jesus was standing. However, before they followed through with their plan, they had to count the cost. They knew they needed permission from the man who owned the house. They also knew they must sacrifice their time and money to repair the roof on this home. The decision was quickly made. Yes, they sacrificed themselves, their time, and their money in order for their friend to be with the Lord Jesus, and they did it all with love. Would you do the same?

They went up to the top of the house, removed some of the tiles on the roof, saw where the Lord Jesus was standing, and carefully lowered the bed which held their dear, paralyzed friend. They were successful! They landed the bed with their dear friend on it right in front of the Savior! That is persistence! They brought their paralyzed friend right to where he needed to be: in front of the Savior.

If we don't have the Lord Jesus Christ in our hearts and lives, we need to be in front of the Savior, the One who died for us, asking him to take away our sins and make us clean.

They had faith in the Lord Jesus Christ. They knew he alone could forgive and heal their friend. When Jesus saw their faith, he said to the paralyzed man, "Son, your sins are forgiven."

Has the Lord Jesus Christ forgiven your sins? Of course, there are those people who do not believe that the Lord Jesus Christ can forgive sins, and sure enough, some of these "religious men" said in their hearts, *How can this man forgive sins? Only God can do that.*

Immediately, the Lord Jesus Christ, knowing that they thought this in their hearts, said, "Why are you thinking these things in your heart? What is easier to say, your sins are forgiven or arise, take up your bed, and walk? But to show you that I have authority on earth to forgive sins because I am God I say, 'Arise, take up your bed, and go your way into your house.'"

Instantly, the paralyzed man got up, took up his bed, and walked before them all. All the people were amazed, and they gave God the glory and the praise saying, "This is truly a miracle."

The paralyzed man was able to get up because he believed the Lord Jesus Christ could heal him and forgive his sins. The once-paralyzed man must have thanked the Lord Jesus and his four friends over and over again.

Do you believe the Lord Jesus Christ can forgive sins? If you say no, your sins will keep you paralyzed. That's how you look before God. It is only when you say yes to the Lord Jesus Christ and ask him to forgive you of your sins can he tell you, "Arise and walk in a new way."

> For by grace you have been saved through faith. And this is not your own doing; it is the gift of God, not a result of works, so that no one may boast.
> Ephesians 2:8-9 (ESV)

What town did this story take place in?
How many friends carried the paralyzed man to the Lord Jesus?
What did they have to do so that the Lord Jesus could see and heal him?
Did the paralyzed man believe that Jesus could heal him?
Did the Lord Jesus heal this paralyzed man?

THE CALL OF MATTHEW

Boys and girls, when the Lord Jesus Christ first started his work on earth, he chose twelve men to be his followers. This is the story of Matthew. The Lord Jesus Christ chose Matthew to follow him.

Boys and girls, Matthew was a tax collector. In the days of the Lord Jesus, a tax collector was hated by the Jewish people. A tax collector was probably Jewish but worked for the Roman government. Many tax collectors would make the people pay them a lot more money than what the tax was. The tax collectors kept the extra money for themselves. Tax collectors became very rich by stealing extra money from the people. Can you see why, boys and girls, the Jewish people hated the tax collectors so much?

According to the Bible, Matthew also had another name. He was also called Levi. Sometimes in the Bible, he is called Matthew, and sometimes he is called Levi.

Let us begin the story according to the Bible. As the Lord Jesus Christ was walking, he saw a tax collector named Matthew sitting at the tax office. The Lord Jesus Christ said to Matthew, "Follow me."

Immediately, Matthew obeyed the Lord Jesus Christ and left his job and all the money and followed the Lord Jesus. Boys and girls, at that moment, Matthew became born again. He had received the Lord Jesus Christ into his heart and into his life.

To show the difference the Lord Jesus Christ had on his life, Matthew gave a big dinner. Matthew invited the Lord Jesus to the dinner. Matthew also invited all his friends (who were also tax collectors and sinners).

He wanted his friends to meet the Lord Jesus, the only One who changed his life forever. Matthew's life would never be the same again! The Lord Jesus Christ came to Matthew's dinner, and all the tax collectors and sinners sat down to eat with the Lord Jesus Christ in Matthew's house.

Boys and girls, in those days, the religious rulers of Israel were called Pharisees. The Pharisees' helpers were called scribes. They were supposed to teach the people about God. But many of the Pharisees and scribes were worse sinners than the tax collectors and sinners at Matthew's house!

Well, boys and girls, when the Pharisees and the scribes heard that the Lord Jesus was having dinner with Matthew and Matthew's friends, they became furious! I'm talking red hot and angry! They spoke many evil things against the Lord Jesus Christ.

The Pharisees and scribes said to the Lord Jesus Christ's followers, "Why do you eat with those terrible tax collectors and sinners?"

The Lord Jesus heard them saying that and then answered the Pharisees and scribes with these words: "They that are well do not need a doctor. They that are sick need a doctor. I did not come to earth to call the righteous, but I came to earth to call the sinners to repentance."

Then the Pharisees and scribes left the Lord Jesus alone. They did not know how to answer him. I am very sure Matthew was glad to have the Lord Jesus at his house that day! The Bible tells us that from that day on, Matthew left his job and became one of the twelve followers! He had made the Lord Jesus Christ his Master and Lord, instead of money. He had a new life! Matthew did the right thing.

Boys and girls, exactly who is a sinner? The Bible tells us in Romans 3:23, "For all have sinned and come short of the glory of God."

Boys and girls, we are all sinners! Each and every one of us! A sinner is a person who does not obey God. If for example, boys and girls, you tell a lie (which we all do), that is sin. It is against God, for sin is disobeying God. God is holy. God never sins.

God loves you so much that he sent his only Son, the Lord Jesus Christ, to die for your sins. If you ask the Lord Jesus Christ to come into your heart and take away your sins, he will! He will come in and give you a clean heart. He will take all your sins away. Now, you can go to heaven! He will give you a home in heaven where you will live with him forever and ever! Boys and girls, would you like that? What will you do with the Lord Jesus Christ?

> For I am not come to call the righteous, but sinners to repentance.
>
> Matthew 9:13b (AKJV)

What did Matthew do for a living?
What was Matthew's other name?
Who ate dinner with Matthew at his house?
Did Matthew ask the Lord Jesus into his heart?
Did Matthew become one of the twelve followers of the Lord Jesus?

POWERLESS MAN

This true story is one of the marvelous miracles that the Lord Jesus Christ performed. We shall see how the Lord Jesus healed a man who had no power to move his body. He couldn't move a leg, an arm, a finger, or any part of his body. It was only after the Lord Jesus Christ came into this man's life that this man could be made well. This powerless man let the Lord Jesus Christ heal him.

There was a special feast taking place at Jerusalem. (Jerusalem is the capital city of the country of Israel.) The Lord Jesus Christ went to Jerusalem. There were many gates around the city of Jerusalem. The Lord Jesus entered the city through the "sheep" gate. (This gate was used to bring sheep into Jerusalem for sacrifice.)

At this gate, there was a pool called Bethesda. This pool of Bethesda had five porches. On these five porches laid many of the sick people which were paralyzed, blind, lame, and had no power or strength in their bodies.

These poor, sick people truly believed with all their heart that an angel would touch the water at a certain time during the year. This gave the water a special healing power. Whoever stepped into the water first after the angel touched it would be healed.

There are people today who believe with all their heart that there are many ways to go to heaven. The Bible teaches that there is only one way to enter into heaven. In fact, it was the Lord Jesus Christ himself who said in John 14:6, "I am the Way, the Truth and the Life. No man comes unto the Father, except by me."

At this pool of Bethesda, there was a certain man who was sick for thirty-eight years. When the Lord Jesus saw him lying there, he had compassion (feelings) for him. Jesus knew (because he is God) that this man had no power or strength in his body for thirty-eight years. He said to the man, "Do you want to be made well?"

The man answered, "Sir, there is no man here to help me into the water when the angel touches the water. While I am trying to get to the water, someone else steps in before me."

The Lord Jesus Christ looked at this poor, powerless man, and with all his love, he said to the man, "Rise, take up your bed, and walk."

Instantly, the man was made well. He took up his bed and walked! He became a new man. No longer was he powerless. He was filled with a new strength in his body and a supernatural strength in his soul. The Lord Jesus not only healed his body, but he also took away this man's sin. This man put his faith in the Lord Jesus Christ and believed in him. He wanted the Lord Jesus to be in control of his life.

This story in the Bible ends with the man telling his own people and friends what the Lord Jesus did for him.

Today, the Lord Jesus Christ is still forgiving and making people new. He can change your life from being powerless to being powerful. What a wonderful friend we have in the Lord Jesus Christ.

> I am come that they might have life, and that they might have it more abundantly.
>
> John 10:10b (AKJV)

In what city did this story take place?
Through what gate did Jesus enter into this city?
What was the name of the pool?
Who did Jesus have compassion on?
Did the Lord Jesus heal this person?

FEEDING OF MULTITUDE

This is a story of how the Lord Jesus Christ performed a miracle and made enough food to feed over five thousand men, women, and children.

The Lord Jesus has just passed over to the other side of the sea of Galilee. Many people knew all about the miracles Jesus had performed: how he healed the sick, made the blind to see, the lame to walk, and many more. They couldn't wait to see the Lord Jesus for themselves. Already, there was a great number of people waiting to meet the Lord Jesus as he came to the other side of the sea of Galilee.

Before the Lord Jesus went to the people, he first took his twelve disciples up into a mountain, and sat with them. When the Lord Jesus is in your heart and life and you feel that the things and people of the world are bothering you, then you also need to get away and be with the Lord for a little while.

You need to spend time with him, you need to speak with him, and you need to let him know how you feel. He will give you strength to go on.

As the Lord Jesus and his disciples were sitting up on that mountain, the Lord Jesus looked up and saw a great number of people coming toward him. The Lord Jesus turned to one of his disciples, Philip, and said, "Where can we buy bread so that all these people can eat?"

The Lord Jesus knew that they had no food with them and being in the country, there was no place near them to buy food. What the Lord Jesus really wanted to know was if Philip had enough faith to believe that the Lord Jesus would be able to satisfy all the people's needs.

Philip did not understand what the Lord Jesus had meant, and he thought the Lord Jesus was talking about buying food to feed all these people. Philip said to the Lord Jesus, "The little bit of money that we have will never feed all these people."

Another disciple, named Andrew (Peter's brother), said to the Lord Jesus, "Here's a little boy with five loaves of bread and two small fishes. But how can these five loaves of bread and two small fishes feed all these people?"

Jesus answered, "Have *everyone* sit down on the grass."

The disciples walked around and had all the people, (which were over five thousand), sit down on the cool, green grass. The Lord Jesus then took the five loaves of bread and the two small fishes and gave thanks to God the Father for the food.

This is why we should also give thanks to God for our food. The Lord Jesus gave us an example for us to follow. The Lord Jesus then asked the disciples to walk around and to give food to all the people until they were all filled. What a big surprise the disciples had when they saw that the food never ran out! Out of five loaves and two small fishes, the Lord Jesus fed over five thousand men, women, and children. In fact, when everyone was full, the disciples gathered up the leftovers, and they filled twelve baskets with bread and fish! Each disciple had a basket of food to eat from. The Lord Jesus did not forget his own.

The Lord Jesus made use of every little piece of bread and fish. Nothing was wasted. Truly, the Lord Jesus Christ is the true Bread of Life!

> He that believeth on me hath everlasting life. I am that bread of life.
>
> John 6:47–48 (AKJV)

Before the Lord Jesus met all the people, where did he take his disciples?

When Jesus saw that the people were hungry, what did he ask Philip?

A little boy had _____ loaves of bread and _____ fishes?

How many people were sitting on the grass waiting for something to eat?

Was the Lord Jesus able to do a miracle and feed all the people?

PETER'S WALK OF FAITH

The Lord Jesus Christ, who is God, had just done a mighty miracle. (A miracle is something so wonderful only God could do it.) There were over five thousand men, women, and children sitting down on the grass. The Lord Jesus Christ felt so sorry for them; he knew he must help them. So with all the love the Lord Jesus had, he healed the sick people of all their diseases. When he finished, he had all the people sit down, and then he fed them. But how could he feed five thousand people? After all, he only had five loaves of bread and two fishes. But that didn't stop the Lord Jesus Christ! He gave thanks for the five loaves of bread and two fishes, and then his twelve followers gave out enough food to feed over five thousand men, women, and children! What a miracle! What a powerful Lord we have!

After he had healed the sick and fed them, he sent them home, healed of their illnesses. He then told his twelve followers to get into a boat and to go to the other side of the sea. He told them he would be with them later. The twelve followers obeyed the Lord Jesus Christ and went in a boat and began to crossover to the other side of the sea.

Meanwhile, the Lord Jesus Christ went up into a mountain to pray to his heavenly Father. Boys and girls, did you know that the Lord Jesus Christ loved to pray? Do you remember to pray to your heavenly Father?

The Lord Jesus Christ stayed praying on the mountain alone until very late in the evening. When the Lord Jesus Christ finished praying, He went to see where his twelve followers were in the boat.

By this time, the twelve followers were in the middle of the sea. They were having a terrible time because the angry waves of the sea were tossing the boat (and them) back and forth, back and forth.

The Bible tells us that between three o'clock in the morning and six o'clock in the morning, the Lord Jesus Christ came to them walking on the water! They were all very scared when they saw the Lord Jesus. They yelled out, "It's a ghost!"

Right away, the Lord Jesus Christ said to them, "Don't be scared. Be happy. It is I. Don't be afraid."

Peter, said, "Lord, if it is you, tell me to come to you."

The Lord Jesus said, "Come."

Peter stepped out of the boat, put his feet on the water, and began to walk on the water! Another mighty miracle! Peter walked right toward the Lord Jesus Christ! As long as Peter looked at the Lord Jesus Christ, he continued to walk on the water.

But poor Peter (just like so many of us) took his eyes off the Lord Jesus. Peter became afraid because the wind was blowing over the sea, making a very loud noise. Peter began to sink down into the water.

Peter cried out, "Lord, save me." Right away, the Lord Jesus stretched out his hand and saved Peter and said to him, "O, you of little faith, why did you doubt?"

After the Lord Jesus and Peter went back into the boat, the wind became calm and quiet. Everyone in the boat fell down before the Lord Jesus Christ and worshipped the Lord Jesus Christ, saying, "It really is true, you are the Son of the living God!"

Yes, boys and girls, truly the Lord Jesus Christ is the Son of God who died on a cross for your sins and my sins. If you cry out to him, "Lord, save me, come into my heart and my life. Please take all my sins away." He will do just that. You will be falling down before him—worshipping and thanking him for that day when he passed your way.

> O you of little faith, why did you doubt?
>
> Matthew 14:31b (ESV)

Where did the Lord Jesus tell his disciples to go while he went up to a mountain to pray?

Did the Lord Jesus spend a lot of time praying up on the mountain?

What did the disciples think they saw walking on the water?

What did Peter say to Jesus while he was sinking down into the water?

Did the Lord Jesus save Peter from drowning?

BLIND MAN

When the Lord Jesus Christ walked on this earth, he performed many miracles. (A miracle is something that is so marvelous, it makes you realize only God could have done it.) This story is just one of the many miracles that the Lord Jesus Christ (who is God) had done. As the Lord Jesus Christ was passing by, he saw a blind man. From the moment this man was born, he was blind.

The Lord Jesus had twelve disciples, who went with him everywhere. When these disciples saw this blind man, they asked the Lord, "Master, did this man sin, or did his parents sin? Is that why he was born blind?"

The Lord Jesus answered, "This man did not sin, neither did his parents sin. This man was born blind so that God could work a miracle in this man's life in order that all could see."

Boys and girls, this man was born blind. He was physically blind. He was also spiritually blind. If you do not have the Lord Jesus Christ in your heart, you are spiritually blind. That means you are lost (you cannot find your way), and you will not go to heaven.

You live in darkness. The Lord Jesus has told us in John 14:6, "I am the Way, the Truth, and the Life. No one comes to the Father except by me." Because of this blind man, the Lord Jesus is going to give everyone a chance to be able to see spiritually and be able to enter into heaven.

The Lord Jesus said, "I must do God's work while I am living and walking on earth. As long as I am in the world, I am the light of the world."

When the Lord Jesus finished speaking, he spat on the ground and made clay. He put the clay on the eyes of the blind man by gently rubbing the man's eyes. Then the Lord Jesus said, "Go and wash in the pool of Siloam."

Many people used this pool of Siloam to wash their clothes or their vegetables or even their children. Once in a while, a shepherd may come to wash his sheep. It is no wonder, then, that the Lord Jesus sent this man to wash in the pool of Siloam. He must wash away the clay from his eyes so that he could see.

The blind man obeyed the Lord, and he went to the pool of Siloam, and he washed his eyes. When he finished washing his eyes, he opened them and received a big surprise. He could see! He was no longer blind. How happy he must have been. The neighbors and others who had seen this once-blind man said, "Isn't that the man who was blind and used to beg?"

Some people said yes, and some people said no, but the blind man said, "I was that blind man that used to beg."

They asked him, "How is it that you could see? What happened?"

When you accept the Lord Jesus Christ into your heart and you really want to please him, people will ask you the same question, "What happened?" That is your chance to tell them about the love of God and how God sent his Son to die on the cross to take away your sin.

The once-blind man answered, "A man named Jesus made clay and rubbed it on my eyes and said to me, 'Go to the pool of Siloam and wash.' I went, and I washed, and I received my sight. I now can see."

They said, "Where is Jesus?"

He said, "I don't know."

Then the people took this man, who could now see, to the Pharisees. (The Pharisees were one of the groups of religious leaders in those days.) It was on the Sabbath or the holy day of rest that the Lord Jesus Christ gave the blind man his sight. According to what the Pharisees taught, you were not to do anything on the Sabbath such as cooking, cleaning, working, and certainly no miracles! Not even if it meant helping another person.

The Pharisees asked him, "How did you receive your sight?"

The man replied, "He put clay on my eyes, I washed, and I see."

Some of the Pharisees said, "This Jesus doesn't come from God because he does not keep the Sabbath."

Others said, "How can a man that you call a sinner do these wonderful miracles?" Some of the Pharisees believed and some of them did not believe.

The Pharisees said to the man, "What do you think of this man who opened your eyes?" The man answered, "He is a prophet."

But the Jews did not believe this man was born blind, and so they sent for his parents. They asked his parents, "Is this man your son? Was he born blind? How is it that he now sees?"

His parents responded, "This is our son, and he was blind when he was born, but why does he see now? We don't know. Who opened his eyes? We do not know. Why don't you ask our son? He is old enough to answer the question. He can speak for himself."

The reason why the parents answered this way is because the Jews had an agreement that whoever says that Jesus is the Messiah, the Savior, would never again be able to worship in the temple. The parents were afraid that they would be thrown out of the temple and would never again be able to worship God there.

The Pharisees would not leave the blind man alone, and again he was brought to them. They told him to give God the praise because this Jesus is just a man and a sinner. The blind man was not afraid of them and said, "Whether he is a sinner or not, I don't know. But one thing I do know—I was blind, but now I see."

Again they said to him, "What did he do? How did he open your eyes?"

The man replied, "I told you already, but you will not listen. Do you want me to tell you again? Will you be his disciples or followers then?"

Then the Pharisees spoke very meanly to him and said, "You are his disciple, but we are Moses's disciples. We know God spoke to Moses, but as for this fellow, this Jesus, we don't even know where he comes from."

The man answered, "Isn't this marvelous? Isn't this something? You don't know where Jesus comes from, and yet he did a miracle and opened my blind eyes, and now I see. We know God does not listen to the wicked person, but if you love, worship, and obey God, God hears you. Tell me, since the beginning of the world, who gives sight to a blind man? If this man did not come from God, he could never have done this wonderful miracle. He could do nothing!"

The Pharisees were mad! They said to the once-blind man, "You were born in sin and now you're going to teach us?"

They threw this man out of the place of worship! When the Lord Jesus heard that the Pharisees threw this man out of the temple, Jesus looked for him. When he found the once-blind man the Lord Jesus said, "Do you believe on the Son of God?"

The man asked, "Who is he, Lord, that I could believe on him?"

Jesus answered, "It is the one that you see now and the one who is talking with you."

He said, "Lord, I believe, and he worshipped the Lord Jesus Christ."

This man was once blind, physically and spiritually, but at the moment he said, "Lord, I believe," he could *see spiritually*. Even though he could never again worship God in the temple (for the Pharisees threw him out), he had something far better. He had the Lord Jesus Christ in his heart, in his mind, and in his soul. He had eternal life.

> I am the light of the world. Whoever follows me will not walk in darkness, but will have the light of life.
>
> John 8:12 (ESV)

What was wrong with this man?
Where did Jesus send him to wash his eyes?
How did the Lord Jesus heal this man?
Who was angry that the Lord Jesus healed this man?
Did this man ask the Lord Jesus into his heart?

JAIRUS'S DAUGHTER

Here is an amazing story of how the Lord Jesus Christ did a mighty miracle and brought back to life a little girl who had died. It all started when the Lord Jesus had come over, by boat, to the other side of the lake. As soon as he stepped out of the boat and onto the dry ground, a man ran up to him and threw himself down at his feet. Who was this man?

This man's name was Jairus. He was one of the leaders of the temple. A temple was the place where the Jewish people would meet to pray and hear God's Word.

There at the feet of the Lord Jesus, Jairus begged the Lord, "My little daughter, only twelve years old, is dying. I pray, come and put your Hands on her so that she may be healed and live."

The Lord Jesus, looking upon this poor man with so much love, followed him. They were not alone. Many, many people followed them. They did not want to miss seeing this miracle!

On the way to the house, some people came running to Jairus, saying, "We have just come from visiting your little girl. She has just died. Why bother the Teacher anymore?"

When the Lord Jesus heard these words, he said to Jairus, "Don't be afraid, only believe, and she shall be made well."

After the Lord Jesus said these words, he did not let anyone follow him any further except his disciples Peter, James, and John. When the Lord came into Jairus's house, he looked around and saw so many people crying. Many of these people were crying very loudly. The Lord said to them, "Why is there so much crying here? The little girl is not dead. She is only sleeping."

When all the people heard this, they stopped crying and started laughing. In fact, they couldn't stop laughing at the Lord

Jesus. He put them all out of the house. He then took Jairus, Jairus's wife, and Peter, James, and John into the room where the little girl was lying.

The Lord Jesus went up to the little girl, put his strong hand around her little, thin hand, and said these words to her, *Talithacumi,* which means "Little girl, I say to you, arise."

Immediately, the child got up and walked. Her parents stood there speechless! They could not say one word! They could not believe their eyes! The Lord Jesus Christ, knowing the people outside did not believe he was the Son of the living God, said to the girl's parents, "Do not tell anyone what was done in this room. Now, go and give her something to eat."

A wonderful miracle had just been done! The day, which had started off with much sadness, had turned into a day full of happiness and joy! Their lives were never the same. The Lord Jesus Christ had come into their home and heart.

When you give your heart to the Lord Jesus Christ, he takes out your old, dead heart and gives you a new, living heart full of joy and happiness. You become like this little girl who was once dead and then alive again.

> This is the promise that he hath promised us, even eternal life.
>
> 1 John 2:25 (AKJV)

Who was Jairus?
Why did he want Jesus to heal his daughter?
How old was his daughter?
Why did the people laugh at the Lord Jesus?
How did Jesus heal the little girl?

THE GREAT SUPPER

This story was told by the Lord Jesus Christ, who was having dinner with the religious leaders, called Pharisees, on the day of worship. There were also some other guests having dinner with the Lord Jesus on that day.

The Lord Jesus Christ wanted to explain to the religious leaders and their guests that the kingdom of heaven lets anyone who wishes to enter heaven to do so. In order to tell them about the deep things that belong to God, the Lord Jesus would tell them stories. These stories were no ordinary stories. They were called parables. (Parables were stories about everyday people, places or things but the meaning of the stories had to do with God, you, your soul and your spiritual life.)

The Lord Jesus is now going to lovingly tell a parable about the kingdom of heaven to the religious leaders and the guests.

Jesus said, "A certain man gave a big dinner. After he had prepared everything—the tables were all set up, the chairs were all in place, and the delicious food was on the tables, ready to be eaten—this certain man said to his servant, 'Go, tell them all to come for everything is now ready.'

"The servant happily obeyed his master and called them to come to this beautiful feast and to share in this time of rejoicing with his master.

"But as the servant invited them to come, one by one, they all made excuses. The first one said, 'I have bought a piece of ground, and I must go and see it. Please excuse me.'

"Another one said, 'I have bought ten bulls, and I want to make sure they are all strong and healthy. Please excuse me.'

"And yet another one said, 'I just married my wife. I cannot come.'

"The servant went back to his master and told him about all these excuses. Then the master of the house became very angry and said to his servants, 'Go out quickly. Go into the streets and to the country roads and bring in the poor, the handicapped, the deaf, the lame, and the blind.'

"To his other servant, the master said, 'Go out into the hedges and the highways and urge them to come so that my house will be full. I tell you that none of those men who were asked and invited first shall taste of my supper in My house.'

"The servants went out, and in they all came: the blind, the deaf, the poor, the ones who cannot walk or talk, and the ones who have no place to live. They all came. Not one had an excuse!

"The master's house was full! He dressed them in the finest white garments—beautiful new clothes. They all sat down in new chairs and ate delicious food of every kind on new tables. They were all laughing, and there were happy faces everywhere. It was a time of rejoicing for them. Once they knew only sadness, but now that they have come to know the master, the sadness went away and happiness flooded their souls.

"When the master came in to see all of his guests, for he knows them all by name, he noticed one man who did not have a beautiful white garment on. He truly wanted to give this man a chance to explain, and so he said, 'Friend, how did you get into the house without a white garment on?'

"The man stood there speechless. He had nothing to say, for he knew he was guilty of trying to enter the master's house the wrong way.

"The master said to his servants, 'Bind him, hand and foot, and throw him into outer darkness where there is crying and weeping and extreme pain.'

"Then the master of the house said, 'Many are called, but few are chosen.'"

The Lord Jesus Christ explained to the religious leaders that religion does not get you to heaven. You must accept God's only Son, the Lord Jesus Christ, into your heart and life to be able to enter heaven. The Bible tells us that there is no other way.

In the parable, the blind, the deaf, the poor, and all the others are those people who do not know everything about religion, but with their little faith, they have accepted the Lord Jesus Christ into their hearts and lives and have been given everlasting life. They are no longer blind, for they now see. They are no longer deaf, for they now have heard the good news of our Lord and Savior, Jesus Christ, and have accepted him.

They are no longer poor but are eternally rich by accepting the Lord Jesus Christ into their hearts and lives. They are no longer lame because they now walk in a new way. They are no longer without a home because they have been given an everlasting home in heaven when they accepted God's only Son into their hearts and lives.

What will you do with God's only Son who died on a cross and shed his blood so that you can enter heaven and live forever? There is a heaven, and there is a hell.

> I will seek that which was lost.
>
> Ezekiel 34:16a (AKJV)

What is a parable?
Who did Jesus tell this parable to?
Who was the master of the house?
What were some of the excuses the people gave for not going to the feast?
Who came to the feast at the master's house?

THE LOST SON

In this story, the Lord Jesus Christ talks to the people of Israel about a lost son who has found his way home again. The Lord Jesus Christ tries to show the people of Israel that they are like this lost son who needs to come back to his Father.

Boys and girls, the Father in this story is God. He is our heavenly Father. We all need him, and he certainly loves us and wants us. Some of us don't have a father on earth, but we have a Father in heaven for sure who is waiting to love us! Won't you let him come in?

Let us begin our story: There was a certain man who had two sons. One day, the youngest son said to his father, "I want everything that belongs to me, and I want it now. I don't want to wait until you die. Give me what belongs to me now!"

And so the father gave his youngest son all that belonged to him. With that, the son packed all his clothes, took his money, and left his father's house! Now only the oldest son was at home with the father.

Meanwhile, the youngest son went to a far country, very far away from where his father lived. In this faraway country, the youngest son used up all the money his father gave him. He used it up by drinking and having friends who drank a lot. He used up all of his father's hard-earned money on a wicked life. Evil men, evil women, drinking, and everything else that wicked people do.

After the youngest son used up all of his father's money, a famine came upon the land he lived in. (Boys and girls, a famine meant there was no food at all.) He became very, very hungry!

Boys and girls, what happened to all of his friends? They all left him. Why? Because he had no money left. These people were not his friends; they just wanted his money. He must have felt very lonely.

Now that he had no money, no friends, and there was a very bad famine in the land, he became very hungry. So he had to find a job. He had to work to get money to be able to eat!

Work? Did you say work? He never ever worked for money before! When he lived at home, his father gave him everything he needed. Now he is on his own, far away from his father and brother, and he needs money very badly in order to live. He needs to eat.

And so, boys and girls, he finds a man who gives him his first job. Do you know what that job was? It was feeding the pigs! He had to feed pigs so that he could eat! He had no choice. He had to do it. He gladly filled his stomach with the same food he fed the pigs because there wasn't anyone who gave him anything to eat.

After a while, when he realized what he was doing, feeding the pigs and gladly eating their food, he thought out loud to himself, *Even in my father's house, the servants have enough good bread to eat and to give to others, and here I am dying because I don't have enough to eat! I will go back to my father's house, and I will say to my father, "Father, I have sinned against heaven and against you. I am not worthy to be called your son. Please make me one of your hired servants."*

He meant every word, and he got up and left his job of feeding the pigs and set off to go back to his father's house. He did not know if his father would take him back or not. He only knew he wanted to go home.

In the meantime, while he was a long way off from his father's house, his father was already outside and saw his son coming. The father felt sorry for his youngest son and the father ran to his son, wrapped his arms around him, and kissed his son.

The youngest son said, "Father, I have *sinned* against heaven, and I have *sinned* against you. I should not be called your son."

But the father would not listen to his son. He loved his son and said to his servants, "Bring me the best robe we have and put it on my youngest son. Put a ring on his hand and shoes on his feet. Take the fattest calf we have, kill it and cook it, for we will eat and be happy. For my son, he was dead and is alive again—he was lost and is found."

All who heard about this news were very happy. Boys and girls, do you remember there were two sons? The oldest son was in the field, and as he came near to the house, he heard music and dancing. So he called one of the servants and asked him, "What is going on?"

The servant said, "Your brother has come home, and your father is making a big party for him because he is back and he is safe."

The oldest son became very angry and would not go into the house. When the father heard about this, the father went to see the oldest son, asking him to please, please come into the house, see your brother and be happy with us.

But the oldest son said to his father, "Dad, I have been with you all through my life. I have served you, and I have done all that you asked me to do. I never said no to you, and yet you have never given me a party with my friends. Instead, as soon as my brother comes home, after all he has done against you by living an evil life and using up your money, you give him a big party! I don't understand!"

And the father answered, "Son, my son, you are always with me, and everything I have is yours. It's only right that we should be happy and have a feast, for your brother was dead. He left us, and is alive again—he has come home. He was lost and is found."

Boys and girls, did you know that God sent his only Son to earth to die on a cross so that you may go to a beautiful place called heaven? If you accept the Lord Jesus Christ into your heart, he will take away all your sins, and he will give you a clean heart. God will then be your Father, and you will belong to him.

There will be a great party in heaven because now you have come home—your real home which is in heaven.

> There is joy in the presence of the angels of God over one sinner that repenteth.
>
> Luke 15:10 (AKJV)

How many sons did the father have?
Which of the sons left home?
What was his first job?
Did he ask his father to forgive him?
What did the father do for him when he came back home?

HE MAKES THE DEAF TO HEAR

The Lord Jesus Christ had just come from two towns called Tyre and Sidon. While there, He performed a miracle.

Boys and girls, a miracle is something so wonderful it makes you realize only God could have done it.

Now, the Lord Jesus was at the sea of Galilee, where a large number of people were waiting for him. Along the sea of Galilee were many fishing towns. The people who lived in these towns fished for a living.

It was by the sea of Galilee that the people brought to the Lord Jesus a deaf man. This deaf man could not hear at all, and he did not speak very well. The people asked the Lord Jesus, "Please put your hand on him and heal him." The Lord Jesus listened to the people. He took this poor deaf man away from everyone. The Lord Jesus wanted to give this man all of his love and attention.

The kind way in which he touched his ears and tongue must have made the poor man understand and believe in a miracle soon to happen.

With all of the love that the Lord Jesus had, he looked at this deaf man, put his fingers in the deaf man's ears, spat and touched the deaf man's tongue. (Remember, he could not hear nor speak very well.)

Then the Lord Jesus Christ looked up to heaven and said to the deaf man, *Ephphatha*, which means "Be opened."

Instantly, the deaf man's ears were opened, and his tongue became free! He was not deaf anymore! He heard every word, and he spoke so clearly not missing a sound! A miracle!

The Lord Jesus said, "Do not say a word about this to anyone." But it was no use. Everyone found out. Many people in all the towns nearby soon found out about this marvelous miracle.

The people praised Jesus saying, "He has done all things well. He makes the deaf to hear and the person who cannot speak, he makes them to speak ever so clearly!"

This deaf man had faith in the Lord Jesus Christ to make him hear and speak. He believed on the Lord Jesus Christ.

Have you heard of how the Lord Jesus Christ has died for you and how he can forgive you of all your sins? If you let him, he will come into your heart and life and make it clean and pure. Then you will be able to speak about him to others and tell them what he has done for you, just as this once-deaf man told many people what the Lord Jesus Christ did for him.

> So then faith cometh by hearing, and hearing by the word of God.
>
> Romans 10:17 (AKJV)

This story took place by the sea of _____?
Who did the people bring to Jesus to heal?
How did Jesus show this man he was going to do a miracle for him?
What word did Jesus say to heal this man?
Did this man tell others about what Jesus did for him?

HEALING OF A CENTURION'S SERVANT

"I say to you, I have not found such great faith not even in Israel." These were the words of the Lord Jesus Christ when he performed a miracle in a town called Capernaum.

Capernaum is a town in Israel, which is near the sea of Galilee. It is a fishing town. The people who lived in this town caught their fish from the sea of Galilee. That is how the people there made a living.

It was during this time that the Lord Jesus Christ lived and walked on earth among the Jewish people in Israel. But because the Jewish people did not obey the one true and living God, God had the Roman people rule over them. The Jewish people were prisoners in their own land.

One of the Roman officers in the Roman army was called a centurion. A centurion in the Roman army had power. He was in charge of a hundred Roman soldiers. He could tell them where to go and what to do and they would obey him. They had to obey him.

This true story is all about how a Roman centurion put his faith in the Lord Jesus Christ. Let's begin: When the Lord Jesus Christ came to Capernaum, a Roman centurion came up to him begging, "Lord, my servant is lying at home paralyzed. He is ready to die."

The Lord Jesus Christ answered, "I will come and heal him."

The centurion said, "Lord I am not worthy, I am such a sinner, that you should come under my roof. But if you would say the word, I know my servant will be healed. I am also a man with power. I have a hundred soldiers under me. If I say to this one, 'Go,' he goes. If I say to that one, 'Come,' he comes. If I say to another one, 'Do this,' he does it."

When the Lord Jesus Christ heard these words, he found it to be so wonderful. The Lord Jesus Christ turned around and said to all the people following him, "Truly, I tell you, I have not found such great faith, not even in Israel."

Then the Lord Jesus Christ looked right at the Roman centurion, and with all the love the Lord Jesus had, he said, "Go your way and as you have believed, so let it be done for you."

The Roman centurion's servant was healed that very same hour.

> And whoever comes to me I will never cast out.
>
> John 6:37b (ESV)

Who ruled over the Jewish people at this time?
A Roman centurion was in charge of _____ soldiers?
What did the Roman centurion ask Jesus to do?
What did Jesus say about the Roman centurion's faith?
Did Jesus heal the Roman centurion's servant?

HEALING OF A LEPER

During the time when the Lord Jesus Christ walked on this earth, there were many lepers. A leper is a person who has a disease called leprosy. Leprosy is a disease which eats away at your skin and body. In those days, they did not know how to make leprosy go away.

As the Lord Jesus Christ was coming into a certain city, a leper walked right up to the Lord Jesus Christ. When the leper was right next to the Lord Jesus Christ, he fell down at the Lord Jesus's feet and began to worship him.

While the leper was kneeling down and worshipping the Lord Jesus Christ, the leper began crying out loud, begging the Lord Jesus Christ to make him better. The leper cried, "Lord, if you will, please make me clean. Please, Lord, heal me."

The Lord Jesus Christ, seeing this poor man full of leprosy with some of his body parts missing (such as his fingers, toes, and nose), looked at this leper and with all the love that the Lord Jesus Christ had, put his hand right on the leper and said to him, "I will make you clean—be clean!"

Children, would you touch a person full of leprosy? Do you believe the Lord Jesus Christ really made this man clean and gave him back all of the parts of his body and his skin?

The Bible says that with God "Nothing is Impossible." (Mark 10:27) God can do anything. The Bible also teaches us that the Lord Jesus Christ is God. Since the Lord Jesus Christ is God, then the Lord Jesus Christ can do anything!

The Lord Jesus Christ can take away all your dirty sins and give you a clean, white heart and life. Because he is God, he can do anything.

The Bible tells us that as soon as the Lord Jesus said, "Be clean," right away the leprosy left the man, and he was clean! The disease was gone and would never come back again! Isn't that wonderful? That is called a miracle.

When the leper saw that his body was new again and that his skin felt just like a baby's skin, he thanked the Lord Jesus Christ. He went everywhere telling everyone what great things the Lord Jesus did for him!

The Lord Jesus Christ can do the same for you, if you will come to him, worship him, and cry out, "Please, help me, Lord. I am such a sinner. I am full of dirty, old sin. Please make me clean."

The Lord Jesus Christ will answer, "Yes, be clean!" He will forgive you right away, and he will come into your heart and life. You will be so happy that you will be telling everyone everywhere what great things the Lord Jesus Christ did for you!

Let us bow our heads and thank him for dying on the cross and for taking away our sins. Let us thank him for giving us a home in heaven where we can live with him forever and ever.

> And the blood of Jesus Christ, his Son, cleanseth us from all sin.
>
> 1 John 1:7b (AKJV)

What is leprosy?
Did a leper ask Jesus to heal him?
What did the leper do when he came right next to Jesus?
Did the leper thank the Lord Jesus for healing him?
Did he tell people everywhere about the great things Jesus did for him?

THE SON OF MAN IS LORD ALSO OF THE SABBATH

Boys and girls, this story took place on the Sabbath. Now the Sabbath was called "The Day of Rest." It was on this day, if you were Jewish, you would go to the place of worship (called the temple) and worship God.

When you returned back home, you would do not work. No cooking, no cleaning, no washing, nothing! You would spend the day resting. Boys and girls, it took God six days to make everything, the earth, the sea, the flowers, the trees, the animals, and man. The Lord God then rested on the seventh day and called it a holy day of rest or the Sabbath.

The Bible tells us that the Lord Jesus Christ is God. That means, boys and girls, that the Lord Jesus Christ made the Sabbath. And because the Lord Jesus Christ made the Sabbath, he was Lord of the Sabbath. The Lord Jesus Christ could do whatever pleased him on the holy day of rest.

This is where our story begins: The Lord Jesus Christ entered into the place of worship on the Sabbath. The Lord Jesus Christ came to teach the people about God. Now, there was a man in the temple whose hand was paralyzed. The hand would not move. The hand was stiff.

When the religious rulers saw this paralyzed man in the temple, they wanted to see what the Lord Jesus Christ would do. The religious rulers hated the Lord Jesus Christ because he went about speaking the truth and doing good.

The religious rulers wanted to see if the Lord Jesus Christ would even think of healing this paralyzed man on the holy day of rest. They hated the Lord Jesus Christ so much. But, boys and girls, the Lord Jesus Christ knew their thoughts. Since the Lord Jesus Christ is God, he could read their minds, and he saw only evil thoughts in their minds.

The Lord Jesus Christ, knowing their wicked thoughts, said to the paralyzed man, "Rise up, and stand up in the middle of all of us."

The paralyzed man obeyed and did exactly as the Lord Jesus Christ told him to do. Then the Lord Jesus Christ said to them, "I will ask you all one thing. Is it wrong on the holy day of rest to do good, or is it wrong on the holy day of rest to do evil, to save a life or to destroy a life?"

After the Lord Jesus Christ said this, he said to the paralyzed man, "Stretch out your hand."

The paralyzed man stretched out his sick hand to the Lord Jesus Christ, and the Lord Jesus did a mighty miracle! He made the sick hand well! It was now as good as his other hand!

The religious leaders were filled with anger, the Bible tells us. They started to talk among themselves what evil they could do to the Lord Jesus Christ. But the Lord Jesus Christ went up into a mountain to pray, and the Lord Jesus Christ continued all night in prayer to God.

Boys and girls, the Lord Jesus Christ can take your heart and life, no matter what it looks like, and make it new! All you have to do is to ask him to come into your heart and take away all your evil thoughts and sins. He will come in and give you a clean heart and life. Then you will be able to begin a new life, just like the once-paralyzed man.

Won't you let him come in? The Lord Jesus Christ promised He would never leave you!

> The son of man is Lord also of the Sabbath.
>
> Luke 6:5 (AKJV)

The Lord Jesus came to teach the people on the Sabbath in the _____?
There was a man whose hand was _____?
Did Jesus heal this man?
Why were the religious leaders angry with Jesus?
Who is Lord of the Sabbath?

HEALING OF BLIND BARTIMAEUS

Boys and girls, do you know what a miracle is? A miracle is something so wonderful that only God could do it. The Lord Jesus Christ did many marvelous miracles while he lived and walked on this earth.

Here is a beautiful story of how the Lord Jesus Christ heard a blind man's cry and how the Lord Jesus Christ, in a powerful way, answered this poor, blind man's cry for help.

Let's begin. As the Lord Jesus Christ came into the city of Jericho, there was a blind man named Bartimaeus sitting by the side of the road begging for food and money. At the same time, there were also a great number of people following the Lord Jesus Christ into the city of Jericho.

The blind man, Bartimaeus, hearing this big crowd of people asked, "What is going on?" (Remember, he is blind.)

The people told him, "Jesus of Nazareth is coming through our city of Jericho."

The blind man immediately cried out, "Jesus, Son of David, have mercy, have pity on me."

But as the blind man Bartimaeus cried out, "Jesus, Son of David, have pity on me," the people told him, "Be quiet!"

But Bartimaeus cried even louder. He wanted the Lord Jesus Christ so much! He needed the Lord Jesus Christ so much!

At that moment, the Lord Jesus Christ stood still and commanded the people to bring blind Bartimaeus to Him.

When Bartimaeus stood before the Lord Jesus Christ, Jesus asked him, "What would you like me to do for you?"

The blind man answered, "Lord, I want to see!"

The Lord Jesus Christ had so much love in his heart for this poor, blind man. To show Bartimaeus how much he loved him, the Lord Jesus Christ put his hand on Bartimaeus's eyes, and immediately, the blind man could see! He was no longer blind! Bartimaeus also believed that the Lord Jesus Christ could do this wonderful miracle because Bartimaeus had faith. Because of Bartimaeus's faith in the Lord Jesus Christ, the Lord Jesus Christ said to him, "Your *faith* has saved you."

Bartimaeus became born-again. He became a new man in the Lord Jesus Christ, and today, Bartimaeus is in heaven with his Lord and Savior. The Lord Jesus Christ is still living today. He is sitting on the right hand side of God, his Father. He still does miracles today. Would you like to have him come into your heart and do a mighty miracle? He can take away all the old, black, sin from your heart and give you a new, clean heart full of love and peace. This joy can only come from asking him into your heart and life. The Lord Jesus Christ loves you so very much! What would you like the Lord Jesus Christ to do for you today?

> Look unto me, and be ye saved, all the ends of the earth; for I am God, and there is none else.
>
> Isaiah 45:22 (AKJV)

Jesus was entering what city?
Who was sitting by the side of the road in this city begging for food and money?
What did he do when he found out that Jesus of Nazareth was passing by?
What did the people tell him?
Did the Lord Jesus heal him?

JESUS LOVES THE LITTLE CHILDREN

Boys and girls, in this true story from the Bible, the Lord Jesus Christ was sitting down. As he was resting, many people brought their babies and young children to him so that he might touch them and bless them.

The Lord Jesus Christ's twelve followers did not understand how much the Lord Jesus loved children and wanted them close to him. Instead, the twelve followers thought the children were bothering him, and they tried with all their strength to stop the children from seeing the Lord Jesus.

But when the Lord Jesus Christ saw what his twelve followers were doing, he became angry at them. He was not happy. He said to his twelve followers, "Let the little children come to me. Do not stop them, for the kingdom of heaven belongs to them."

Then the Lord Jesus Christ took all the children he could hold and put his big arms around them, and he put his Hand on them, and he blessed each and every child.

Boys and girls, do you see how much the Lord Jesus Christ loves you? Oh, receive him today and ask him to come into your heart. He will come into your heart and into your life. He will hold you in his arms and he will love you. You will be blessed by him because you will belong to him forever and ever.

Let us pray: "Dear Lord, we thank you so very much for loving all the children of the world. We thank you that you died on the cross for our sins and that if we let you come into our hearts, you will give us a new, clean heart and a beautiful home in heaven. We will be able to live with you forever and ever. Thank you, dear Lord, so very much."

> Whoever does not receive the kingdom of God like a child shall not enter it.
>
> Luke 18:17 (ESV)

What was the Lord Jesus doing at the beginning of this story?
Many people brought their _____ and _____ to Jesus so that he may bless them?
Why did Jesus's twelve followers try to stop the people?
What did Jesus tell his twelve followers?
Does Jesus love the little children?

WIDOW OF NAIN

Boys and girls, do you know what the word compassion means? *Compassion* means "to feel sorry for someone who is sad and suffering and needs help."

The Lord Jesus Christ had real compassion on a poor, lonely woman. Because the Lord Jesus Christ is God, he is able to do something so wonderful for this poor, old woman. No one else in the whole world could help her with her suffering.

The Lord Jesus Christ, his disciples (or followers), and many people were entering into a city called Nain. To enter the city of Nain, you must go through the gate of the city. As they all came to the gate of the city, the Lord Jesus Christ, his followers, and all the people with him saw that a funeral was taking place in Nain that day. Someone had just died.

As the Lord Jesus Christ and the people watched, they saw that it was a young man who had just died. The Lord Jesus Christ also saw a poor, lonely, old woman crying. This very sad woman was also a widow. (A widow is a woman whose husband had died.)

Everyone soon found out that the young man who died was the only son of this widow. How sad! First, her husband died, and now her only son is dead also.

Do you feel sorry for her? The Lord Jesus Christ did. She was so sad and so lost in her sorrow, and there was no one, not one person, she could turn to for love and help in her time of need.

But the Lord Jesus Christ knew this. He knows everything. He is God. He was right there to help her in her time of need. He is the only one who could help her! The Lord Jesus Christ immediately walked over to this dear, sad woman, and he put his loving arms around her. With all of the love that the Lord Jesus had, he said unto her, "Please don't cry." To show her the power of his love, he was going to change her world forever!

He walked over to her dead son's coffin, and he touched the coffin! At that moment, everything stopped! The people stood still! They were wondering, "What is the Lord Jesus Christ going to do? What else could he do? After all, the young man is dead, and it's too late."

It is never too late for the Lord Jesus Christ to do a wonderful miracle. Because the Lord Jesus Christ is God, He could do anything! All eyes were on the Lord Jesus Christ. The Lord Jesus touched the dead man's coffin, and he said, "Young man, I say to you, Rise."

Immediately, the young man rose up from the dead, and he sat up in his coffin and began talking!

Everyone must have been so shocked and so surprised to see this mighty miracle happen right before their eyes! What could they say? They brought the young man to his dear, old mother. After seeing this beautiful miracle and seeing her only son alive again, she praised God and was so happy! Her joy returned to her. All the sorrow, loneliness, and pain were gone!

There was a deep and holy respect for the Lord Jesus Christ. All the people, especially the widow, began to praise God, "Certainly, God has visited his people."

What a Son-filled day that was! The Son of God, the Lord Jesus Christ, healing the son of a widow. What else could you say but "To God be the glory."

I'm sure many people saw the true and real compassion the Lord Jesus Christ had for this lonely widow, and they gave their hearts and lives to the Lord Jesus Christ!

The Bible tells us, "Nothing is impossible for the Lord Jesus Christ!" (Mark 10:27) Boys and girls, how about you? Are you sad today? Feeling lonely? Feeling lost? Need a friend—a real and true friend? Why not let the Lord Jesus Christ come into your heart and life? He will give you so much happiness that, just like the widow, you will be thanking him over and over again! Not only on earth, but you will be thanking him also in heaven, for you will be with him forever and ever. What a real and true compassionate friend we have in the Lord Jesus Christ!

God is love.

1 John 4:16b (AKJV)

In what city did this story take place?
Boys and girls, what does the word "compassion" mean?
Who did Jesus have compassion for?
What was the miracle that Jesus did?
Did the people praise God for this miracle?

THE MASTER SPEAKS!

Boys and girls, this is a story from the Bible about the Lord Jesus Christ and his followers. This story really happened.

On a certain day, the Lord Jesus Christ, and his twelve followers went into a boat. When they all filled the boat, the Lord Jesus Christ said to them, "Let us go over to the other side of the lake." And so, the boat took off to go to the other side. As they were going along in the boat, the Lord Jesus Christ fell asleep. He must have been very tired.

While he was sleeping, a big, black, storm came whipping over the lake, making the water angry and tossing the boat back and forth. The boat became filled with water! All the twelve followers of the Lord Jesus Christ became afraid. They thought they were going to die!

They ran to the Lord Jesus Christ and woke him up, saying, "Master, we are going to die. The boat is going down into the water!"

Boys and girls, do you think the Lord Jesus Christ is going to let them all die? The Bible tells us in 1 Peter 5:7, "Casting all your care upon him, for he careth for you."

The Master of the sea and land (the Lord Jesus Christ), stood up in the boat and told the wind to go away and said to the sea, "Peace, be still."

Right away, the storm stopped! The wind went away, and the water became quiet again. Imagine that, boys and girls! Who could do that? Only God! The Lord Jesus Christ then turned to his followers and said to them, "Why are you so afraid? Where is your faith?"

They were afraid to answer the Lord Jesus Christ. Instead, they said to each other, "Wow! What kind of man is this, for he commanded even the winds and the water to obey him, and they did!"

Boys and girls, it tells us in the Bible that the Lord Jesus Christ is the same yesterday, today, and forever. He still commands the wind and the water to obey him. But he did something even greater! He left a beautiful place called heaven to come here to earth, and at the age of thirty-three, he died on a cross for your sins so that you can go to heaven. Who could do that? Only God could do that! That's how much he loves you!

Won't you let him into your heart and life? He will take away all your sins, and you will be saved, and you will belong to him. Then he will begin to work powerfully in your life. You will be amazed at what the Master can do for you.

Believe on the Lord Jesus Christ, and you shall be saved.

Acts 16:31 (AKJV)

Where was Jesus and his followers going in the boat?
Jesus was so tired he fell _____ in the boat?
What came whipping over the lake?
What did the followers of Jesus do?
What did Jesus tell the wind and the sea?

THE TEN LEPERS

Boys and girls, we are going to read a true story from the Bible. The story is about ten men who had leprosy. You can find this story in the Bible, in the book of Luke 17:11–19.

This story is about the Lord Jesus Christ, and ten men who were lepers. Boys and girls, leprosy is a disease that you can get from another person. Leprosy slowly eats away the outside part of your body. Leprosy can eat away your nose, your fingers, your ears, your toes, your skin, and all parts of the outside of the body. In the day that the Lord Jesus Christ walked on this earth, there was no cure for leprosy.

There is another disease that can eat away at your life very slowly. It starts off little and gets bigger and bigger as time goes by. That disease is called sin. It will eat away at your life little by little, and it will destroy you at the end of your life.

Everyone has this disease called sin. The Bible tells us in Romans 3:23, "For all have sinned and come short of the glory of God."

In Romans 6:23, it tells us, "For the wages of sin is death."

Boys and girls, these ten men who had leprosy were very sad, and they were very sick. They knew they had no hope of living. They knew leprosy was going to kill them. They had no hope, that is, until the Lord Jesus Christ walked their way and met with them!

The story begins: And it came to pass that the Lord Jesus Christ was on his way to Jerusalem, which is the main city in the country of Israel. The Lord Jesus Christ passed through the middle of the country of Samaria and Galilee before going to Jerusalem.

Many Jewish people and many Arab people hated the people of Samaria. The people from Samaria were called Samaritans. The reason the Samaritans were hated was because they were half Jewish and half Arab. But the Lord Jesus Christ, who knows all things, knew he had to go to Samaria and Galilee. The Lord Jesus loves all people. The Lord Jesus has no favorites.

As the Lord Jesus Christ entered into this certain village, the ten lepers met the Lord Jesus Christ. The ten men stayed away because they did not want to give the leprosy to the Lord Jesus Christ.

But, boys and girls, these ten lepers did not know that the Lord Jesus Christ, who is God, is our Creator. He made us. There is no way that the Lord Jesus Christ could ever catch leprosy or any other kind of disease. God is holy. God never sleeps. God never lies. God is perfect. The Lord Jesus Christ is God.

When the ten lepers saw the Lord Jesus Christ, they raised their voices and said, "Master, have mercy on us."

And when the Lord Jesus Christ saw these ten poor men filled with the disease, the Lord Jesus Christ said to them, "Go, show yourselves to the priests of Israel."

Boys and girls, in those days, if you had leprosy or any disease, you would go to the Jewish priests who lived in the temple. The temple was the place of worshipping God. The Jewish priests would look on the disease you had, and they would either say you had leprosy and put you away from the people or say you are clean, you do not have leprosy. They would let you live with the people again.

That is why the Lord Jesus Christ said to them, "Go, show yourselves to the priests."

The Bible tells us, boys and girls, that as the ten lepers were going to see the Jewish priests, the Lord Jesus Christ did a mighty miracle! He took away all their leprosy from them as they were walking to the temple to see the Jewish priests! The Lord Jesus

Christ cleansed them. What a wonderful miracle! Only God could do that!

These ten lepers who had no hope of living on earth were now filled with hope! They were not going to die of leprosy! They would live!

The Bible tells us that there were ten men who had leprosy. But when the Lord Jesus Christ healed all the ten men, only one came back to the Lord Jesus Christ and, with a loud voice, glorified God! Only one gave thanks to God! This one man fell down on his face at the feet of the Lord Jesus Christ and gave the Lord Jesus Christ thanks. And this one man was a Samaritan! He was half Jewish and half Arab, hated by both the Jewish people and the Arab people!

The Lord Jesus Christ said to this man, "Didn't I take away the disease of leprosy from ten men? But where are the nine? They have not returned here to give thanks to God, only one, this stranger, came back to give thanks and to worship God."

The Lord Jesus Christ said to this man, "Get up and go your way, for your faith has made you well!"

How happy the man must have been! The Lord Jesus Christ must have been surprised that only one came back to thank him. The Lord Jesus Christ must have felt sad that the other nine refused to thank him for the gift of life and not death by leprosy. Only one came back, a Samaritan, but the Lord Jesus Christ said to him, "Your faith has made you well."

The Samaritan leper believed and knew the Lord Jesus Christ was the Savior of the whole world when he saw his leprosy was gone. Because of that faith in the Lord Jesus Christ, knowing that the Lord Jesus was God, the Messiah, the Savior of our sins, that man was born again. He would now have a home in heaven and live forever with the Lord Jesus Christ when he died. The leper had much to be thankful for!

Boys and girls, will you walk the way that one leper did right back to the Lord Jesus Christ, falling down on his face at the feet of the Lord Jesus and confessing the Lord Jesus as Savior of the world and giving thanks to him? Or will you be like the other nine lepers who walked away from the Lord Jesus Christ and walked right into a lost eternity called hell? The choice is up to you.

> Whosoever shall call upon the name of the Lord shall be saved.
>
> Romans 10:13 (KJV)

What book of the Bible will you find this story?
Why didn't the lepers get close to Jesus?
How many lepers did Jesus heal and make clean?
How many lepers came back to thank and worship the Lord Jesus?
Jesus said to this leper, "Your _____ has made you well?"

THE POWER OF PRAYER

Do you know, boys and girls, that when you pray, many wonderful and powerful things happen?

First, you must ask the Lord Jesus Christ to come into your heart and take away all your sins. Then he becomes the captain of your life. You can then begin to talk to him everyday. Talking to the Lord is called prayer. Oh, how the Lord loves when you pray to him. It can be about anything: school, your home, your friends, your family or whatever you want.

Prayer is such a beautiful way to talk to the Lord. Sometimes, your prayer is answered right away, and sometimes your prayer is answered after a while. But the most important part of prayer is to keep talking to the Lord Jesus everyday. The Bible tells us, boys and girls, that God hears our every prayer.

This is a story told by the Lord Jesus Christ about a woman who would not give up until she got what she needed. This story will teach us about how important it is to keep coming to the Lord Jesus Christ with our needs in prayer. Let's begin. Jesus said, "There was a judge who lived in a city. This judge did not obey God. He did not respect God or man or woman or child. But in the same city, there lived a widow.

"Every day, this widow went to see this judge because there was a person in her life who kept giving her trouble. This person would not let her alone. When this widow stood before the judge, she said, "Give me justice and help me against my enemy." But the judge would not listen to her.

"Day after day after day, this poor widow would appear before the judge, begging him for help with her enemy. But day after day after day, the judge refused to give her what she requested, and the widow went back to her home feeling so sad. But she refused to let that stop her from seeing the judge one more time.

"She would not give up. The next morning, there she was standing before the judge with her request. The Bible states that after some time had passed, the judge could no longer take listening to this widow any longer. The judge said to himself, *Even though I don't care about God or anyone, I have to help this widow because she won't leave me alone. I am getting so tired of her coming to me every single day.* And with that, the judge finally gave her help from her enemy!"

Now, boys and girls, the judge did not love God or man, and yet he helped the poor widow with her problem.

God loves you very much and would love to spend time with you in prayer.

Oh, it's wonderful and marvelous, this beautiful tool called prayer. Many powerful things happen when you pray and call upon the name of our almighty God!

> Whatever you ask in prayer, believe that you have received it, and it will be yours.
>
> Mark 11:24 (ESV)

_____ is a beautiful way to talk to God?
When you _____, you can talk to God about anything?
Who did this widow go to see about her problem?
Why did he finally help her?
Do you know that God loves you?

ZACCHEUS

The Lord Jesus Christ had just entered a town in Israel called Jericho. The reason the Lord Jesus came to this town was to see a little man named Zaccheus. But this little man had no idea that the Lord Jesus was going to visit with him today. Let's see what happens when they meet each other.

There was a little man named Zaccheus who lived in Jericho, which is in the country of Israel. At this time, the Jewish people were prisoners in their own country under the Roman people. The Jewish people had to do whatever the Roman people told them to do.

Now Zaccheus was Jewish, but he worked for the Romans as a tax collector. He took money from the Jewish people to give to the Romans. The Jewish people did not like Zaccheus. Not only did he take their money and give it to the Romans, but he took more than he should have from his own people and kept it for himself. He was very rich yet very lonely.

No one liked Zaccheus. No one ever said to him, "Good morning, Zaccheus. How are you on this beautiful day?" or "Zaccheus, would you like to have dinner with us today?" He had no friends. That is, until the Lord Jesus Christ came to the town where this little man, Zaccheus, this hated tax collector, lived and worked.

When everyone found out that the Lord Jesus was coming to Jericho, they all ran to meet him. They all wanted to see the Lord Jesus because he could make a blind man see and a deaf man hear.

Of course, Zaccheus was always the last to find out anything because he had no friends to tell him anything. But when he did find out by listening to others talking about it, he also ran to meet the Lord Jesus. But by the time he got there, there were too many people in front of him. And that was not Zaccheus's only problem—he had another big problem. The Bible tells us that Zaccheus was a little man. So how was he going to see past all those people?

Why, the answer is so easy! He ran and climbed up a sycamore tree! He had the best seat of all. He could watch every step the Lord Jesus took as he entered into the town of Jericho.

There was Zaccheus sitting way up high in the sycamore tree, and way down there at the bottom of the tree stood the Lord Jesus Christ. He was looking right up at Zaccheus. The Lord Jesus Christ knew where to find Zaccheus. And what the Lord Jesus said to Zaccheus shocked all the people.

The Lord Jesus said, "Zaccheus, come down, for today I must stay at your house."

Zaccheus was so happy that someone was coming to his home. He came down from that tree so quickly, and he had the biggest smile on his face! He was so excited!

All the people of Jericho became very upset, and they said to each other, "Jesus is going to visit the house of a sinner!"

Boys and girls, the Bible says that we are all sinners. We all need the Lord Jesus Christ to come into our hearts and take away our sins and make us clean.

While the Lord Jesus was with Zaccheus in his house, a wonderful thing happened. Zaccheus asked the Lord Jesus Christ to come into his heart and life. Zaccheus's loneliness went away. Zaccheus had a friend now.

Then Zaccheus told the Lord Jesus, "Lord, half of everything I have I will give to the poor. And if I took money from any person and kept it for myself, I will give that person their money back, and I will give back four times more than I took."

The Lord Jesus said to his new friend, "Zaccheus, *today*, salvation has come to this house. You truly are, by putting your trust in me, a son of Abraham who believed on me."

Boys and girls, it wasn't the money that saved Zaccheus, for he gave back half of all his money; it was the fact that Zaccheus put his trust in the Lord Jesus Christ. Zaccheus believed that the Lord Jesus Christ alone could save him and give him a clean heart, a new life, and everlasting joy. The world never gave this to Zaccheus.

> For the Son of Man is come to seek and to save that which is lost.
>
> Luke 19:10 (AKJV)

What did Zaccheus do for a living?
Why didn't Zaccheus have any friends?
When Jesus came to his town, where was Zaccheus?
Did Jesus have dinner with Zaccheus?
Did he ask the Lord Jesus into his heart?

THE GOOD SAMARITAN

Boys and girls, do you know what the word kindness means? *Kindness* means "to show love to someone by being nice to that person or even helping that person."

It can be as easy as saying "Good Morning" to the person who lives next door to you or helping an old man or woman by carrying their heavy bags of food up the stairs. Can you think of another way to be kind to someone?

The Lord Jesus Christ knew what it meant to be kind. He told us a story in the Bible about kindness. He wants us to learn what it means to be kind, and then he wants us to be kind to each other. Not just to our very best friend or to our family, but to all people. Let's begin.

A certain man was on his way from the city of Jerusalem to the city of Jericho. Both Jerusalem and Jericho are in the country of Israel. While he was travelling from Jerusalem to Jericho, he was attacked by a group of thieves. These thieves took all the man's clothing away from him. They also hurt him very badly. After attacking him, they ran away, and they left the man on the ground bleeding. The man was left to die on the cold, hard ground.

Not long afterward, along came a priest. The priest saw this badly beaten man lying on the ground. What do you think the priest did? The Bible tells us that he looked at this poor dying man, and then he crossed the street and kept on walking. He walked away from the hurting man. The priest pretended that nothing happened. He didn't care. A little while later, along came a Levite. This Levite looked at the bleeding man lying on the ground, and what do you think he did?

The Bible tells us that he did the very same thing that the priest did. He crossed over to the other side, and he kept on walking. He didn't care if the man lived or died. But the priest and the Levite should have cared. They both knew the religious rules. But they could not care because they did not have the Lord God in their hearts!

They could show no love, only a cold, hard stare. After a little time had passed, along came a Samaritan. (A Samaritan is a person who is half Jewish and half Arab. The Jewish people and the Arab people were always fighting with each other. Because of this fighting between them, the Jewish people hated the Samaritans, and the Arab people hated the Samaritans. They both thought it a terrible thing to be a Samaritan.)

When this certain Samaritan saw this half-dead man lying on the ground, what do you think he did, boys and girls? The Bible tells us he had *compassion* on this dying man. He showed love toward this badly beaten, helpless man. He wanted to help him. And he did help him. He went over to the bleeding man, and he touched him. He took out some bottles of oil and wine and poured the oil and wine into the man's sores. Then he bound up the man's wounds. He put the sick man on his very own donkey, and he brought the man to an inn (place of rest). There at the inn, the good Samaritan took care of the man.

He cleaned the man's sores, bound up the man's wounds, gave the man a place to rest his tired, hurting body, fed the man with good food so that the man could get his strength back, and then the man fell into a deep, restful sleep. All these things are needed to be made strong and well again. And the good Samaritan made sure the man received all of these necessary things.

The following day, the good Samaritan had to go away for a little while, but he said to the innkeeper, "Here is some money. Take care of him. If you spend more money than I gave you, when I come back, I will pay you."

Boys and girls, which man was the kindest? Yes, the good Samaritan was. I am sure the sick man never forgot the kindness of the good Samaritan.

The Lord Jesus Christ wants you to be kind to people just like the good Samaritan was to the dying man. Let us bow our heads and ask the Lord Jesus to give us a kind, soft heart so that we can be a good Samaritan.

> Be ye kind one to another, tenderhearted, forgiving one another, even as God, for Christ's sake, hath forgiven you.
>
> Ephesians 4:32 (AKJV)

Where did this story take place?
Who attacked this man while he was travelling?
A _____ and a _____ saw this man badly beaten lying on the ground and passed him by?
Who helped this badly beaten man?
Who told this story?

THE WOMAN AT THE WELL

Boys and girls, do you remember how we just read the story about the Good Samaritan? Do you remember the part about how everyone hated the Samaritans because they were half Jewish and half Arab? The Jewish and the Arab people thought it was a terrible thing to be a Samaritan.

But the Lord Jesus Christ loved the Samaritans. He made them, and he had to go to their country called Samaria to see them.

When the Lord Jesus Christ came into the country of Samaria, he went to a city there in Samaria called Sychar. It was in this city that Jacob gave Joseph, his son, a piece of land. Remember the story of Joseph? He was sold as a slave by his brothers, and God raised him up to be second-in-command of all the land of Egypt. (Egypt at that time was the most powerful country on earth.)

Now, there was in the city of Sychar, a well called Jacob's Well. The Lord Jesus Christ, being tired from his journey, rested, and sat by Jacob's well. It was about six o'clock in the evening when this happened.

As the Lord Jesus Christ was resting by the well, a woman from Samaria came to the well to get water. The Lord Jesus said to her, "Give me some water to drink." (The Lord Jesus Christ was alone because his disciples were in another city buying food.)

The woman of Samaria answered the Lord Jesus Christ and said, "How is it that you, a Jew, ask me, a woman and a Samaritan for a drink of water?"

Boys and girls, she knew that the Jews hated the Samaritans, but she didn't know that she was talking to the Lord Jesus Christ.

She was not saved. She did not have the Lord Jesus Christ in her heart or in her life.

But the Lord Jesus Christ was going to change all of that!

The Lord Jesus answered her and said, "If only you knew the gift God has for you and if only you knew who you were talking to right now, you would say to me, 'Give me water, Lord,' and I would give you living water, and you would never be thirsty again."

The poor Samaritan woman did not know that the Lord Jesus was talking about her soul and going to heaven. She thought he was talking about the water from the well. She answered, "Sir, you don't have anything to get the water out of the deep well, so how can you give me that living water? Are you greater than Jacob who gave us this well and drank from it himself and gave water to his children and cattle?"

But the Lord Jesus Christ had one thing on his mind, and that was this Samaritan's soul! She needed a new life—she needed everlasting life! She needed to be born again. She needed the Lord Jesus Christ! The Bible tells us, children, in Psalms 49:8, "A soul is very precious to God." The Lord Jesus Christ loves you very much, and he loved this Samaritan woman and wanted her to know she needed eternal life.

The Lord Jesus answered her, "Whoever drinks from this well will be thirsty again. You will need to keep coming back to this well for more water, but whoever drinks of the water that I will give him will never be thirsty again, for I will give him a well of everlasting water springing up into everlasting life."

The Samaritan woman still did not see the sin in her life and in her heart.

She was spiritually blind. Instead, she was thinking about regular drinking water and thought, *Wow, I won't have to ever come to this well again. That would be great!* So she said to the Lord Jesus Christ, "Sir, give me this water so that I won't be thirsty anymore and have to come to this well."

The Lord Jesus Christ wanted this woman's soul, and he did not change the subject, but instead, he said to her, "Go, call your husband and come here."

The woman answered, "I have no husband."

The Lord Jesus said to her, "You have said the truth, 'I have no husband,' for you have had five husbands, and the man you are living with now is not your husband."

Now, children, her spiritual eyes are starting to open, and she said, "Sir, I can see you are a prophet." (A prophet is a messenger of God.) "Our fathers worshipped in this mountain, and you say Jerusalem is the place of worship."

The Lord Jesus Christ patiently and lovingly answered her, "Woman, I tell you there is going to come a time when you will not worship God here in this mountain or in Jerusalem. You don't know who you are worshipping, for right now, salvation is for the Jews, but the time will come when *all* people who are the true worshippers will worship God the Father in spirit and in truth. God the Father is looking for those people to worship him. God is a spirit, and they that worship him must worship him in spirit and in truth."

The Samaritan woman said to the Lord Jesus, "I know the Messiah, the Savior of the world, is coming, who is called Christ. When he comes, he will tell us all things."

Children, this is the reason the Lord Jesus Christ needed to go to Samaria, for it was at this point the Lord Jesus said with all the love he had, "I am the Messiah, the Savior of the whole world. I am Christ. I am he."

When the Samaritan woman heard these words, she dropped her jar of water suddenly and ran so quickly into the city and said to all the men, "Come, see a man who told me all the things that I did. Is not this the Christ?"

The men followed her to the Lord Jesus Christ. In the meantime, do you remember that the followers of the Lord Jesus were in another city buying food? Well, they have returned, and they couldn't believe what they saw! Here was the Lord Jesus Christ talking to a woman and a Samaritan woman at that! No one does that! But they aren't God who loves us all.

When they came to him, they said, "Come now and eat." But the Lord Jesus Christ answered his twelve followers, "My food is to do the will of my Father and to finish his work. Don't we say there are still four more months before the food is fully grown, and then we are ready to pick it at harvest time? Behold I say to you, 'Lift up your eyes and look on the people's lost souls, for they are ready to receive me into their hearts and lives. They need to be saved now!'"

When the Lord Jesus Christ finished speaking these words to his followers, the Samaritans, along with the woman, came to the Lord Jesus Christ. They accepted him into their hearts and lives as their personal Savior and Lord, just like the Samaritan woman did. They begged the Lord to stay with them a couple of days, and the Lord did. He stayed two more days. Many more Samaritans were saved—not because of what the woman had said, but because they listened to the words of the Lord Jesus Christ and said, "For a truth, he is the Christ, the Savior of the world." They became saved, born again, just like the Samaritan woman at the well.

Now, boys and girls, you have heard the words of this story taken right from the Bible. What will you do with the Lord Jesus Christ? Oh, accept him today before it is too late.

> Is not this the Christ?
>
> John 4:29b (AKJV)

What country did Jesus need to pass through?
The _____ and the _____ did not like each other?
Where was Jesus when he met the Samaritan woman?
Did Jesus tell her he was the Savior of the world?
Did the Samaritan woman ask Jesus into her heart?

THE RAISING OF LAZARUS FROM THE DEAD

When the Lord Jesus Christ lived on this earth, he would often go to many towns and villages in the country of Israel. He would preach the good news of how he came to save them from their sins. He would heal them of their many sicknesses and diseases. He would feed the hungry, love and hold the children, and help the poor and the lost—the ones who could not help themselves.

He would tell them that he is the Light of the World, and that if anyone followed him, they would no longer walk in darkness but have the light of life. He would tell them he is the Bread of Life, and that if anyone tasted of him, they would never be hungry again. If they would ask the Lord Jesus Christ to forgive them of their sins and ask him into their hearts and lives as their own Lord and Savior, they would be given a clean heart, a new life in Christ, a reason to live, and a home in heaven waiting for them.

In one of these villages named Bethany, the Lord Jesus had some very good friends. Their names were Lazarus, Mary, and Martha. They were a family: a brother and two sisters. The Lord Jesus would stay with them, eat with them, and talk with them. The Lord Jesus Christ loved them very much.

One day, while the Lord Jesus was in another village, word came to him that his friend, Lazarus, was very sick. But instead of going to him right away, the Lord Jesus did something else. He said, "This sickness is to bring honor to God so that the Son of God will receive the praise for it." Then he said he would stay another two days in the village before leaving.

Why would the Lord Jesus stay two more days when he knew Lazarus was very sick? We know he loved Lazarus. We shall see.

After two days passed, the Lord Jesus said to his twelve followers, "Let us go into Judea again." His followers answered him, "But, Lord, they are going to kill you there. Don't you remember what happened last time in Judea? Why do you want to go there again?"

The Lord Jesus answered, "Our friend, Lazarus, is sleeping, but I will go and wake him up from his sleep."

When you have the Lord Jesus Christ in your heart and life and you pass away on this earth, the Bible says you are only sleeping because your soul is with the Lord in heaven.

But the followers of the Lord Jesus Christ did not understand what the Lord Jesus meant when he said Lazarus is sleeping, and so the Lord Jesus had to tell them plainly, "Lazarus is dead. And I am glad that I was not there when he was dying so that you will all believe. Now, let us go."

As they were coming near to the village of Bethany where Lazarus, Mary, and Martha lived, Martha ran out to meet the Lord Jesus. Martha said to the Lord Jesus Christ, "Lord, if you had been here, then my brother would not have died. But I know, Lord, that if you ask of God, God will answer you and will give you what you have asked."

The Lord Jesus looked at Martha with love and said to her, "Your brother shall rise again. Your brother will live again, Martha."

Martha said, "I know that on that last day when you come again, my brother will rise again on that Resurrection Day."

The Lord Jesus said to Martha, "I am the Resurrection and the Life. Whoever lives and believes in me shall never die. Do you believe this?"

Martha answered, "Yes, Lord, I believe you are the Christ, the Son of God who should come into the world." Martha then left and whispered secretly to her sister, Mary, "The master is come, and he is asking for you."

Mary ran out of the town of Bethany, and when she saw the Lord Jesus Christ standing there, she fell on her feet and said, "Lord, if you had only been here, then my brother would not have died."

When the Lord Jesus saw Mary crying and the other Jewish people crying because dear Lazarus was dead, the Lord Jesus felt sorry for them and said, "Tell me, where have you put him to rest?"

They said, "Lord, come and see."

And Jesus cried. Then the people said, "How he loved Lazarus!"

Now Lazarus was buried in a cave, and a stone covered the opening of the cave. The Lord Jesus said, "Take away the stone from the opening of the cave."

Martha said, "But Lord, his body stinks. He has been dead for four days."

The Lord answered and said to Martha, "Didn't I say that if you would only believe, you will see the great and mighty things that God will do?"

So they took away the stone from the opening of the cave where Lazarus was buried.

The Lord Jesus lifted up his eyes toward heaven and said, "Father, thank you for hearing me. And I know that you always hear me, but because of these people who stand by, I said it that they may believe that you have sent me."

And then the Lord Jesus Christ, the Son of the living God, cried out with a loud, clear voice, "Lazarus, come out of the grave."

Lazarus, who was dead, came out of the grave with graveclothes on his body and a cloth bound around his face.

The Lord Jesus Christ said to the people, "Loose him, and let him go."

How do you think the people felt when they saw Lazarus alive again? Do you think they were surprised? Didn't the Lord

Jesus say, "If you would only believe, you would see the great and mighty things that God will do?"

What a powerful miracle the Lord Jesus Christ did that day! Many of the Jewish people believed on the Lord Jesus Christ after they saw Lazarus come out of the grave.

Boys and girls, who can bring a person back to life again? Who is like the Lord?

> Call to me and I will answer you, and I will tell you great and mighty things, which you do not know.
>
> Jeremiah 33:3 (NASB)

What were the names of Jesus's three friends?
What was the name of the village that Jesus's friends lived in?
What happened to Lazarus?
Did the Lord Jesus cry when he found out about his friend Lazarus?
What was the mighty miracle Jesus did for his friend Lazarus?

THE WIDOW'S MITES

Boys and girls, this beautiful story took place during the time the Lord Jesus Christ (who is God) walked on this earth. The Lord Jesus was visiting a city called Jerusalem, which is in the country called Israel.

When the Lord Jesus Christ entered the big city of Jerusalem, he went straight to the temple. (A temple is a place where the people worshipped God.)

In the temple, they have a place called the treasury. That is where the people put their money in for the temple. With this money, I am sure they would buy special things needed for the temple such as candles, candleholders, special paper to write the Scriptures on, and much more. They probably used the money also to keep the temple looking nice.

When the Lord Jesus Christ was in the temple, He decided to sit down right across from the treasury.

While the Lord Jesus was sitting there, he watched many different people putting their money into the treasury. The rich people threw a lot of money into the treasury.

I wonder, boys and girls, what the Lord Jesus Christ was thinking about when all these people put some of their money into the treasury?

After he saw many of the rich people putting their money into the treasury, along came a very poor widow. Boys and girls, a widow is a woman whose husband has died. She is now living alone on earth without her husband.

When it was her turn at the treasury, the Lord Jesus Christ kept his eyes on her. She wasn't rich, she didn't have much, and so she could only put mites into the treasury. (In those days, a mite was the smallest amount of money like the penny is for us today.)

Yet, the Lord Jesus Christ saw in her something very different. What do you think the Lord Jesus saw?

The Bible tells us because the Lord Jesus Christ is God, he can look right into a person's heart. Boys and girls, the Lord Jesus is looking deep inside your heart. What do you think he sees?

The Lord Jesus saw something special in this poor widow's heart. He called his twelve followers together and told them what he saw in her heart. He said, "Truly, I say to you, this poor widow gave all that she had. She needed this money to live, and yet she gave it to God. The others who are rich have more money at home, but not this widow. She did not hold back one mite from God."

Just think, boys and girls, how God must have blessed her and kept his loving hand over her. In heaven, one day, she will receive a big reward because she gave out of the goodness of her heart. She gave to God because she wanted to give, not because she had to give. That's what made her different from the others.

I am sure in heaven she will be told this beautiful verse from Matthew 25:21, "Well done, you good and faithful servant. You have been faithful over a few things. I will make you ruler over many things. Enter now into the joy of your Lord." What a happy day that will be for her! Boys and girls, will it also be a happy day for you? Oh, ask him to come into your heart right now. He will come in and give you a new and clean heart. He will live in your heart, and he will give you a new life on earth and a beautiful home in heaven.

> God loveth a cheerful giver.
>
> 2 Corinthians 9:7b (AKJV)

What was the name of the city where Jesus was in this story? When Jesus entered this city, where did he go first?

Where did Jesus sit in this place?
Why was Jesus watching all the people?
What did Jesus say was special about the widow woman?

WORSHIPPING THE LORD JESUS CHRIST

Boys and girls, we just finished reading about how the Lord Jesus Christ raised his good friend, Lazarus, from the dead. Only God can raise a body from the dead, and since the Bible tells us that the Lord Jesus Christ is God, that is how we know he alone could do such a powerful and mighty miracle!

In this story, the Lord Jesus Christ is now visiting Lazarus and his sisters, Mary and Martha, and others with his followers in the home of Simon. Simon lives in a place in Israel called Bethany.

Lazarus has been raised from the dead by the Lord Jesus Christ and is living again. Lazarus's sister, Martha, was busy serving dinner to the Lord Jesus Christ. While Martha was serving dinner, Lazarus was one of many at the table sitting, eating, and talking to the Lord Jesus Christ.

Boys and girls, do you remember that Lazarus had two sisters? Where was his sister Mary, and what was she doing while Martha was serving dinner?

The Bible tells us that she came to the table, and right where the Lord Jesus Christ sat, she bowed down before him. She took a pound of beautiful-smelling perfume, and she poured it and worked it into the precious feet of the Lord Jesus Christ. This perfume cost a lot of money.

After she finished putting it on the Lord Jesus Christ's feet, she wiped it all off with her long hair, and the house was filled with the smell of this perfume.

She really loved the Lord Jesus Christ, and this was her way of worshipping and showing him just how much she loved him.

Boys and girls, do you love the Lord Jesus Christ? He loves you very much. He died on a cross for your sins so that you can go to heaven and live with him forever and ever.

There was a follower of the Lord Jesus Christ named Judas Iscariot. He did not love the Lord Jesus Christ the way Mary did. All he cared about was the money. Because this perfume was expensive, Judas Iscariot was very angry that the money did not go to feed and take care of the poor people.

The Bible tells us, boys and girls, that Judas Iscariot did not care about the poor people either. The Bible says he was a thief, and what he wanted was the money. That's all he could think about! He wanted to keep the money and use it for himself.

So when Judas Iscariot yelled out, "Why wasn't this money given to the poor people?" the Lord Jesus Christ answered Judas and said, "Let her alone. I am going to die and be buried soon. This is why she is doing this. Judas, the poor people will always be here, but I will not. You will not always have me. Leave her alone. Truly, I say to you, 'Wherever this good news about me is preached throughout the whole world, what she did today will be remembered.'"

Boys and girls, God never lies. You can find this story about Mary and how she worshipped the Lord Jesus Christ in the Bible, in the gospel called John, chapter 12, verses 1–8. And Judas Iscariot? He never changed. As a matter of fact, when the Lord Jesus Christ was going to die, Judas Iscariot sold the Lord Jesus Christ for thirty pieces of silver—the price of a slave.

Boys and girls, what are you going to do with the Lord Jesus Christ?

> Behold, the Lamb of God, who takes away the sin of the world!
>
> John 1:29b (ESV)

Jesus is visiting with his friends and followers in the house of _____?

Who poured a pound of beautiful-smelling perfume over Jesus's feet?

What did this person use to wipe Jesus's feet with?

Who was angry that this money did not help the poor?

Did Jesus say she did the right thing?

MY SAVIOR, MY LORD, THE KING

This is a beautiful story about the Lord Jesus Christ entering Jerusalem. Jerusalem was the biggest and most crowded city in all of Israel. Everyone from all the different towns and villages in Israel were coming to Jerusalem to celebrate the Passover. Do you remember the story of the Passover? It happened many, many years before the Lord Jesus Christ was born.

The Jewish people were slaves in the land of Egypt. They were treated very meanly by the Egyptian people. God chose Moses to be the leader of the Jewish people. Under God's direction, Moses took the Jewish people out of Egypt and brought them to a beautiful land that was flowing with milk and honey. It was called the Promised Land.

God was going to make the Jewish people into a powerful country. God loved the Jewish people, and he wanted to bless them.

Every year since that special time, the Jewish people went to Jerusalem to remember and to celebrate that wonderful day. The Lord Jesus Christ was also on his way to Jerusalem.

Just before the Lord Jesus Christ came to Jerusalem, He told two of his disciples to go to a certain village, and in that village, they will find a young donkey. No man, woman, or child has ever sat or ridden on this young donkey.

The Lord Jesus said, "I want you to untie the young donkey and bring it back to me. If anyone asks you 'What are you doing?' you tell them, 'The Lord Jesus Christ needs this donkey.'"

The two followers of the Lord Jesus Christ obeyed the Lord and did exactly what he said. In fact, everything happened just the way the Lord Jesus Christ had said. The disciples of the Lord took off their coats and put them over the young donkey. Then they put the Lord Jesus Christ on the donkey, and they entered the big city of Jerusalem. As the Lord Jesus Christ was riding on the donkey, many people took off their coats and threw them on the ground so that the donkey would not step in the dirt or in the mud.

Many, many, many people took branches from a tree called the Palm tree. (It is a common tree in Israel.) They took the branches from the Palm tree and spread them all over the ground for the Lord Jesus Christ.

All of these people (and there were many), then followed him into the big city of Jerusalem. They all began saying with a very loud voice, "Hosanna to the Son of David! Blessed is he that comes in the name of the Lord. Hosanna in the highest!" (*Hosanna* means "praise.")

All the people rejoiced and praised God for all the mighty works the Lord Jesus Christ had done. They were so happy!

It was a beautiful day, and all the people worshipped the Lord Jesus Christ!

Do you remember to thank and worship the Lord Jesus Christ? You should. He died on a cross so that you can have all your sins taken away. If you ask the Lord Jesus Christ to come into your heart and life, he will give you a clean heart, and you will be able to live forever and ever in heaven with your Savior, your master, the king, the Lord Jesus Christ!

> This is the LORD's doing; it is marvelous in our eyes. This is the day which the LORD hath made; we will rejoice and be glad in it.
>
> Psalms 118:23–24 (AKJV)

In what city did this story take place?
Jesus came into the city riding on a _____?

The people took branches from the _____ tree?
What were the people saying?
Were the people happy?

DEATH, BURIAL, AND RESURRECTION OF THE LORD JESUS CHRIST

Not long after the Passover ended, the enemies of the Lord Jesus Christ began their plan to kill him. The Lord Jesus Christ knew who hated him. The Lord Jesus Christ also knew he had to die on a hard, wooden cross for our sins in order for us to live with him in heaven forever and ever.

The Lord Jesus Christ had twelve followers. One of the twelve followers was named Judas Iscariot. He was going to turn against the Lord Jesus even though he walked and talked with the Lord for three years. Judas Iscariot heard the Lord Jesus speak, and he saw many people healed and made completely well by the Lord Jesus Christ. But Judas Iscariot loved something much more than the Lord Jesus, and that, boys and girls, was *money*.

One day, Judas Iscariot decided to visit the enemies of the Lord Jesus. Many of them were Pharisees and scribes. Judas said to them, "What will you give me if I deliver the Lord Jesus Christ into your hands?"

They answered and said, "We will give you thirty pieces of silver."

In those days, thirty pieces of silver was the price of a slave. That is what they thought of the Lord Jesus.

Judas Iscariot agreed to the thirty pieces of silver and said to them, "I will take you to him in the night. I will go right up to the Lord Jesus and give him a kiss on his cheek so that you may know exactly who he is."

The enemies of the Lord Jesus Christ liked that idea! They all said yes. They all agreed to Judas Iscariot's evil plan.

That night, they put their evil plan into action. Judas Iscariot led the Pharisees, scribes, and chief priests right to the place where the Lord Jesus was staying. Judas went right up the Lord Jesus Christ and said, "Hail, Master," and then kissed him on the cheek.

Jesus said to Judas, "Friend, why are you come"?

Boys and girls, at that moment, the Lord Jesus was giving Judas Iscariot a chance to change his mind about going through with this very wicked plan of killing the Lord Jesus, but Judas Iscariot did *not* change his mind or his heart.

The Bible tells us that the enemies of the Lord Jesus came with soldiers, and the soldiers put their hands on the Lord Jesus and took him away with them.

At that point, another follower of the Lord Jesus, Simon Peter, took his sword and cut off the high priest's servant's ear! Wow! The servant's name was Malchus.

Jesus said to Peter, "Put away your sword. I must die for the sins of the world. I am the good shepherd who gives his life for the sheep. Whosoever follows me shall not walk in darkness but shall have the light of life. I am the light of the world." The Lord Jesus then touched Malchus's ear and healed him.

Amazing! Jesus does all things well!

Jesus said to the Pharisees, the scribes, and the chief priests, "You have come after me like a thief. I taught in the temple openly and in front of all the people everyday. I was with all of you everyday in the temple teaching, and not one of you took me. You come in the night, when it is dark, and no one can see what you are doing, to take me?"

The Bible tells us that all the followers of the Lord Jesus Christ were so afraid that they all ran away. The Lord Jesus was left alone with these evil men, but God was with him.

According to Jewish law, there was only one high priest at a time. But these were evil times, and there were two high priests. One was named Annas and the other high priest was named Caiaphas. They took Jesus to Annas first, and then they tied Jesus up and sent him to the other high priest named Caiaphas.

In the meantime, Simon Peter (one of the twelve followers of the Lord Jesus), was following Jesus from faraway.

Now when all the enemies of the Lord Jesus came together (the Pharisees, chief priests, elders, and all the council members of the temple), they had people lie about the Lord Jesus. After these false witnesses lied about things the Lord Jesus said, Caiaphas (one of the two high priests), stood up and said to Jesus, "Don't you have anything to say? Can't you hear what they are saying against you?"

The Bible states that the Lord Jesus stayed quiet.

Caiaphas said to Jesus, "Tell us, are you the Christ, the Son of God?"

The Lord Jesus answered, "You say that I am." (I am is God's name.)

Then Caiaphas, the high priest, said, "He is guilty of death because he made himself equal to God."

The Bible tells us that they spat in Jesus's face, and they hit him hard with their hands. They said to the Lord Jesus, "Tell us now, who hit you if you are God?"

Boys and girls, do you remember that one of the followers of the Lord Jesus named Simon Peter was following Jesus from faraway? Three people at three different times, and three different places said to Simon Peter, "You are one of Jesus's followers." Three times, Simon Peter said, "No, I am not." Three times he lied and said, "I don't know him." Simon Peter denied the Lord Jesus Christ three times. After the third time, the rooster crowed. Simon Peter then remembered Jesus saying to him, "Before the rooster crows, you will say you never knew me three times." Peter then left, crying.

When the morning came, all the enemies of Jesus said, "We will put him to death." They tied the Lord Jesus and led him away to the Roman Governor who ruled over the land of Israel. His name was Pontius Pilate.

Remember Judas Iscariot? He was the one who turned against the Lord Jesus for thirty pieces of silver. When Judas Iscariot saw that the Lord Jesus was being condemned to death, he tried to give back the thirty pieces of silver, but the Pharisees, the chief priests, the scribes, and the councilmen told Judas, "We are not taking back your money." Judas Iscariot threw the money down on the ground, ran out, and hanged himself.

The chief priests took the thirty pieces of silver from off the ground and used it to buy land to bury strangers in. They called it the field of blood.

Boys and girls, if Judas Iscariot had really known the Lord Jesus Christ, he would have known that the Lord would have forgiven him. How sad! Judas Iscariot walked and talked with the Lord Jesus for three years. Judas saw Jesus forgive many people of their sins.

Now Jesus is in front of the Roman governor, Pontius Pilate, in a place called the hall of judgment. The Bible tells us it was very early in the morning. The chief priests stayed outside.

Pilate went out to them and said, "What are you accusing this man of?"

They said, "He is a criminal, and that is why we have brought him to you."

Pilate answered, "Take him and judge him yourself according to your Jewish laws." They said, "It is not in our law to put any man to death."

Pontius Pilate was a *Roman* governor. The Roman's way of putting a person to death was by putting that person on a hard, wooden cross to die. The Bible tells us that the Lord Jesus Christ died the death of a criminal even though he did nothing wrong.

Then Pontius Pilate entered into the hall of judgment and said to Jesus, "Are you the king of the Jews?"

Jesus said, "Are these your words, or are other people telling you this about me?"

Pilate said, "Am I Jewish? Your own nation and the chief priests have delivered you to me. What did you do?"

The Lord Jesus Christ said, "My kingdom is not of this world. If my kingdom were of this world, my servants would fight for me. My kingdom is not from here."

Pilate answered, "Are you a king"?

Jesus said, "Yes, you say I am a king. This is the reason I was born. The reason I came into the world is to show you the truth. Everyone that is of truth hears my voice."

Pilate said, "What is truth?"

Boys and girls, Pilate did not know nor could he see that Jesus Christ is King of kings and Lord of lords.

Pilate went back out to the chief priests and said, "I find no fault at all in him."

The chief priests said, "We have no king but Caesar." Caesar was the King of Rome. When Pilate heard that, he became afraid. He was afraid of losing his job. He was the Roman governor over Israel.

So he offered them a choice. He said, "I know at your Passover, you have a custom that I should release to you one of your prisoners. Do you want me to release unto you, Jesus, the king of the Jews?"

They all cried out saying, "No, not this man, but Barabbas." Now Barabbas was a robber. Pilate then asked, "What shall I do with this man called Jesus?" They answered, "Crucify him. Crucify him."

When Pilate saw that he could do nothing more, he took water and washed his hands before all the people, saying, "I am innocent of the blood of this good man. See to this yourselves."

The people answered, "His blood be on us and our children."

Pilate released Barabbas to the people. Pilate had Jesus whipped, and then Pilate delivered Jesus over to be crucified.

Boys and girls, we are all guilty of sin. The Bible tells us in Romans 3:23, "All have sinned and come short of the glory of God."

The Roman soldiers took Jesus and put a crown of thorns on his head, a purple robe on his body, and a stick in his hand. They made fun of him, bowing their knees and saying, "Hail, King of the Jews." Then they spat on him and hit him very hard with their hands. They also hit him over the head with the stick that was in his hand.

The Lord Jesus Christ came out wearing the crown of thorns on his head and the purple robe for all to see.

Pilate said, "Behold the man."

The chief priests and officers cried out, "Crucify him, crucify him."

Pilate said, "You crucify him."

They answered, "He has to die because he said he is the Son of God."

When Pilate heard that, he became very afraid. He asked Jesus, "Where do you come from?"

The Lord Jesus Christ did not answer Pilate.

Pilate said, "Don't you know I have the power to kill you or let you go?"

Jesus said, "You have no power over me at all except that God is giving it to you."

But the chief priests and many of the people cried out even more, "Crucify him, crucify him!"

Pilate then let them take the Lord Jesus to be crucified on the hard, wooden cross. The soldiers took off the crown of thorns from Jesus's head and the purple robe from his body. They put his clothes back on him.

As the Roman soldiers led Jesus away to be crucified, they chose a man named Simon who came from a place called Cyrene to carry Jesus's cross. They laid the cross on Simon so that he might bear it and carry it for the Lord Jesus Christ.

They led Jesus to the place called *Golgotha*, which means "the place of a skull." They laid the Lord Jesus on the cross and put nails in his hands and in his feet. They lifted him up on that hard, wooden cross, and then with a boom, they lowered the cross into the ground. And there he hung for the whole world to see. The Lord Jesus Christ hung on that cross for you and for me. Oh, the pain he felt and went through for us!

Pilate wrote a title, and the Roman soldiers put this sign over the cross where Jesus hung. It said, "Jesus of Nazareth, King of the Jews." It was written in Hebrew, Greek, and Latin. They were the three major languages at that time.

The chief priests of the Jews said to Pilate, "Do not say 'King of the Jews,' but say that he said he is King of the Jews."

Pilate said to them, "What I have written, I have written."

While the Lord Jesus Christ was dying on the cross, the Roman soldiers were gambling for his coat. The Lord Jesus's coat was entirely made from top to bottom with only one piece of material!

Boys and girls, the Bible tells us in Psalms 22:18, "They took my coat and gambled for it."

There were two thieves also dying on the cross for their own sins.

The Lord Jesus Christ had no sin in Him, but He died for our sins on the cross so that we may have everlasting life and go to heaven.

One thief was on the left cross, and the other thief was on the right cross. The Lord Jesus was on the middle cross right in between both of them.

One of the thieves said to Jesus, "If you are the Christ, save yourself and us."

But the other thief said, "Don't you fear God? We deserve to die. We are thieves. We have sinned. But this man has done nothing wrong." And then that same thief said to Jesus, "Lord, remember me when you come into your kingdom." Jesus answered, "Truly, I say to you, today you will be with me in paradise."

Can you see, boys and girls, how much the Lord Jesus loves us? Even when he was dying on the cross, he was willing to save people from their sins. Yes, even while the Lord Jesus was dying on the cross.

There, at the bottom of that hard, wooden cross was Jesus's mother, Mary. John, another follower of the Lord Jesus Christ, was also there next to Mary. When Jesus saw His mother and John standing by the cross, the Lord Jesus said to Mary, "Woman, behold your son." Jesus then said to John, "John, behold your mother." From that hour on, John took Jesus's mother to live with him. John obeyed the Lord Jesus.

Now from the sixth hour until the ninth hour, there was darkness over all the land. The Bible tells us that at about the ninth hour, Jesus cried out with a loud voice saying, "Eli, Eli, lama sabachtani?" That is "My God, my God, why have you forsaken me?"

Then Jesus cried out again with a loud voice and gave up the spirit. Jesus died.

Some miracles began to happen after the Lord Jesus died. The veil in the temple was torn in two from top to bottom. That veil was there to separate the people from the high priest and the holiest of holies where only the high priest could enter into. But after the Lord Jesus Christ died, the veil was torn in two from top to bottom. The veil was not needed any longer because the Lord Jesus Christ has now become your high priest, and you can go straight to him to have your sins forgiven. He loves you so much.

One of the commanders of the Roman soldiers called a centurion was there at the bottom of the cross where Jesus died. He was watching Jesus. When Jesus died, there was a big earthquake. When the Roman centurion felt this big earthquake, he became very afraid and said, "Truly, this was the Son of God."

Many women and other people were there when Jesus died. They were all so very sad. They went away crying after they saw him die.

There was a rich man named Joseph who lived in the city called Arimathaea. He was a follower of the Lord Jesus Christ. He went to Pilate and begged for the body of Jesus so that he may bury him. Pilate commanded the body of Jesus to be given over to Joseph. Joseph of Arimathaea and Nicodemus, two men who loved and followed Jesus, wrapped Jesus's body in a clean, linen cloth with spices and laid the Lord Jesus's body in Joseph's own new grave which was cut out of the rock. He then rolled a great stone to the door of the grave and they both left. The grave was in a garden.

Two women, one named Mary Magdalene and another named Mary stayed near the grave where Jesus was buried for a while and then they also left.

The chief priests and the religious rulers of Israel went to see Pontius Pilate. Boys and girls, do you remember them all? They told Pilate that Jesus said that after three days, he would rise again from the dead.

They said to Pilate, "Command the Roman soldiers to watch over the grave so that Jesus's followers will not steal his body in the night and then tell everyone that he rose from the dead. If this happens, it will be worse than when he was alive."

Pilate agreed and put Roman soldiers by the grave to make sure Jesus would stay in the ground.

The Lord Jesus Christ is God, and no one can stop God!

Bright and early on the first day of the week, there was a great earthquake! The angel of the Lord came down from heaven, rolled back the stone from the door of the grave, and sat on the stone. His face was shining brightly, and his clothes were as white as snow. When the Roman soldiers saw the angel, they all began to shake. They could not stop shaking. They were full of fear. The Bible tells us that they all became as dead men.

There were two women there, one was Mary Magdalene and the other woman was named Mary.

The angel spoke to these two women, saying, "Do not be afraid. I know you are looking for Jesus who was crucified. He is not here, for he is risen from the dead just as he said. Come and see the place where the Lord lay. Go now quickly and tell his followers that he is risen from the dead *just as he said.*"

The two women left quickly with much joy to tell the other followers that Jesus had risen from the dead. He's alive!

The Lord Jesus Christ himself met the two women on the way to Galilee and said, "All hail." The two women came to the Lord Jesus and held him by his feet and worshipped him. The Lord Jesus said to these two faithful women, "Do not be afraid. Go, tell my followers in Galilee that they shall all see me."

Boys and girls, could you even begin to imagine the feelings of joy that these two women felt after seeing the Lord Jesus Christ alive?

Before the Lord Jesus showed himself to his followers, the Bible tells us that Jesus first went to see Simon Peter. Do you remember that it was Simon Peter who denied the Lord Jesus three times? The Bible tells us in Luke 24:34, "The Lord is risen indeed and has appeared to Peter." The Lord Jesus forgave Peter for denying Him three times. The Lord Jesus Christ loved Peter, and Peter loved the Lord.

God used Peter in mighty ways to heal sick people and to teach people about the Lord Jesus Christ. Many people asked the Lord Jesus to come into their hearts and into their lives.

Then the eleven followers went into Galilee and up into a mountain to meet the Lord Jesus. There they saw the Lord Jesus Christ! He's alive! He's alive! They bowed down, and they worshipped him.

The Lord Jesus Christ said to them, "All power is given to me in heaven and in earth. Go, all of you now, and teach all nations about me baptizing them in the name of the Father, the Son, and the Holy Spirit. Teach them to do the things I commanded you, and Lo, I am with you always even to the end of the world. Amen."

Over five hundred people, at one time, saw the Lord Jesus before he went up into heaven. Today, the Lord Jesus Christ is seated on the right side of his heavenly Father. He said he will come back soon for those who love him and have accepted him into their hearts. Oh, receive him today into your heart.

> Christ died for our sins according to the Scriptures and that he was buried and that he rose again the third day according to the Scriptures.
>
> 1 Corinthians 15:3b–4 (AKJV)

Who died on the cross for our sins?
What was the name of the Roman Governor?
Who denied knowing Jesus three times?
Did the Lord Jesus forgive him?
Over _____ people, at once, saw the Lord Jesus before he went up into heaven?

THE ROAD TO EMMAUS

Dear children, this is a true story about the Lord Jesus Christ. The Lord Jesus Christ was crucified (nailed to a cross made out of wood). The Lord Jesus Christ died on that cross for our sins. He was buried, and after the third day, according to the Bible, the Lord Jesus Christ arose from the dead.

He is now living and seated on the right hand of God, his heavenly Father. This story took place right after the Lord Jesus Christ arose from the dead. Everyone who had come to know and love the Lord Jesus Christ was so sad! They thought they would never see him again. Their whole world came apart the day the Lord Jesus Christ died.

Boys and girls, in Israel, there is a village called Emmaus. Two of the followers of the Lord Jesus Christ were walking together on the road which led to the village of Emmaus.

These two followers of the Lord Jesus Christ were talking about all the things that happened to the Lord Jesus Christ, such as how he died so cruelly on a wooden cross between two thieves and how he was buried in a brand-new grave which belonged to a rich man named Joseph. Joseph loved the Lord Jesus Christ.

I guess, boys and girls, they thought they would never see the Lord Jesus Christ again. Wouldn't we feel the same way?

While they were talking with each other about these things which happened to the Lord Jesus Christ, what do you think happened?

Well, boys and girls, the Bible tells us that the Lord Jesus himself came to them and walked with them on the road to Emmaus! And do you know what? The two followers of the Lord Jesus Christ did not know it was the Lord Jesus who joined them! They could not see with their eyes that it was indeed the Lord Jesus Christ.

The Lord Jesus said to them, "What are you two talking about while you are walking? Why are you both so sad?"

One of the followers of the Lord Jesus Christ named Cleopas answered the Lord Jesus and said, "Are you a stranger to Jerusalem? Don't you know the things which happened here?" (The Lord Jesus Christ died on a cross in a place outside the camp of Jerusalem called *Golgotha*, which means "the place of the skull.")

The Lord Jesus said, "What things happened here?"

The two followers answered, "Everything concerning Jesus of Nazareth, who was a prophet, mighty in miracles and mighty in preaching and teaching before God and all the people.

"The chief priests of the Jewish people and our rulers delivered the Lord Jesus Christ to be killed on a cross between two thieves.

"We are so sad because we thought and hoped that the Lord Jesus Christ was our Messiah, our Savior, our Redeemer, for all of Israel. And besides all of this, today is the third day since these terrible things were done to the Lord Jesus."

Do you remember boys and girls, the Lord Jesus Christ said he would rise from the dead on the third day?

The two followers continued talking to the Lord Jesus Christ and said, "Certain women of our group amazed us! They went early to the grave where the Lord Jesus was buried. They did not find the Lord Jesus's body! But they did see angels who told them, 'The Lord Jesus Christ is alive!'

"Some of the other people who were with us ran to the grave, and they did not see the body of the Lord Jesus either, but they also did not see any angels as the women did."

Then the Lord Jesus said to his two followers, "O, foolish ones and slow of heart not to believe all that the prophets have spoken! Didn't you read in the Holy Writings of the prophets how the Lord Jesus Christ would have to suffer these things and then enter into his glory?"

Boys and girls, the Lord Jesus explained to the two followers, beginning at Moses and all the prophets, everything about himself and all that would and must happen so that we may enter heaven.

When the two followers of the Lord Jesus and the Lord Jesus Christ himself came to the village of Emmaus, the Lord Jesus kept on walking. The two followers begged the Lord Jesus saying, "Please stay with us, for evening is near, and the day is far gone."

The Lord Jesus stayed with them. They still did not know it was the Lord Jesus Christ himself who was with them all this time.

And it came to pass as the Lord Jesus Christ sat eating with them; the Lord Jesus took bread and blessed it and broke it and gave it to them.

At that moment, boys and girls, their eyes were opened, and they recognized the Lord Jesus Christ. They knew at that moment it was the Lord himself.

The Lord Jesus vanished from them. He disappeared from them. The two followers said to each other, "Did not our heart burn within us while he talked with us along the way and while he opened to us the Holy Scriptures—the Holy Writings about himself!"

Boys and girls, why would the Lord Jesus Christ suffer so much and then die on a cross for us? There must be a reason. John 3:16 tells us, "For God so loved the world that he gave his only begotten Son that whosoever believes in him should not perish but have everlasting life."

> Did not our hearts burn within us while he talked to us on the road, while he opened to us the Scriptures?
>
> Luke 24:32 (ESV)

Lois M. Bitler

The two followers were on the road to _____?
Why were they sad?
Who appeared to them and walked with them on this road?
Did they ask this person to stay the night?
At the end of the story, did they recognize who the person was?

WALKING AND TALKING AND PRAISING GOD!

This story took place after the Lord Jesus Christ had died and is now in heaven. He gave power to his disciples to heal the sick people and to show them the way to everlasting life through the Lord Jesus Christ.

While on earth, the Lord Jesus Christ had twelve disciples. Their names were: Peter, Andrew, James, John, Philip, Bartholomew, Matthew, Thomas, James, the son of Alpheus; Simon, and Judas, the son of James; and Judas Iscariot.

Here is a true story of how two of the disciples named Peter and John had done a mighty miracle and healed a man who could not walk.

Peter and John were in Jerusalem. It was about three o'clock in the afternoon. Peter and John were on their way to the temple. (A temple is a place of worship for the Jewish people.) They were going to pray to God there.

At the same time that Peter and John were going to the temple, a certain man, who was lame from birth, was being carried to the gate of the temple. This certain man, from the moment he was born, could not walk.

The Bible tells us that, everyday, he lay at the gate begging for money. He needed money to buy food. And that's exactly what he was doing one day until he saw Peter and John. He didn't know who they were, what they did, or that they had a very special person in their life.

The only thing this certain lame man did know was that he needed money to live. So when Peter and John passed by, he said to them, "Money for the lame man, money for the lame man."

Peter and John stopped and put their eyes right on this sad, lame man, and they said to him, "Look at us." The lame man obeyed and looked at Peter and John, thinking he would get money from them.

But Peter said, "Silver and gold, I have none, but what I have, I give to you. In the name of Jesus Christ of Nazareth, rise up and walk."

And Peter took the lame man by the right hand and lifted him up. Immediately, the lame man's feet and ankle bones received strength. This lame man was walking now! A miracle!

He went with Peter and John into the temple. He was walking, leaping, and praising God!

All the people saw him walking and praising God. They knew it was the same man who begged for money.

The people were filled with wonder and amazement. And the once-lamed man? The last they saw of him, he was with Peter and John, walking and leaping and praising God!

> Silver and gold have I none; but such as I have give I thee: In the name of Jesus Christ of Nazareth rise up and walk.
>
> Acts 3:6 (AKJV)

Can you name three disciples of the Lord Jesus?
What two disciples were in Jerusalem?
Who asked them for money?
What was wrong with this man?
After he was healed, the man was _____ and _____ and _____ God!

REJOICING ALL THE WAY!

This Bible story is about one of the twelve followers of the Lord Jesus Christ named Philip. This story takes place after the Lord Jesus Christ died and rose again the third day from the dead. The Lord Jesus Christ now lives in heaven and seated on the right hand of God, his Father.

Philip had just finished preaching about the Lord Jesus Christ in the city of Samaria. God sent an angel to tell Philip, "Arise, and go south toward the way that goes down from Jerusalem to a place called Gaza." Now Gaza was a desert. Philip obeyed and did exactly as the angel had told him.

Boys and girls, remember what we read about Gaza? It was a desert. You won't find many people living in the desert. But Philip, when he came to Gaza, saw an eunuch from the country called Ethiopia. The eunuch had much power which was given to him by Queen Candace of Ethiopia. The eunuch was in charge of all the queen's treasure.

The Bible tells us, boys and girls, that the eunuch had come to Jerusalem to worship, and now he was on his way home again to Ethiopia.

While he was going home, the eunuch was sitting in his chariot, reading the book of the Bible called Isaiah.

Then the Holy Spirit said to Philip, "Go near to the eunuch. Go right up to his chariot."

Boys and girls, Philip obeyed! In fact, the Bible tells us that Philip ran to the eunuch! He heard the eunuch reading from the book of Isaiah, the prophet. Philip said to the eunuch, "Do you understand what you are reading?"

The eunuch answered, "How can I understand unless someone helps me?" The eunuch then asked Philip to help him understand the Word of God.

Now, the place in the Bible the eunuch was reading said this: "He was led as a sheep to the slaughter; and like a lamb dumb before his shearers so he opened not his mouth.

In his humiliation, his judgment was taken away and who shall declare his generation? For his life is taken from the earth."

The eunuch said, "I beg of you, who is the prophet Isaiah talking about? Is Isaiah the prophet speaking about himself, or is he speaking about some other man?"

Then Philip opened his mouth, and at the exact same place where the eunuch started to read, Philip preached to the eunuch about the Lord Jesus Christ!

What a wonderful opportunity Philip had to preach about our Savior and Lord, Jesus Christ!

As Philip and the eunuch traveled together, they came to a certain water. The eunuch said to Philip, "See, here is water. What is stopping me from being baptized?"

Philip said, "If you believe with all your heart in the Lord Jesus Christ, you may be baptized."

The eunuch answered, "I believe that Jesus Christ is the Son of God."

Boys and girls, at that moment, the eunuch became born-again—born from above.

The eunuch commanded the chariot to stand still, and Philip and the eunuch both went down in the water. Philip had the joy of baptizing the eunuch.

When they came up out of the water, the Holy Spirit took Philip away to preach somewhere else about the Lord Jesus Christ. The eunuch never saw Philip again. The Bible tells us that the eunuch went on his way back to Ethiopia rejoicing all the way!

Boys and girls, wouldn't you like to be as happy as the eunuch was? You can. All you have to do is ask the Lord Jesus Christ into your heart and life and to forgive you of all your sins. The Lord Jesus Christ will enter your life and your heart. He will take away all your old, dirty sins, and he will give you a clean heart, and you will be born again, born from above! Now that's what I call true happiness!

> Neither is there salvation in any other; for there is none other name under heaven given among men, whereby we must be saved.
>
> Acts 4:12 (AKJV)

Was Philip one of the twelve disciples?
Who told Philip to go to Gaza?
What book of the Bible was the eunuch reading?
Did Philip help the eunuch to understand what he was reading?
Did the eunuch believe that Jesus Christ is the Son of God?

SAUL OF TARSUS BECOMES PAUL THE APOSTLE

This is a true story of how one man gave his heart and life to the Lord Jesus Christ in a most unusual way. His name is Saul, and he came from a city called Tarsus. He was a very smart man. He knew all about the Jewish religion. He obeyed all the Jewish rules. He was a religious leader and belonged to a Jewish group called the Pharisees. The Pharisees were very careful to follow every rule in the Jewish law. They walked around with long robes and long beards with their rules tied to their robes, making sure the people obeyed them.

Many times they forgot, though, how to treat a person with love and compassion. Saul of Tarsus was living when the Lord Jesus Christ was taken back to heaven. The Lord Jesus Christ had already died, was buried, rose again, and now lives in heaven.

When the Lord Jesus Christ was living on earth, he often spoke with the Pharisees, explaining to them that it doesn't matter how many rules you follow. If you do not accept God's Son into your hearts and lives, you will not go to heaven. They hated the Lord Jesus Christ. They thought their way was the right way.

In the meantime, because Saul was a Pharisee, he was going to try to kill all the Christians (ones who believed in the Lord Jesus Christ as their Savior and Lord). In fact, the first Christian to be stoned to death was Stephen (a very godly man who truly loved God and the Lord Jesus Christ). It was Saul who gave the order to have Stephen stoned to death.

Saul thought he was doing the right thing, but God knew he wasn't! After Stephen died, Saul went to the high priest, asking him to give him letters so that he may go to Damascus, to the temple, and take away all the Christian men and women and bring them bound to Jerusalem. He wanted to stone them just as he had Stephen stoned to death.

Saul of Tarsus was angry! He was yelling and threatening to kill all the Christians. (Again, believing with all his heart that he was doing the right thing.) God knew what Saul was up to, and was Saul of Tarsus in for a big surprise!

As Saul and his men traveled near Damascus, there suddenly shone a bright light all around Saul. He fell to the ground, and he heard a voice from heaven, saying, "Saul, Saul why are you persecuting me?"

Saul said, "Who are you, Lord?"

And the Lord said, "I am Jesus, whom you are persecuting. It is impossible to fight me."

Saul was scared! In fact, he was trembling! He never had an experience like this one before!

While he was trembling, he said, "Lord, what do you want me to do?"

The Lord said to him, "Get up and go into the city, and there you will find out what you must do."

Now the men who traveled with him were speechless! They must have been shaking in their shoes! They heard a voice but saw no man! Saul rose up from the ground, and when he opened his eyes, he could not see. He was blind. The Word of God tells us that for three days, he could not see. He did not eat or drink anything for those three days. The men who traveled with Saul led him by the hand into Damascus. At Damascus, there was a certain disciple named Ananias. The Lord appeared to Ananias and said, "Ananias."

Ananias answered, "Here I am, Lord."

The Lord said, "Go to the street called Straight. At that street, go to the house of Judas. Ask for Saul of Tarsus, for he is praying.

He saw you in a vision coming to him and putting your hand on him so that he can again receive his sight."

It is difficult, at times, to follow God's directions even though we know we must. We need to understand that God loves us very much, and he knows what is best for us.

Ananias said to the Lord, "Lord, I have heard many evil things about this man and what he is doing to the born-again Christians at Jerusalem. He has authority from the chief priests to kill us."

But the Lord answered, "Go! This man is my chosen instrument to carry my name before the Gentiles and their kings and before the people of Israel. I will show him how much he must suffer for my name."

Ananias obeyed the Lord. He went to the street called Straight. He went into the house of Judas, and when he saw Saul, he said, "Brother Saul, the Lord Jesus appeared to me and told me to come here so that you may, once again, receive your sight and be filled with the Holy Spirit, the Power of God."

Immediately, the scales fell from his eyes, and he received his sight and was baptized. He began to eat again, and his strength came back to him. Saul stayed with the disciples at Damascus for a little while.

He immediately began to preach the good news of our Lord and Savior, Jesus Christ.

God changed Saul's name to Paul (*Paul* means "Little"). He meant little to the world, but he did great things for God through the strength of the Lord Jesus Christ. Paul became the first missionary and truly brought the good news of our Lord Jesus Christ to the Gentiles.

> That at the name of Jesus every knee should bow and that every tongue should confess that Jesus Christ is Lord, to the glory of God, the Father.
>
> Philippians 2:10a-11 (AKJV)

After Saul saw a bright light and fell off his horse, who spoke to him?
Saul was blind for ____ days?
Who did God send to heal Saul so he could see again?
God changed Saul's name to _____?
He became the first _____?

DORCAS: A TRUE FRIEND OF WIDOWS

Boys and girls, this story takes place after the Lord Jesus Christ died on the cross for our sins and has gone back to heaven. The Lord Jesus Christ is now seated on the right hand of God, his heavenly Father, in heaven.

The name of the woman in this story is called Dorcas. She was also called Tabitha. Dorcas was a mighty servant of the living God. God used Dorcas in a wonderful way to help cheer and encourage the widows where she lived.

The Bible teaches us to be thoughtful and kind to widows. Dorcas obeyed that commandment. Do you know any widows you can be kind to today?

Dorcas, (also called Tabitha), lived in a place called Joppa. The Bible tells us that Dorcas was full of good works for the Lord Jesus Christ. She loved the Lord Jesus Christ. Dorcas gave many gifts to the poor, and she helped the widows by making clothes for them to wear.

One day, Dorcas became very sick. She became so sick that she passed away.

Dorcas had died. The people who loved Dorcas washed her body, and they laid her body in an upper room.

Boys and girls, it was the custom in those days to lay a dead person's body in a room of the house. Today, we have funeral homes, but I am sure in many parts of the world they still follow the old custom.

Now the disciples had heard that Peter was in a place called Lydda. Lydda was very near to Joppa where Dorcas had lived. The disciples sent two men to Lydda to see Peter. They wanted Peter to come with them in a hurry back to Joppa.

Boys and girls, do you remember the disciple Peter? When the Lord Jesus Christ lived on this earth, the Lord Jesus Christ chose Peter to be one of his twelve followers. Peter walked with the Lord Jesus Christ for three years on this earth. Then the Lord Jesus Christ died on a hard, wooden cross for your sins and for my sins. Some of the people remembered that Peter was with the Lord Jesus Christ while he was alive on earth, but Peter, being so afraid, told the people three times that he did not know the Lord Jesus Christ at all. After three days, the Lord Jesus Christ rose up from the dead, and Peter asked the Lord to forgive him, and the Lord Jesus Christ said, "Yes, Peter, I forgive you."

Now when the two men spoke to Peter at Lydda about Dorcas, Peter got up and went with them. When they came to Dorcas's home, they took Peter to the upper room where Dorcas's body lay. All the widows stood by Peter, crying and showing Peter the coats and clothes Dorcas had made for them while she was living. How the widows truly loved Dorcas!

Peter asked everyone to leave the room. Peter then kneeled down and prayed. Turning to Dorcas, (who was also known as Tabitha), Peter said, "Tabitha, get up." And she opened her eyes! When she saw Peter, she sat up!

Boys and girls, it wasn't Peter who raised up Dorcas from the dead—it was God! Peter had to kneel down and pray to God for God to raise up Dorcas from the dead. Peter was used by God in a mighty way.

Peter gave Dorcas his hand and lifted her up. Peter then called all the saints and all the widows to come and see Dorcas alive! Wow! What a mighty miracle!

The good news about Dorcas spread through all of Joppa, and many people believed in the Lord Jesus Christ and were saved that day!

The Bible teaches us that Jesus is the only way to heaven. Won't you ask him today to come into your heart and into your life? You will be thanking him over and over again for the day you let the perfect Son of God, the Lord Jesus Christ, into your life.

> Come now, and let us reason together, saith the LORD: though your sins be as scarlet, they shall be as white as snow; though they be red like crimson, they shall be as wool.
>
> Isaiah 1:18 (AKJV)

What was Dorcas's other name?
Dorcas was a _____?
Why were all the women sad?
What did the women show Peter when he arrived at Dorcas's house?
Was it God or Peter that raised Dorcas from the dead?

GOD'S ANSWER TO PRAYER

This story took place after the Lord Jesus Christ had died and is now in heaven. He gave power to his twelve followers to heal the sick and to show others the way to everlasting life through the Lord Jesus Christ.

One of the Lord Jesus's followers was named Peter. Peter went to many places in Israel, telling the Jewish people about the Lord Jesus Christ. The king at that time was named King Herod. He was a wicked king. He hated the Lord Jesus Christ, his twelve followers, and everyone who believed in the Lord Jesus Christ as their personal Savior and Lord.

King Herod killed one of the followers named James with a sword, and now he took hold of Peter and put him in jail. He had sixteen soldiers to watch Peter in prison. King Herod was planning to do something evil to Peter. He was going to keep Peter in prison till after Easter and then bring him before all the people. He wanted Peter killed.

Now many people had asked the Lord Jesus Christ into their hearts. They were called Christians. Every moment of the day ever since the Christians heard about Peter being in jail, they prayed to the Lord for his safety. They wanted the Lord to set Peter free from prison if that was the Lord's will. Day and night, prayers went up to the Lord in heaven for Peter.

Boys and girls, do you remember to pray to the Lord? He would love to hear what you would like to tell him. Because of these prayers made by the Christians in the church, God answered them in a most powerful way!

On the day when King Herod was going to bring Peter out of prison, God moved that night! Peter was sleeping (bound in chains) between two soldiers, and the soldiers guarding the prison door, but that didn't stop God from working!

An angel of the Lord came to Peter, and a light shone brightly in that dark, cold prison. The angel hit Peter on the side and raised him up, saying, "Arise quickly!" Peter's chains fell off from his hands!

The angel said to Peter, "Get dressed and put your sandals on your feet." Peter obeyed.

The angel then told Peter, "Put on your outer coat and follow me."

Peter did everything the angel told him, but he thought he was dreaming. Peter did not know this was really happening.

Now the soldiers didn't see a thing! They didn't hear anything! They were all in a deep sleep!

Boys and girls, who could only have done this miracle? That's correct. Only God.

There is no one mightier than God!

After the angel and Peter went past the first and second group of soldiers, they came to the iron gate of the city. Would you like to hear another miracle? The iron gate opened by itself! The angel and Peter walked right out of the city and passed through a street. Immediately, the angel left Peter.

Right at that moment, Peter realized all of this was true and happening to him. Peter said, "Now I know for sure that the Lord God has sent his angel and has delivered me out of the hands of wicked King Herod and from everything the Jewish people would have done to me!"

Peter must have been so thankful to God and so happy! Boys and girls, would you have felt that same way?

Peter went to the house of Mary, the mother of John. John was also called Mark.

It was at this house that many Christians were gathered together and praying for Peter to be set free, if it was the will of

God. Peter came to the door of the house and started knocking. A young girl, named Rhoda, went to the door.

When she heard Peter's voice, she did not open the door for him. Instead, she was so happy, she ran back to tell the Christians that Peter was standing at the door, waiting to be let in.

The Christians, who were all praying for Peter to be set free, did not believe what Rhoda told them. Instead, they said to her, "You're crazy." But Rhoda kept on insisting and telling them, "Peter is at the door."

Then the Christians said, "It is Peter's angel." But Peter continued to knock, and finally, when they opened the door and saw for themselves that it was Peter, they were truly surprised! They couldn't believe it!

Boys and girls, aren't we the same way? We ask the Lord to help us with something or we ask him for something, and then when he gives it to us, we just can't believe it! We are no different than the Christians were with Peter.

Peter, realizing they couldn't believe it was him, put up his hand and told them to please be quiet. Peter then told all of them how the Lord God had brought him out of the jail.

Peter said, "Now go and tell these things to James and the other followers of the Lord Jesus Christ."

Then Peter left them and went to another place to serve the Lord Jesus Christ.

Remember wicked King Herod? When King Herod found out that Peter was gone and was nowhere to be found, he questioned each of the soldiers. The soldiers could not give King Herod an answer, and so, just like that, King Herod had all the soldiers who watched over Peter in jail put to death!

The Bible tells us, boys and girls, that soon after, God took King Herod's life in a terrible way. King Herod was eaten by worms. He was an evil king and a very wicked man.

Boys and girls, have you ever prayed to the Lord Jesus Christ and asked him to come into your heart? He will answer your prayer, and he will come in and live there. He will become your best friend, if you let him.

> For the eyes of the Lord are over the righteous, and his ears are open unto their prayers.
>
> 1 Peter 3:12a (AKJV)

What was the name of the king in this story?
Did this king put Peter in prison?
Who led Peter out of prison?
When Peter was knocking at the door, who answered it?
Were the Christians praying for Peter?

A CHANGED HEART

Boys and girls, do you know who was the first missionary? Do you know who was the first person who went to the Gentiles with the good news of our Savior?

If you said Paul, you are correct. Very good! God used Paul in a great and mighty way to spread the wonderful and true story of the Lord Jesus Christ to all the people.

In this true story from the Bible, Paul, the first missionary, had a friend named Silas. He, too, loved the Lord Jesus Christ very much. Together, Paul and Silas went everywhere, talking to everyone about how much God loved them and how the Lord Jesus Christ died on the cross for their sins.

As Paul and Silas went to pray one morning, a certain young girl followed them and cried out loud, "These men are the servants of the most high God who can show us the way to be saved."

She followed Paul and Silas around for many days, making it very hard for them to preach about the Lord Jesus Christ to the people. This certain young girl had an evil spirit in her, and the evil spirit would not leave her alone. It was the evil spirit that was making her do these things.

An evil spirit is from the devil. An evil spirit does not come from God. Finally, after a few days, Paul and Silas could not take this evil spirit any longer, so Paul, in a strong voice, said to the evil spirit, "I command you in the name of the Lord Jesus Christ to come out of her."

Right away, the evil spirit left her. It ran away. The girl became herself again. But the girl was owned by two men, her masters.

They made money from her when she had the evil spirit in her. They became very angry when Paul commanded the evil spirit to leave her, and it did!

The two men took Paul and Silas to the marketplace and brought them before the rulers of the land. All the people went against Paul and Silas. The rulers took their clothes off, and Paul and Silas were beaten many times by the soldiers.

After the soldiers beat Paul and Silas, they threw them in jail. They put them in the deepest, darkest part of the jail. They put their feet in chains, and the rulers commanded the jailkeeper to make sure they would not escape!

Now, you would think this would make Paul and Silas very sad. But they weren't. The Bible tells us that Paul and Silas were praying and singing songs to God at midnight! In fact, all the prisoners heard them!

They were so happy because they knew God would never forget them; no, not even in the deepest part of the jail. They put their trust in the Lord Jesus Christ. These men had faith in God.

Because of their faith, God did a wonderful thing: a miracle! Suddenly, there was an earthquake, the jail shook, and right away, all the doors of the jail opened, and everyone's chains fell off! All the prisoners were free! Wow!

Remember the jailkeeper? What command did the rulers give him? He was told by the rulers to make sure they did not escape! In those days, if the jailkeeper lost one prisoner, the jailkeeper would be put to death!

Well, the jailkeeper was sleeping when all of this happened, and when he opened his eyes and saw how all the doors of the jail were opened and the prisoners set free, he took out his sword to kill himself.

Just at that moment, Paul saw the jailkeeper with the sword in his hand, and Paul cried out, "Don't kill yourself, for we are all here."

The jailkeeper got a light and walked in, and when he saw Paul and Silas, he fell to his feet. He brought Paul and Silas out of that deep, dark pit and took them to his house and to his family. He took care of them by washing their wounds.

The jailkeeper then said to Paul and Silas, "Sirs, what must I do to be saved?"

Paul and Silas happily answered, "Believe on the Lord Jesus Christ, and you shall be saved and your family too."

They then told the jailkeeper and his family all about the Lord Jesus Christ, and they all received the Lord Jesus Christ into their hearts and into their lives. They all became saved. At that same hour, they were all baptized. They all became one in the Lord Jesus Christ—the family of God.

After they were all baptized, the jailkeeper took Paul and Silas back to his home, and he gave them food to eat. They all rejoiced and were so very thankful and so very happy for giving their hearts and lives to the Lord Jesus Christ!

You, too, can have the Lord Jesus Christ come into your heart. It's so simple! Ask him to take away your sins and give you a clean heart. He will, you know. He will come into your heart and life forever. You will be so happy you invited him in.

> Sirs, what must I do to be saved? Believe on the Lord Jesus Christ, and thou shalt be saved.
>
> Acts 16:30b-31a (AKJV)

Who was the first missionary?
_____ and _____ went everywhere telling people about Jesus.
Why did they put them in jail?
God sent an _____ and the doors of the jail opened!
Did the jailkeeper and his whole family ask the Lord Jesus to come into their hearts?

> Behold, I make all things new.
>
> Revelation 21:5a (AKJV)

e|LIVE

listen|imagine|view|experience

AUDIO BOOK DOWNLOAD INCLUDED WITH THIS BOOK!

In your hands you hold a complete digital entertainment package. In addition to the paper version, you receive a free download of the audio version of this book. Simply use the code listed below when visiting our website. Once downloaded to your computer, you can listen to the book through your computer's speakers, burn it to an audio CD or save the file to your portable music device (such as Apple's popular iPod) and listen on the go!

How to get your free audio book digital download:

1. Visit www.tatepublishing.com and click on the e|LIVE logo on the home page.
2. Enter the following coupon code:
   de04-049f-b727-7aac-a08e-02c4-d7f8-a601
3. Download the audio book from your e|LIVE digital locker and begin enjoying your new digital entertainment package today!